Crown Court Practice & Procedure

Tolley Publishing Company Limited

Lawyers Practice & Procedure Series

Crown Court Practice & Procedure

by Kris Gledhill
BA (Oxon), LL M (Virginia), Barrister

Tolley Publishing Company Limited
A UNITED NEWSPAPERS PUBLICATION

ISBN 0 85459 753-0

First published 1993

Published by
Tolley Publishing Company Limited
Tolley House
2 Addiscombe Road
Croydon
Surrey
CR9 5AF
081-686 9141

© Kris Gledhill 1993

Typeset in Great Britain by
Action Typesetting Limited, Russell Street, Gloucester

Printed and bound in Great Britain by
Hobbs the Printers, Southampton

Preface

The purpose of this book is to provide a simple guide to the procedures under which the Crown Court operates. I hope it is sufficiently detailed to be of value to the practitioner who appears regularly in the Crown Court; it should be of value to someone who appears there infrequently or is at the start of their career. It aims to give practical advice also to solicitors and their employees who prepare cases for trial.

The appearance of necessary detail does not, I hope, prevent the book being used by others regularly involved in the activities of the Crown Court—probation officers, police personnel, court reporters and so on —and also members of the wider public who may want to know how the Crown Court operates.

All authors are inevitably grateful to certain people. I will limit my specific thanks to four: Anthony Heaton-Armstrong, who introduced me as the potential author of the book; Irene Kaplan, who commissioned the book; Alan Radford, who edited the book from the publisher's viewpoint; and Joanne Richards, who provided some useful assistance.

Finally, can I apologise for the use throughout the book of the masculine case. The professional opinion of the publishers was that the interests of readability in a book of this nature mandate the use of male pronouns.

Kris Gledhill
1 Pelham Close
Camberwell
London SE5 8LW

Contents

Part II: The Crown Court as an Appellate Tribunal

Part III: Trial on Indictment

Contents

Table of Statutes

Table of Statutory Instruments

Table of Statutory Instruments

Table of Cases

PART I:
THE JURISDICTION OF THE CROWN COURT

Chapter 1

Jurisdiction

1. Introduction

The Crown Court is part of the Supreme Court of England and Wales and, pursuant to s 46(1) of the Supreme Court Act 1981, has sole jurisdiction in respect of trials on indictment. It has appellate functions in respect of most cases heard by magistrates' courts, and is also the court which in some circumstances will sentence defendants convicted in the magistrates' court. Appellate jurisdiction is covered in Chapter 2.

(a) Categorisation of offences

Criminal offences are split into three categories, as defined in Schedule 1 to the Interpretation Act 1978. An indictable-only offence is one which, in the case of adult defendants charged with such offences, must be tried on indictment and therefore in the Crown Court. A summary-only offence must be tried in the magistrates' court. The third category is of "either-way" offences; defendants charged with such offences always have the option to be tried on indictment, though the case may be dealt with in the magistrates' court if both the defendant and the magistrates' court agree.

To this simple classification must be added two riders. There are certain circumstances in which summary-only offences can be heard by the Crown Court. In addition, with respect to defendants aged under 18, they will generally be tried summarily in the youth court even if charged with an indictable-only or either-way offence.

In order to decide into which category of offence a particular allegation falls, one must first determine whether the offence is common law or statutory. Common law offences are indictable-only unless there has been a statutory provision affecting this. If the offence is created by statute, the statute or a subsequent statute will indicate into which category the offence falls.

(b) Territorial jurisdiction

The Crown Court is a single entity, though it sits in different locations throughout England and Wales. It has jurisdiction in respect of an offence the *actus reus* of which is completed in England and Wales. This can cause problems in respect of inchoate offences. An attempt is triable in the jurisdiction if the completed offence would be: see *DPP* v *Stonehouse* [1978] AC 55. A conspiracy can be tried in England and Wales provided the conspirators perform an act pursuant to the conspiracy in the jurisdiction: see *DPP* v *Doot* [1973] AC 807.

Sections 1 to 6 of the Criminal Justice Act 1993 introduce special rules in relation to the main offences of dishonesty under the Theft Acts 1968 and 1978 and the Forgery and Counterfeiting Act 1981, and inchoate offences of a like nature. Briefly, a person may be guilty of one of the substantive offences covered by the Act if any "relevant event" occurs in England or Wales. A "relevant event" is "any act or omission or other event (including any result of one or more acts or omissions) proof of which is required for conviction of the offence". There are similar provisions to extend jurisdiction over the relevant inchoate offences where there is any real connection with England and Wales.

There are other statutory provisions which may extend territorial jurisdiction to offences committed outside England and Wales. For example, British subjects may be prosecuted for murder or manslaughter committed abroad; bigamy is similarly extended (ss 9 and 57 of the Offences Against the Person Act 1861). The European Convention on the Suppression of Terrorism 1977, which was brought into effect by the Suppression of Terrorism Act 1978, provides for the trial in the jurisdiction of terrorists who are accused of terrorist acts in any convention country.

(c) Parties

(i) The accused; corporate liability

The accused is the person charged with the offence alleged. This will invariably be an individual. However, an incorporated company is a legal person, and a statute may define an offence in such a manner as to make the company liable to prosecution. Typically, these are offences of strict liability. A company does not have a mind of its own, and so cannot be said to have the necessary *mens rea* when such is required. However, a company can be identified with the natural persons who are responsible for the exercise of the powers of the corporation (under its memorandum and articles of association, or as a result of action taken by the directors or the members in general meeting), and their state of mind can be imputed to the company. (See *P&O European Ferries (Dover) Limited* [1991] Crim LR 695, relating to corporate liability for manslaughter.)

(ii) The Crown Prosecution Service; the Director of Public Prosecutions

The prosecution will usually be conducted through the Crown Prosecution Service, headed by the Director of Public Prosecutions, which takes over every prosecution instituted on behalf of a police force (except for various minor motoring matters). Some offences can only be prosecuted if the DPP consents at the outset. The police can always consult the CPS before charging any particular offence: they might, for example, want guidance on whether there is sufficient evidence in respect of a given case.

(iii) Other prosecutors

Other public bodies have responsibilities for prosecutions: the Serious Fraud Office, the Inland Revenue, the Post Office and so on. A private person may also commence a prosecution which is not within the exclusive ambit of a given prosecuting authority. However, in such a circumstance, s 6(2) of the Prosecution of Offences Act provides that:

> "Where criminal proceedings are instituted in circumstances in which the Director is not under a duty to take over their conduct, he may nevertheless do so at any stage".

The Director may act in order to then prosecute the offence charged, or in order to stop the prosecution by discontinuing it.

(iv) Role of the Attorney-General

The Attorney-General may also become involved in the prosecution of certain offences. The DPP is answerable to the Attorney-General, who issues guidelines on various matters to Crown Prosecutors. In addition, some offences can only be prosecuted if the Attorney-General consents to the prosecution—usually where public policy issues are raised. The Attorney-General also has power to enter a *nolle prosequi* to terminate a prosecution on indictment when it is not in the public interest for it to be continued (for example, where a defendant has become physically or mentally unfit to be prosecuted further).

(v) Rights of Audience

The Crown Court is one of the courts where barristers in private practice retain a monopoly, though this is being reviewed under the machinery of the Courts and Legal Services Act 1990. Solicitors may be granted rights of audience pursuant to directions issued by the Lord Chancellor under s 83 of the Supreme Court Act 1981. A Practice Direction of 26 August 1988 [1988] 1 WLR 1427 allows solicitors to appear at the Crown Courts in Caernarvon, Barnstaple, Truro and Doncaster in respect of appeals from magistrates' courts, committals for sentence, civil matters and trials on indictment of class 4 offences (on which see below). There are similar rights of audience at Lincoln Crown Court in respect of proceedings from certain magistrates' courts.

There are general rights of audience for solicitors in all Crown Courts in respect of appeals from magistrates' courts and committals for sentence: Practice Direction of 9 February 1972 [1972] 1 WLR 307. In some Crown Court centres, solicitors and other employees of solicitors' firms may appear in respect of business conducted in chambers (on which see Chapter 6).

2. Committal for trial

(a) Basic principles

The Crown Court's jurisdiction to try a case on indictment rests on compliance with s 2 of the Administration of Justice (Miscellaneous Provisions) Act 1933. A bill of indictment is valid only if:

(i) the person charged has been committed for trial by a magistrates' court,

(ii) the offence is specified in a notice of transfer, or

(iii) a voluntary bill of indictment is preferred by the Court of Appeal or with the consent of the High Court.

Committal for trial is the most common method. What happens at the committal can have an impact on the proceedings in the Crown Court.

A committal will be held in two circumstances: first, if an adult is charged with an indictable-only offence, the case must be tried in the Crown Court; secondly, if it is an either-way offence and the magistrates declined jurisdiction or, the magistrates having accepted jurisdiction, the accused did not consent to summary jurisdiction. In these cases, the method whereby the case moves from the magistrates' court to the Crown Court is the committal for trial.

It is important to know what happened in the magistrates' court for purposes of costs if the defendant is convicted. For example, if an accused adult is charged with robbery (which is indictable-only) and is found guilty of theft by the jury or enters a plea of guilty to theft which is accepted in the Crown Court, it might be unjust to make him bear the full cost of bringing the case to the Crown Court because the option of dealing with the case summarily and without a trial was not open. Similarly, if the magistrates declined jurisdiction on a simple domestic burglary without any aggravating feature (not in accordance with the *Mode of Trial Guidelines* [1990] 1 WLR 1459) this factor can be used for mitigation—since being committed to the Crown Court is more of an ordeal—and to argue against paying the full costs after a guilty plea or finding of guilt.

A committal may involve a consideration of the evidence pursuant to s 6(1) of the Magistrates' Courts Act 1980, or it may proceed without consideration of the evidence (under s 6(2) of the Act). The latter is more common. A single lay magistrate, sitting as an examining justice, has jurisdiction to commit a case to the Crown Court; it does not matter whether the alleged offence occurred within the county in which the court sits (provided the English courts have jurisdiction). The hearing must be in open court unless the interests of justice demand otherwise. The defendant must be present unless it is not practicable because of his disorderly conduct or ill health; in the latter case, the defendant must be represented and have consented to proceedings in his absence.

(b) Joinder of defendants and charges at committal

On occasion, there may be more than one charge and/or more than one defendant. What happens at the committal is not binding on the Crown Court. Nevertheless, defendants should only be committed together if the allegations against them are sufficiently connected that it would be appropriate to draft a single indictment. Similarly, a series of charges against one defendant should be committed together only if the charges would appear on the same indictment in the Crown Court.

(c) Juveniles in the Crown Court

The question as to the joinder of defendants merits particular attention when those under the age of 18 are involved. Under s 24 of the Magistrates' Courts Act 1980, juveniles charged with offences other than homicide are to be tried summarily unless there are special circumstances. One of the circumstances is where the juvenile is charged jointly with an adult and it is in the interests of justice to commit both for trial—this involves weighing the general principle that jointly charged individuals ought to be tried (and, if convicted, sentenced) together against the principle that juveniles should be diverted from the adult criminal justice system where possible.

The statutory scheme of retaining summary trial for juveniles charged with indictable offences does not apply to offences of homicide, and a juvenile charged with such shall be committed to the Crown Court and tried on indictment. Homicide, which is not defined in the statute, clearly encompasses murder and manslaughter. It is not clear whether it also includes such offences as infanticide, attempts, or causing death by dangerous driving or careless driving whilst intoxicated. It is submitted that homicide should be strictly interpreted to cover only murder and manslaughter. The aim of the legislation, it is to be noted, is to keep juveniles out of the adult system wherever possible. Although the maximum sentence for infanticide is as for manslaughter, current sentencing practice makes it plain that therapeutic sentences are the norm. With respect to causing death by dangerous driving or by careless driving whilst intoxicated, the maximum sentence is ten years' detention and, by this benchmark, the offence is no more serious than other offences which are heard summarily in the youth court even though they would be indictable only if committed by an adult (such as robbery). This latter argument applies also to attempts.

This does not mean that juveniles charged with a serious offence involving death will necessarily be dealt with by the magistrates; it simply means that they will not automatically be sent to the Crown Court. The magistrates may decline jurisdiction in their discretion when the juvenile before them is aged over 14 and is charged with an offence which carries a maximum term of imprisonment of over 14 years in the case of an adult; or charged with causing death by dangerous driving or careless driving whilst under the influence of drugs or alcohol, or when the juvenile is aged 16 or 17 and is charged with indecent assault. Such a juvenile may be ordered to be detained for a period of up to the maximum prison term under s 53(2) of the Children and Young Persons Act 1933, but only by a Crown Court and only if convicted on indictment. Consequently, if the offence is such that the juvenile may have to be detained for longer than the maxima possible following a summary trial, the juvenile will have to be committed for trial.

(d) The standard of proof required for a committal

The test to be applied in deciding whether to commit is not entirely clear. Section 6(1) of the Magistrates' Courts Act 1980 requires committal if there is "sufficient evidence to put the accused on trial by jury". There is little assistance in case law to interpret what this means. The accepted practice is that this simply requires that there be a case to answer. This is commonly thought to be a low standard of proof. However, it should be recalled that the decision to commit is a judicial decision, that being compelled to stand trial is a considerable civil disability, and that the magistrates have an important function in ensuring that the prosecution have sufficient evidence to justify proceedings. It is worth noting in this connection that paragraph 4 of the *Code for Crown Prosecutors*, which is headed "The Evidential Sufficiency Criteria", indicates that the prosecution should not be continued unless there is a realistic prospect of conviction; the Code expressly disavows proceedings where there is only a bare *prima facie* case.

There is further confusion if one accepts that the test is whether there is a case to answer. This test in turn rests upon the *Practice Direction (Submission of No Case)* [1962] 1 WLR 227 (which expressly relates to summary trials) or the Court of Appeal's ruling in *Galbraith* [1981] 1 WLR 1039 (which expressly refers to the duties of the Crown Court judge at the end of the prosecution case in the trial on indictment).

It is unfortunate that it is not clear which one is appropriate, because the tests are different. Both would agree that the case ought to go no further if there is no evidence to prove an essential element of the *actus reus* or *mens rea*. In such a case, it would be appropriate for the defence to allow the prosecution evidence to be read before the submissions are made. When, however, the case turns on the reliability of a witness, the Practice Direction would allow examining justices to decline to commit where the evidence has been discredited by cross-examination or shown to be manifestly unreliable so that no reasonable tribunal could safely convict on it. The *Galbraith* test indicates that where the matter turns on matters such as reliability which are properly for the jury, the case should proceed.

It is submitted that the Practice Direction, with its wider discretion, is to be preferred because justices, unlike Crown Court judges, are empowered to decide on questions of fact as well as questions of law.

(e) Committal without consideration of the evidence

It has been possible to have a committal without consideration of the evidence only since the Criminal Justice Act of 1967; a committal where the evidence is considered is commonly called an "old-style" committal and must be held unless the following conditions are met:

(i) the evidence is in the form of written statements; each statement must be signed by its maker, and be in the appropriate form to comply with s 102 of the Magistrates' Courts Act 1980;

(ii) a copy of each statement must be served on the defence (one copy for each defendant);

(iii) each accused must be represented;

(iv) the accused's lawyer must not wish to make a submission that there is insufficient evidence for a committal. The defence consequently admits that there is a case to answer in the Crown Court.

Rule 6 of The Magistrates' Courts Rules 1981 sets out the procedure:

(i) the court is told that the evidence is in statements, copies of which have been given to the defence;

(ii) the charge on which it is proposed that the accused be committed is then written down (if it has not already been done) and read to the accused. This is important, particularly with respect to costs, in case the Crown later puts a lesser charge on the indictment or the accused is found guilty of a lesser charge;

(iii) the court asks whether there is any objection to any of the statements or a desire to make a submission that there is insufficient evidence;

(iv) the alibi notice is given unless it is unnecessary. This warns the defendant that evidence of an alibi or supporting witnesses may not be permitted at the Crown Court unless particulars are given then or within seven days to the prosecution. If the notice requirement is not complied with, the leave of the trial judge is required. If the alibi notice is not given, leave must be given; and

(v)   the accused is then committed for trial.

(f) "Old-style" committal—appropriate occasions

It is appropriate to request an old-style committal where there is a realistic possibility of the examining justices finding that there is no case to answer, or it is felt that there are tactical advantages to be gained by testing a witness before the trial or eliciting facts not revealed in the statement.

Special considerations apply to cases which turn on identification. The Attorney-General, in written answers to Parliamentary Questions, has indicated that the prosecution ought to call the identifying witness at the committal and give the defence a chance to cross-examine the witness, put forward alibi evidence and so on. This should not be done if both sides feel that it is not necessary and the court agrees.

The tactical reasons for requesting (or not) an old-style committal depend on the facts of each case. Typical arguments against are that it might allow prosecution witnesses to rehearse their evidence or become more at ease with giving evidence, or it might reveal to the prosecution weaknesses in their case which they might be able to shore up before the trial on indictment. Typical arguments in favour are that prosecution witnesses might give evidence which differs from their statements to the police and which might change again at the trial, opening up the witness to attack in the trial as to consistency and hence credibility; similarly, potential lines of cross-examination can be probed and assessed. It is by no means true to say that a paper committal should always be agreed because there is a case to answer.

(g) Procedure at an "old-style" committal

If the defence do not consent to a committal under s 6(2) of the Magistrates' Courts Act, it is for the prosecution to decide which witnesses they propose to rely on to furnish sufficient evidence to commit; there is no requirement that all the witnesses whom the prosecution propose to call at the trial be made available at the committal. Of course, the defence can indicate which statements they will not consent to being read out. In certain circumstances, it may be appropriate to have all statements read: this will apply where the defence wish to submit that the prosecution evidence, even when taken at its highest and not challenged, does not disclose sufficient evidence to commit.

The procedure at an old-style committal is governed by rule 7 of the Magistrates' Courts Rules 1981; the rule is supplemented by the court's inherent jurisdiction to control its own procedure when the rule is silent.

(i)   The prosecution may make an opening speech; this is desirable to indicate how the case is put.

(ii)   The prosecution then read such statements as meet the requirements of s 102 of the Magistrates' Courts Act 1980, including the consent of all the parties to the reading of the statement; or they call such witnesses as they feel necessary; oral evidence is taken down by the clerk of the court and signed by the witness, and is referred to as a deposition.

(iii)   The defence may submit that the case should not be committed; the court has a discretion to allow the prosecution to reply.

(iv)   If the submission succeeds, the defendant is discharged. This is not an acquittal: the prosecution may bring the case again, though it would be more usual to seek a voluntary bill of indictment (see later) if they believe the examining justices were wrong.

(v)   If the submission fails, the charge is read to the accused (having been put in writing if it is not already in writing).

(vi)   If appropriate, the alibi warning is given.

(vii)   The accused may give evidence and call witnesses. If the accused exercises this right, the defence advocate may make a submission before or after defence evidence is called; if the defendant gives evidence and calls witnesses, the court may allow submissions both before and after the defence evidence is given. If the defence advocate is allowed two submissions, the prosecutor must be allowed to be heard before the second defence submission.

(viii) The court then decides whether or not to commit.

(h) Ancillary matters

There are several ancillary matters dealt with at the committal.

(i) Publicity

It is unlawful to report the evidence at committal proceedings unless all the accused apply to have reporting restrictions lifted (because, for example, they hope that favourable witnesses to the incident may come forward, or potential alibi witnesses may recall being with the accused at the appropriate time). If there is more than one defendant and one objects to an application to lift reporting restrictions, then restrictions are lifted only if it is in the interests of justice to do so. This might be relevant at the Crown Court if an application is to be made to move to another trial venue because of publicity.

(ii) Witness orders

Examining justices are required under the Criminal Procedure (Attendance of Witnesses) Act 1965 to order that the witnesses attend at the Crown Court. The order will be conditional on further notice being given if the evidence in a witness's statement is unlikely to be required or unlikely to be disputed. The order is technically one for the court on the basis of representations by the parties: in practice, the order is based on the request of the defence. It is to be noted that if all witnesses are conditionally bound, the Crown Court listing office may list the case on the basis that a guilty plea is to be entered. Of course, there are circumstances where the facts of the case mean that it is not necessary to cross-examine prosecution witnesses. In such cases, the court listing should be informed that the case will require time for a trial even though all the prosecution's witnesses are conditionally bound. Most Crown Courts will, in any event, request information from the defendant's representatives as to the likely plea so as to assist the court in disposing of the case efficiently.

(iii) Venue

The committal must be to a named Crown Court. This is a decision to be made after account has been taken of the convenience of the defence and prosecution (including their witnesses), the expediting of the trial, and directions given by the Lord Chief Justice (s 7 of the Magistrates' Courts Act 1980).

The Practice Direction (Crown Court Business: Classification) of 2 November 1987 [1987] 1 WLR 1671 splits indictable offences into four categories. Classes 1 and 2 cover a number of specified serious offences (including murder, manslaughter and rape); class 4 offences are all either-way offences and certain indictable-only offences (including robbery, wounding or causing grievous bodily harm with intent, and conspiracy to commit offences other than those in classes 1 and 2); other indictable-only offences are in class 3.

Paragraph 2 of the Practice Direction requires magistrates' courts to commit offences in classes 1 to 3 to the most convenient location of the Crown Court where a High Court judge regularly sits; class 4 offences are to be sent to the most convenient location. In deciding the test of "most convenient" the magistrates take account of the factors in the statute and the locations specified by the presiding judge of the Crown Court circuit covering the petty sessional area of the particular magistrates' court. Applications for change of venue are usually dealt with in the Crown Court (see Chapter 3).

(iv) Bail or custody

The question of bail is considered at the committal. There is no automatic right to make a fresh bail application if the accused is in custody and has exhausted his or her automatic entitlement to fully argued applications: *Slough Justices, ex parte Duncan* (1982) 75 Cr App R 384. However, it will usually be possible to find a new consideration in consequence of the committal—the court will be in a better position to assess the seriousness of the allegation, the defence will be in a position to argue the strengths of the prosecution case, and so on.

(v) Legal aid

If the defendant is legally aided, unless the grant was a "through order" covering both the proceedings at the magistrates' court and any trial on indictment, application should be made to extend legal aid to cover the proceedings at the Crown Court. This will usually be done as a matter of course, subject to changes in means. Some magistrates feel that the fundamental right to jury trial does not merit state-assisted legal representation if the charge is trivial or simple; unfortunately, they do have a discretion not to extend legal aid, thus making it necessary to apply to the Crown Court for legal aid. Section 22 of the Legal Aid Act 1988, which lists the factors which are to be taken into account in determining whether it is in the interests of justice to grant legal aid, applies equally to proceedings in the Crown Court as in the magistrates' court. Consequently, if legal aid was granted in the lower court, there is no proper reason for its not being available in the Crown Court.

(i) Committal of summary offences

It is possible for an offence which is classified as summary-only to be committed to the Crown Court. There are two separate provisions. Under s 41 of the Criminal Justice Act 1988, if the magistrates commit an accused for trial on an either-way offence, a summary offence which arises from the same or connected circumstances may also be committed to the Crown Court. There is no provision for this to occur if the main offence is indictable-only. In addition, the summary offence must be punishable by imprisonment or involve obligatory or discretionary disqualification from driving. On committal the proceedings in the magistrates' court are treated as if they had been adjourned *sine die*.

The summary offences committed pursuant to s 41 will not be tried in the Crown Court. The Crown Court may deal with them if the accused enters a guilty plea; otherwise, after the trial on indictment of the either-way matter is completed, the information relating to the summary offence can be reinstated in the lower court.

Certain summary offences—common assault, taking a motor vehicle without authority, driving whilst disqualified, and criminal damage involving less than £2,000—may be included on an indictment and tried by the jury. This is allowed by s 40 of the Criminal Justice Act 1988, which requires that the summary offence be founded on the same facts or evidence as the indictable offence, or that it be part of a series of offences of the same or similar character. This section applies when the main offence is either-way or indictable-only.

If the summary offence is committed under s 41 when it could have been committed under s 40, the prosecution may include it in the indictment. Of course, the simple fact that the offence is committed under s 40 and appears on the draft indictment used at the committal stage does not mean that it will necessarily appear on the indictment; that is a matter for the person who drafts the indictment.

3. Notice of transfer—serious fraud cases

(a) Action by the prosecution and the magistrates' court

In serious fraud cases, the prosecution can bypass the need for a committal by giving a notice of transfer. This is governed by the Criminal Justice Act 1987 (ss 4 to 6) and regulations made under the Act (SI 1988 No 1691 and 1695). The prosecution give notice that there is sufficient evidence to justify a trial and that the fraud is so serious and complex that the management of the case should without delay be taken over by the Crown Court. The notice can be served at any time before the commencement of committal proceedings; obviously, it should be given as soon as possible after charge.

The notice should also specify the location of the Crown Court selected for the trial (which should be done in accordance with normal principles, regard being had to the convenience of the parties and witnesses, the expediting of the trial and any practice directions, including the Practice Note of 16 December 1992 [1993] 1 All ER 41, which specifies the Crown Court centres which have the appropriate facilities) and the charges. Appended to the notice should be a statement of the evidence: this requirement does not mandate service of witness statements, though it is to be hoped that such copies will always be served.

The notice of transfer is served on the magistrates' court which is dealing with the case (or, if the notice is served before the first appearance, which would usually deal with the case), the Crown Court selected and the accused. Once the notice has been served, the magistrates' jurisdiction ceases except with respect to legal aid (which may be granted and/or extended to cover the Crown Court proceedings) and bail. If the defendant is on bail, the notice may state that he is not required to attend at the magistrates' court; if it does not so state, the duty to attend remains and a further decision on bail will be taken at the hearing. A defendant in custody at the time the notice is issued will be ordered to be kept in custody until the first appearance at the Crown Court. This will be done the next time his case is before the magistrates.

The magistrates are also required to make witness orders under the Criminal Procedure (Attendance of Witnesses) Act 1965, though it is difficult to see how they should decide whether the order should be full or conditional. In practice, this is unlikely to cause any problem because there will be a pre-trial review in the Crown Court at which witness orders can be decided. The bill of indictment is to be preferred by the prosecution within 28 days of the notice of transfer.

(b) The defendant's right to challenge the case before trial

If a notice of transfer is issued, the defendant loses the right to test the evidence of the prosecution by way of an old-style committal. The decision to issue a notice of transfer may not be challenged in any court: s 4(3) of the Act. There is a limited substitute. It is possible to apply to the Crown Court to have the charges dismissed, in accordance with the Act and the regulations. The application can be oral or in writing, though it would be unusual for applications in cases of such importance to be completed without an oral hearing.

(c) The test for the judge on an application to dismiss

The test for the judge who is considering an application to have the charges dismissed is whether there is sufficient evidence for a jury properly to convict the accused. This is similar to the *Galbraith* test for whether or not there is a case to answer (see Chapter 6). Thus, when making his decision on the application, there is no mandate for a judge to take account of witness credibility or other matters which are generally for the jury. It is often said that lay juries are not able properly to follow complicated fraud trials. Since that has not been proved, it would not be right to use this allegation as a ground for allowing a judge to intervene in the jury's province.

(d) The procedure for an application to dismiss

There are standard forms for the various applications which may be made in the course of determination of an application to dismiss.

(i) Notice of intention to make an application

A written notice of intention to apply to have the case dismissed must be served on the appropriate officer of the Crown Court to which the case has been transferred, and the prosecution and any co-accused. This should be done within 28 days of the notice of transfer, though this can be extended by the court on written application; the application to extend time should give grounds, and the decision of the judge will give reasons. The application to extend time should be served by the applicant on the prosecution and co-accused. There is no express provision for allowing the prosecution and co-accused to make submissions on whether time should be extended; however, it should be permissible in accordance with the court's power to regulate its own procedures when statutes and regulations are silent.

It is possible for the application to be in writing. Whether or not the application is oral or written, the applicant shall furnish any statements or documents relied upon; this is to be served on the prosecution and any co-accused.

(ii) Defence request for oral application or to present oral evidence

If the defendant wishes that an oral application for dismissal be made, the notice of application should so indicate. If the applicant wishes oral evidence to be given, the application should seek the leave of the court on the application form. Oral evidence may not be given without the leave of the court; the judge's decision to grant or not grant leave shall be given to all parties. The judge may order that oral evidence be given even if leave is not requested.

(iii) Prosecution request for oral hearing

If the accused is content with a written application, the prosecution can nevertheless apply for an oral hearing; this should be done within seven days of receipt of the application, and should state the grounds. This time limit can be extended on application with grounds. The judge's decision on the prosecution application is to be in writing and served on all parties.

(iv) Prosecution request to present oral evidence

If the accused requests an oral hearing, the prosecution may apply to present oral evidence; this should be done within seven days of receipt of the notice of intention to make an oral application. The names of the proposed witnesses and the grounds for calling them should be stated; the time limit can be extended by the court. Again, the judge's decision on the prosecution application is to be in writing and served on all parties. However, the rules also grant the judge the power to give leave to call oral evidence even if the above procedure has not been followed. There is no provision for the accused (or the co-accused) to respond to either of these prosecution applications. However, it would seem just that the Crown Court be able to invite such comments by virtue of its power to regulate its own proceedings.

There is no provision for the prosecution to apply first for an oral hearing and, on being granted that, to apply for leave to present oral evidence. It does not seem appropriate that the court should be prohibited from allowing the two applications if it is just in the particular circumstances of the case. However, given that the aim behind the changes in the preliminary stages of a major fraud trial was to reduce delay by preventing the defence from being able to insist on oral evidence being called, it will only be in exceptional circumstances that the prosecution will succeed in applying for leave to call oral evidence.

(v) Prosecution comments and evidence

The prosecution may serve on the court and all parties written comments or further evidence (statements or documents) in response to the notice of application (or written application). This should be done within 14 days of receipt of the material on which the accused relies, though the time limit may be extended.

(vi) Decision

The Crown Court judge's decision on an application to dismiss ought to be amenable to judicial review on the application of an interested party. If the defendant's application is successful, the prosecution are able to continue proceedings only if they obtain a voluntary bill of indictment from the High Court (s 6(5) of the Criminal Justice Act 1987).

4. Notice of transfer—young witnesses

(a) Offences covered

The notice of transfer system was extended by s 53 of the Criminal Justice Act 1991 to cover a vast range of violent and sexual offences. The offences covered are those in respect of which witnesses under the age of 14 may give evidence in the Crown Court through a live television link (under s 32 of the Criminal Justice Act 1988—see Chapter 3). Violent offences include any offence involving an assault or injury or threat of injury (and attempting, conspiring or participating in such an offence). Sexual offences include offences relating to indecent photographs of children under the Protection of Children Act 1978.

(b) Pre-conditions

A notice of transfer may issue if the following conditions are met:

(i)   a child is alleged to be a victim or witness and will be called at trial;

(ii) the Director of Public Prosecutions (whose functions are exercised by a Crown Prosecutor) is of the opinion that there is sufficient evidence to commit—which is somewhat otiose as the prosecution should not be continued unless the Crown Prosecutor is of the opinion that there is a realistic prospect of a conviction;

(iii) the transfer is necessary to avoid prejudice to the welfare of the child.

The decision of the Director of Public Prosecutions to issue a notice of transfer may not be challenged in any court.

(c) Definition of child

The definition of "child" varies:

(i)   if the offence is one of violence, a child is someone under the age of 14 at the time of the notice of transfer;

(ii) if the offence is a sexual offence (including indecent photographs of children under 16), a child is someone under 17;

(iii) if the child's evidence has been recorded on video tape under the provisions of s 32A of the Criminal Justice Act 1988 (as introduced by s 54 of the Criminal Justice Act 1991), and the child was under the age of 14 or 17 (as the case may be) when the video was made, a child is someone under the age of 15 or 18 respectively.

(d) Procedural provisions

The procedural provisions for use of the notice in the circumstances of this Act are contained in Schedule 6 to the Act. These provisions mirror those applicable to serious fraud cases, with the addition of special provisions relating to the reporting of the hearing of an application to dismiss the charges (para 6 of Schedule 6). The court to which the case is transferred must be one able to hear evidence through live television link facilities: the appropriate courts are listed in the Practice Direction of 31 July 1992 (1992) 95 Cr App R 354.

5. Voluntary bills of indictment

(a) Use of the procedure

A bill of indictment may be preferred by the direction or with the consent of a High Court judge, pursuant to s 2 of the Administration of Justice (Miscellaneous Provisions) Act 1933. *The Practice Direction (Crime: Voluntary Bills)* [1990] 1 WLR 1633 makes it plain that the procedure should be used only where the interests of justice require it: it should not be used instead of committal for trial for reasons of administrative convenience. However, the decision of the High Court judge to direct that a voluntary bill be preferred cannot be challenged in the Crown Court and will not be challenged by the Court of Appeal, provided that the judge acted within his jurisdiction. Similarly, the decision of a High Court judge is not amenable to judicial review.

(b) Application

The Indictment Rules of 1971, supplemented by the Practice Direction, require a signed application by the prosecutor or his solicitor, accompanied by the proposed bill of indictment; the latter requirement is met if the bill is available before the judge makes his decision.

The application states whether there have been any previous applications and/or any committal proceedings, and the result of the same. If there have not been any committal proceedings, the reason why the voluntary bill procedure is being used should be stated. If there have been committal proceedings which resulted in a committal, it should be stated why it is proposed to use a voluntary bill rather than relying on the committal (which will usually be because the magistrates declined to commit on all charges).

Witness statements and documentary exhibits should be appended to the application; if there has been a committal, the committal bundle and any additional statements should be used. There should also be a summary of the evidence or some other document which identifies the counts (if any) in the draft indictment on which the accused has been committed for trial, and identifies the place in the bundle of statements and exhibits which contains the evidence to every count on the draft indictment: the application should state that the evidence will be available at trial and to the best of the applicant's knowledge is substantially a true case. If there has been a committal, the application shall also contain a copy of the charges on which the examining justices committed the defendant and a copy of any charges on which they refused to commit.

(c) Affidavit

In the infrequent cases where the application is not by the Director of Public Prosecutions or a Crown Prosecutor, the application should be accompanied by an affidavit verifying that the statements are true to the best of the deponent's belief.

(d) Determination of application

The judge will determine the application in writing and usually without the presence of the applicant or witnesses, though he can require their attendance in chambers. The proposed defendant will not be present. In accordance with the decision in *Raymond* [1981] QB 910, it seems that the High Court judge may in exceptional cases invite written representations by the defendant as to whether the prosecution should be allowed to proceed by voluntary bill rather than committal. There is no authority to the effect that a defendant may make representations as to whether a case to answer is made out. This is rather anomalous since it effectively means that a decision of great importance about a person's life can be taken *ex parte*.

(e) Power of the Court of Appeal

It is worth noting that the Court of Appeal also has the power to order a defendant to stand trial on indictment if it quashes a conviction on appeal.

6. Committal for sentence

In certain circumstances, the magistrates' court which has found a defendant guilty or in front of which a guilty plea has been entered may send the defendant to the Crown Court for sentence. There are several statutory provisions under which the magistrates can act. Some of these powers relate to specific sentences.

(a) Breach of a Crown Court conditional discharge

If the defendant commits an offence within the period of a conditional discharge imposed by a Crown Court, the breach can only be dealt with by the Crown Court: Powers of Criminal Courts Act 1973, s 1B (as inserted by Part I of Schedule 1 to the Criminal Justice Act 1991).

(b) Breach of a Crown Court community sentence

Similarly, if someone given a community sentence imposed by a Crown Court breaches the order, the provisions of Schedule 2 to the Criminal Justice Act 1991 come into effect. Community sentences are probation orders, community service orders or curfew orders and, no doubt, also combination orders; though combination orders are not specifically mentioned in the schedule, they consist of a probation order and a community service order, and a person can be brought to court if they breach either order.

A person accused of breaching an order will be brought in front of the magistrates. If the magistrates are satisfied that an order has been breached without reasonable excuse, one option available is to commit the person to the Crown Court. A certificate signed by a magistrate certifying the failure to comply with the order is admissible in evidence before the Crown Court. If the relevant failure is admitted or proved to the satisfaction of the Crown Court, the Crown Court has a number of options open, including revocation of the order and resentencing the offender for the original offence.

It should be noted that, pursuant to paragraph 5 of Schedule 2, conviction of a further offence does not amount to a failure to comply with an order. However, there is power to revoke an order if to do so would be in the interests of justice in the light of the circumstances which have arisen since the order was made—which includes the circumstance of a further offence being committed. There is a specific provision allowing revocation of an order if a custodial sentence is subsequently imposed on an offender (see paragraphs 7 to 10 of Schedule 2). If the original order was imposed by a Crown Court, the offender may be committed by the magistrates to the Crown Court.

(c) Breach of a Crown Court suspended sentence

If the defendant is convicted by magistrates of an offence which could carry a sentence of imprisonment, and the offence occurred during the time that the defendant was subject to a suspended sentence of imprisonment imposed by a Crown Court, the magistrates have two options: s 24 of the Powers of Criminal Courts Act 1973. They can sentence for the new offence and notify the chief clerk of the Crown Court of the conviction. It is then for the Crown Court to decide whether to summons (or issue a warrant for the arrest of) the defendant to deal with the breach of the suspended sentence.

The other option is for the magistrates to commit the defendant to the Crown Court for sentence for the offence which is in breach of the suspended sentence; the Crown Court can deal with the breach and the fresh offence. The committal for breach of the suspended sentence will be under s 24 of the Powers of Criminal Courts Act 1973; the committal for sentence for the offence which breaches the suspended sentence will be under s 56 of the Criminal Justice Act 1967 (see below).

(d) Prisoner released before expiry of term

Under Part II of the Criminal Justice Act 1991, there is a duty to release prisoners after they have served a proportion of their sentence. (This is covered more fully in Chapter 7.) If a released prisoner commits an imprisonable offence during the period before he would have been released if he had served his full term, the court which sentences him may order a return to prison for any part of a period equivalent to the time between the date of the fresh offence and the end of his full term. A magistrates' court cannot order a return to prison for a period exceeding six months; but it may commit the person to the Crown Court for sentence, under s 40 of the Criminal Justice Act 1991.

(e) Power to commit in respect of a mentally unwell offender

One of the sentences available for an offender who is suffering from mental illness, mental impairment or a psychopathic disorder is a hospital order under s 37 of the Mental Health Act 1983; this power is available to magistrates, and places the offender in the same position as any person detained under the civil provisions of the Act. Section 41 of the Act allows the imposition of extra restrictions in respect of those convicted of an offence if such is necessary to protect the public from serious harm. Such restriction orders may be imposed only by a Crown Court. Consequently, s 43 of the Mental Health Act 1983 allows magistrates to commit an offender over the age of 14 to the Crown Court if they feel that a restriction order ought to be considered.

(f) General power to commit

Where the magistrates have accepted jurisdiction over an either-way offence, and there is then a conviction or plea of guilty, the defendant may be committed for sentence by the Crown Court if the offence or its combination with associated offences means that it merits punishment in excess of the powers of the magistrates. A similar power exists if the protection of the public from an offender aged at least 21 convicted of a violent or sexual offence requires the imposition of a sentence greater than that which the magistrates can impose. Both powers are contained in s 38 of the Magistrates' Courts Act 1980 (as amended by s 25 of the Criminal Justice Act 1991 and s 66 of the Criminal Justice Act 1993).

(g) Committal for sentence of youths

The youth court may commit for sentence a defendant aged 15 or over if it feels that the defendant who has been convicted of an either-way or indictable-only offence merits a greater term of detention than that which it can order. This power is of limited significance because a Crown Court can impose only 12 months' detention, whereas the youth court can impose up to 6 months' detention for one indictable offence and a total of 12 months' detention (by way of two consecutive terms of 6 months) if there are two or more offences in front of the court which carry custodial sentences. The Crown Court's power to order detention under s 53 of the Children and Young Persons Act 1933 can only be exercised following trial on indictment.

(h) Supplementary power to commit

If an offender is committed under any of the above powers, any other offence which is in front of the magistrates for sentence may also be committed under s 56 of the Criminal Justice Act 1967. This is obviously sensible since it allows the offender to be sentenced for all outstanding matters on one occasion.

PART II:

THE CROWN COURT AS AN APPELLATE TRIBUNAL

Chapter 2

Appeals to the Crown Court from the magistrates' court

1. Introduction

The Crown Court also has jurisdiction to hear appeals from the magistrates' court in criminal and various civil matters dealing with licences granted by the justices.

A person who wishes to challenge a decision of a magistrates' court may take several possible courses of action, depending on the circumstances. Broadly speaking, the defendant may appeal to the Crown Court against a conviction or a sentence, a refusal to grant bail, or a decision relating to custody time limits. If the conviction by the magistrates was wrong in law or in excess of jurisdiction, then an appeal to the High Court by way of case stated is possible; the High Court also has jurisdiction over bail matters. In addition, a person with *locus standi* may apply for judicial review of the actions of a magistrates' court if proper procedures have not been followed or jurisdiction has been exceeded. In respect of the latter, there is an overlap with the use of the case stated method of appeal.

The prosecution may appeal to the High Court by way of case stated if an acquittal was wrong in law, and may make use of judicial review. They may also apply to the Crown Court or the High Court with respect to bail.

In licensing matters, any person aggrieved by a decision of the licensing justices may appeal to the Crown Court.

2. Appeal to the Crown Court against conviction or sentence

(a) Right of appeal

A person convicted by the magistrates may appeal against that finding to the Crown Court (Magistrates' Courts Act 1980, s 108). The provisions of s 13 of the Powers of Criminal Courts Act 1973, the effect of which is that a finding of guilt which has led to an order of probation or an absolute or conditional discharge shall not rank as a conviction, do not prevent an appeal against conviction where the lower court has dealt with the person convicted in that manner.

A person may also appeal against sentence; this applies whether or not there is also an appeal against conviction.

The rights to appeal apply whether the offence is either-way or summary-only. Youth court findings of guilt and sentences may also be appealed to the Crown Court.

(b) Limited right of appeal against conviction following guilty plea

The fact that a defendant pleaded guilty in the magistrates' court is not a bar to an appeal against conviction, but the right of appeal is limited to exceptional circumstances. The right to appeal against sentence is not limited following a guilty plea.

(i) Equivocal pleas

If the plea of guilty was equivocal when made (being followed, before sentencing, by an explanation which amounts to a defence), the conviction can be set aside by the Crown Court and the case remitted to the magistrates' court for hearing as a not guilty plea.

(ii) Plea under duress

Similarly, if it transpires that the plea was entered under duress, the case can be remitted for hearing: *Huntingdon Crown Court, ex parte Jordan* [1981] QB 857.

(iii) Crown Court finding binds magistrates

The Crown Court's decision that the plea was equivocal or made under duress is binding on the lower court, which cannot refuse to hear the case on the basis that the accused has already pleaded guilty: *Plymouth Justices, ex parte Hart* [1986] QB 950.

(c) Notice of appeal to the Crown Court in criminal matters

Part III of the Crown Court Rules 1982 governs the procedure on appeals in criminal matters. A written notice must be given to the clerk of the magistrates and the prosecutor, and also to the appropriate officer of the Crown Court (usually the chief clerk of the Crown Court to which cases are normally committed for trial or sentence). There is no prescribed form set out in the rules, though most magistrates' courts will have an accepted standard form. The rules simply state that the notice shall be in writing and shall indicate whether the appeal is against conviction, sentence or both.

(d) Stating the grounds of appeal

There is no requirement to state the grounds of appeal. Whether the appellant should or should not state the grounds depends on the facts of every case. To do so might save time in certain cases, thereby reducing costs; or it might encourage the prosecution not to oppose the appeal if the grounds are compelling. The latter situation often applies in the case of a defendant who was convicted in his absence and who can show that he was elsewhere at the time of the incident in respect of which he has been convicted. In other cases, stating the grounds of appeal might allow the prosecution to prepare their case more fully, which might be to the detriment of the appellant.

(e) Time limits for filing the notice of appeal

The notice is to be served (personally or by post) within 21 days of the decision against which there is an appeal. If the case is adjourned for reports prior to sentencing, the 21 days run from the date of sentence rather than the date of conviction, even if the appeal is against conviction only. If the court defers sentence, the 21-day time limit for the appeal against conviction is calculated from the date of deferment rather than from the date of the ultimate sentence. Naturally, the limit on the time for appealing against sentence runs from the date of the ultimate sentence. There can be no appeal against the decision to defer sentence, because that requires the consent of the person subject to the deferment.

(f) Extending the time limit

It is possible to apply to the Crown Court to extend the 21-day time limit. The application can be made after the 21 days have expired; it must be in writing and should be sent to the appropriate officer of the Crown Court. The grounds for the application must be given. Since the merits of the appeal are relevant, the grounds of appeal should be given; this is particularly so when it is possible to adduce evidence before the Crown Court which was not available during the trial in the magistrates' court.

The judge who makes the decision may allow the applicant to make oral representations. There is no set procedure for this, nor any guidance in case law. The reasons for refusing an application need not be given—and there is no procedure for appealing against the refusal to extend time. An applicant who is aggrieved by a refusal might be able to challenge the decision by way of judicial review. If the application is granted, the court notifies the appellant and the clerk to the magistrates.

(g) Appealing against conviction before the sentence is imposed

It is not clear whether, if sentencing is adjourned, one can appeal against the conviction before the sentence is imposed. The argument against this is that the notice of appeal must state whether it is against conviction or sentence or both, which is not possible until after sentence has been imposed. However, the rules contemplate the possibility of an appeal against conviction when there has not yet been a sentence, namely when sentence is deferred. The Magistrates' Courts Act 1980 clearly allows someone to appeal against conviction without appealing against sentence. The Crown Court Rules set out a clear time limit for an appeal. It is difficult to see how this can be read as a mandatory provision preventing appeal until after sentence has been handed down. The rule in the Crown Court is that the time limit with respect to any appeal against conviction starts on the day of conviction, not the date of sentence; this again indicates that the different rule applicable to the magistrates' court is not mandatory. If a defendant is remanded in custody before the sentence is imposed, it is important that he is able to appeal against the conviction immediately.

(h) Listing of the appeal

Once the notice of appeal is received by the Crown Court, the court gives notice of the time and place of the hearing to the appellant, other parties to the appeal and the clerk to the magistrates.

(i) Preparation of the appeal

The hearing in the Crown Court is a hearing *de novo*; the court is not seeking to discover whether the magistrates made an appealable mistake, but is asked to consider the matter afresh on the basis of whatever evidence is produced and representations made to it. The Crown Court will not necessarily know what occurred in the magistrates' court.

Consequently, the preparation of the case involves doing whatever would be done to prepare the case the first time around. Of course, if it became apparent that the case was lost in the magistrates' court because a piece of evidence was missing, steps can be taken to locate that evidence and have it available for the appeal hearing.

It may be appropriate to obtain the notes of the court clerk as to what happened in the court below. These must be supplied to a defendant who is in receipt of legal aid, pursuant to regulation 42 of the Legal Aid in Criminal and Care Proceedings (General) Regulations 1989 (SI 1989 No 344). Where an appellant who is not receiving legal aid requests a copy of the notes, his request is to be viewed sympathetically: *R v Clerk to Highbury Corner Justices, ex p Hussain* [1986] 1 WLR 1266. In any event, a clerk may be summonsed to attend at the Crown Court and to produce the notes of evidence pursuant to s 2 of the Criminal Procedure (Attendance of Witnesses) Act 1965.

(j) Bail pending appeal

Under s 113 of the Magistrates' Courts Act 1980, a magistrates' court may grant bail to someone who has been convicted and given a custodial sentence when that person has filed a notice of appeal to the

Crown Court or requested that the magistrates state a case for the opinion of the High Court (see below). It may be important to file a notice of appeal very quickly after conviction in order to make a bail application.

Section 81 of the Supreme Court Act 1981 provides that the Crown Court has jurisdiction to grant bail to a person appealing against sentence or conviction and sentence. Since any custodial sentence handed down by a magistrates' court is likely to be comparatively short (and in reality will be half the sentence announced, given the duty of the Home Secretary to release short-term prisoners after one-half of their sentence), there is a risk that an appellant will have served the entirety of his sentence before the appeal is heard: if the appellant is in custody until such time as the appeal is heard, there is an obvious risk of injustice if the appeal is successful. A way of avoiding this is to release the appellant on bail until such time as the appeal can be heard.

3. Hearing of appeals in criminal cases

(a) Constitution of the court

The court consists of a professional judge (from High Court judge down to assistant recorder) and between two and four justices of the peace who were not connected with the case in the court below. The usual number is two. If the appeal is from the youth court, the justices must be justices who sit in youth courts. Under rule 4 of the Crown Court Rules 1982, the Crown Court may sit with one justice (or one youth court justice in an appropriate case) if the judge finds that the court cannot be properly constituted without unreasonable delay. The court acts by majority, though in practice there will be deference to the professional judge on matters of law.

(b) Abandoning appeal

An appeal may be abandoned with the leave of the Crown Court or by giving written notice at least three working days before the date set for the hearing; notice of abandonment is to be given to those who have received the notice of appeal.

(c) Appeals against sentence

The procedure is as if the appellant had entered a guilty plea to a matter committed to the Crown Court. The advocate for the prosecution (the respondent) will introduce the matter and outline the basis of the allegation against the appellant, introduce antecedents and previous convictions to the extent that they are relevant (and point out matters of mitigation if the appellant is unrepresented). Then the appellant (or his advocate) will make a speech in mitigation, outlining the facts upon which the plea was based (if it was a guilty plea in the lower court) or commenting on the evidence if the case was contested in front of the magistrates and pressing such other matters as are thought appropriate in mitigation. If the factual basis of the criminality is in question, the principles in *Newton* (1982) 4 Cr App R (S) 388 apply (see below).

It should be noted that, pursuant to s 3 of the Criminal Justice Act 1991, if an offender was given a custodial or community sentence without the court considering a pre-sentence report, it is necessary for the Crown Court on appeal to obtain such a report (see Chapter 7). There is a clear argument for bail pending appeal in such a circumstance. Since the appeal cannot be heard until such time as there is a pre-sentence report, and such a report will usually take at least three weeks to prepare, this should be a sufficient argument in favour of bail pending appeal.

(d) Appeals against conviction and sentence

(i) General

When the appeal is against conviction and sentence, the case proceeds as if it were a contested summary trial. Counsel for the prosecution (the respondent) will make an opening speech and call the evidence; thereafter, the defence may make a submission of no case to answer and, if appropriate, then call evidence and make a closing speech.

The principles with respect to adjournments, summonses for witnesses, the right of the appellant to be present and so on apply equally to appeals as to trials on indictment. Some matters are necessarily different because of the constitution of the court. Since the tribunal of fact is comprised of the same personnel as the tribunal of law, there is no procedure equivalent to the judge determining matters of law in the absence of the jury (see Chapter 6).

(ii) Admissibility of evidence

(a) General

It is a matter for the court as to how disputes concerning the admissibility of evidence are resolved, though it should always be mindful of what is fair to the appellant and should hear representations as to the appropriate procedure. There is no set rule for when the court will rule on the question of admissibility, except perhaps with respect to confessions.

In other circumstances—submissions under s 78 of the Police and Criminal Evidence Act 1984 or at common law—the court may hear all the evidence, including that which is disputed, and ask the advocates to make submissions as to the disputed evidence at the end of the prosecution case, or may decide the issue at the outset. The issue of admissibility should usually be decided before the accused's case is heard so that the appellant knows the case he faces. Indeed, it will usually be fairer to the accused to have the issue of admissibility decided at the outset, so that the extent of necessary cross-examination is known to the appellant. The only reason for not having a separate trial within a trial is that if the evidence is ruled admissible in a *voir dire* it will have to be heard again. This, however, is a matter of administrative convenience and consequently of limited force compared with what is fair to the appellant. In any event, disputed evidence which is ruled admissible can no doubt be heard expeditiously the second time around.

(b) Confessions

Section 76(2) of the Police and Criminal Evidence Act 1984 provides:

> "If, in any proceedings where the prosecution *proposes* to give in evidence a confession made by an accused person, it is represented to the court that the confession was or may have been obtained (a) by oppression of the person who made it; or (b) in consequence of anything said or done which was likely, in the circumstances existing at the time, to render unreliable any confession which might be made by him in consequence thereof, the court *shall not* allow the confession to be given in evidence"

except to the extent that the prosecution prove that there was no oppression or unreliability (author's italics). This seems to suggest that the confession shall not be admitted in evidence until after the *voir dire* has been held. However, the Divisional Court has decided in *Liverpool Juvenile Court, ex p R* [1988] 1 QB 1 that in a summary trial the defendant may raise an attack on a confession at any stage; it is only if the defence raise the question of the admissibility of the confession before the close of the prosecution case that the trial within the trial must be held. Of course, the defence should raise the question, by way of cross-examination, before the end of the prosecution case. It is only if defence evidence unexpectedly raises doubts as to the admissibility of the confession that the question will arise of there having been no *voir dire* before the prosecution evidence is given.

(e) Failure of the appellant to attend

Under s 122 of the Magistrates' Courts Act 1980, an absent party represented by a legal representative is deemed to be present unless a statute or a condition of any recognizance expressly requires attendance. A similar rule applies to the Crown Court: *R v Croydon Crown Court, ex p Clair* (1986) 83 Cr App R 202.

(f) The role of the prosecution in meritorious appeals

In respect of sentence, the prosecution takes no view, and must remain objective: it will assist the court with information requested, but no more. In case of appeals against conviction, there is a view that the prosecution is under a duty to argue that the decision of the court

31

below in convicting the appellant was the correct decision. This view is not correct.

The prosecution remains under a duty at all times to be fair to the accused person. If this means that, on consideration of the evidence, the prosecution takes the view that the court below was mistaken, it should be prepared to offer no opposition to the appeal. For example, if a dock identification occurred in the magistrates' court which the advocate for the prosecution would not allow to occur at the Crown Court, or if other evidence was admitted in the court below which the Crown now accepts was not admissible, and if the absence of that evidence means that the case against the appellant will not properly survive a submission of no case to answer, the prosecution should offer no response to the appeal. There is no merit in asking the Crown Court to make the same mistake as the magistrates' court.

(g) Powers of the Crown Court on appeal in criminal matters

Section 48 of the Supreme Court Act 1981 gives the Crown Court the power to "confirm, reverse or vary any part of the decision appealed against ... or remit the matter". The power to remit is appropriate when the Crown Court determines that a plea of guilty was equivocal. It is held that an appeal against conviction necessarily involves an appeal against sentence as well, and the power to vary any part of the decision of the magistrates' court includes the power to increase sentence. Some judges will allow the appeal against sentence to be withdrawn upon the failure of the appellant to overturn the conviction: however, sentence is technically at large, subject to the requirement that it does not exceed the maximum that could have been imposed by the magistrates.

The Crown Court may also deal with the question of costs as if the case had been a trial on indictment. If the appellant loses, he may be ordered to pay the costs incurred by the prosecution. A successful appellant may be awarded costs from central funds (to the extent that legal aid does not cover the matter).

4. Appeal to the Crown Court in civil matters

(a) Liquor licensing

The Crown Court is also the venue for appeals on licensing matters. Section 21 of the Licensing Act 1964 provides for appeals against decisions made by the licensing justices, including the grant or refusal to grant a new licence for the sale of liquor, the refusal to renew or transfer an existing licence, or decisions relating to conditions of an on-licence. The right to appeal is given to a "person aggrieved". When the appeal is against a refusal to grant a licence, this will primarily be the applicant; it will also include an owner or mortgagee of licensed premises. A person aggrieved by the decision to grant a new licence must have appeared before the licensing justices as an objector.

(b) Procedure for appealing

The procedure for appeal is set out in s 22 of the Licensing Act 1964, as supplemented by the Crown Court Rules. It is similar to that for criminal cases. The applicant must give notice within 21 days to the clerk to the licensing justices; under the Crown Court Rules this time limit may be extended by the Crown Court, as with criminal matters. In contrast to the procedure relating to criminal cases, there is a requirement that written grounds of appeal be given.

The notice is to be given to the clerk to the magistrates, who is responsible for sending the notice to the appropriate officer of the Crown Court (usually the chief clerk); the officer of the Crown Court, in turn, is responsible for listing the case for hearing. If the appeal is against the grant of a licence, the notice shall be given to the person granted the licence. In addition, under the Crown Court Rules, any other party to the appeal shall be served with the notice; this will include an objector to the grant of a licence when the appeal is against the refusal to grant a licence. The clerk to the justices is obliged to record the names and addresses of objectors and, in the event of an appeal, forward the names to the chief clerk of the Crown Court along with the notice of appeal.

(c) Special hours certificates

There are separate statutory provisions relating to special hours certificates, under ss 76 ff of the Licensing Act 1964. The appeal provisions are set out in s 81B of the Act and in the Crown Court Rules. The procedure is essentially the same. However, the definition of a "person aggrieved" in the case of a decision not to revoke a special hours certificate or not to impose a condition on a certificate is restricted to the chief officer of police.

(d) Other instances

There are various other instances of appellate jurisdiction. For example, s 50 of the Licensing Act 1964 provides for an appeal against the refusal of a magistrates' court to register premises as a club (or renew an existing registration) or the decision to revoke a registration, or against a decision about conditions relating to the sale of liquor in a club. Where the club appeals, objectors to the granting of the certificate shall be parties to the appeal.

Magistrates are also responsible for the granting of licences for betting offices and bookmakers. The refusal to grant or renew such a licence may be appealed to the Crown Court, as may the decision of magistrates to cancel a bookmaker's permit on the application of the police. This right of appeal is granted by Schedule 1 to the Betting, Gaming and Lotteries Act 1963. There is a similar right under Schedule 2 to the Act relating to the refusal by a district council to register a pools promoter, or a decision to revoke a registration; and, under

Schedule 3, where a district council revokes a licence for betting on racetracks.

There are also rights of appeal relating to the licensing of premises for the public performance of plays (Theatres Act 1968), licences under the Gaming Act 1968, the Lotteries and Amusements Act 1976, the Local Government (Miscellaneous Provisions) Act 1982 (which relates to public entertainments, sex shops and cinemas) and the Cinemas Act 1985. In all these cases, the procedure is similar to that for alcohol licences; the main difference from criminal cases is the requirement that written grounds of appeal be given.

(e) Rehearing

Appeals are, according to long-standing practice, by way of a rehearing. The Crown Court Rules require that in liquor licensing and betting licensing cases, there shall be a judge and four justices who are members of a licensing committee; two of the justices shall be justices for the petty sessional area in which the premises are located.

5. Challenging the decision of the Crown Court in an appeal

There are two ways in which the decision of the Crown Court can be challenged. The court's conclusions on questions of law and jurisdiction can be questioned by way of "case stated" to the Divisional Court; an application for judicial review by the High Court can also be made. Both procedures are open to any party to the appeal.

(a) Application to state a case

The procedure for stating a case is contained in rule 26 of the Crown Court Rules 1982. A written application must be made to the correct officer of the court (usually the chief clerk) within 21 days, and a copy served on all parties who appeared in the Crown Court. The court may extend this and all other time limits mentioned in the rules. The grounds for the application must be given. The application will be forwarded to the judge who presided over the Crown Court hearing.

(b) Refusal to state a case

The judge may refuse to state a case if the application is frivolous; the applicant may ask for the reasons for refusal to be stated, allowing for an application for judicial review and an order of mandamus to require the judge to state a case.

(c) Draft statement

If the judge decides to state a case, a written notice to that effect will be served on the applicant who must then draft a case within 21 days of receipt of the notice and send it to the court and all the parties. The statement of the case should include the facts, the submissions made (including authorities referred to), the decision of the court, and the question for the High Court to answer.

(d) Further action

The other parties have 21 days from receipt of the draft case to:

(a) indicate that they will not participate further, or

(b) agree with the draft presented by the applicant, or

(c) present an alternative case.

The judge will then state a case. There is no specific provision for the amendment of the statement of the case by the judge, although the High Court may in the course of hearing the appeal by way of case stated remit the case for it to be restated in accordance with the High Court's decision.

The above procedure may be modified by the judge, who may also require the applicant to provide a recognizance or sureties that the application will be prosecuted expeditiously.

(e) Action in the High Court

Pursuant to rule 1 of Order 56 of the Rules of the Supreme Court, the applicant shall enter the matter for hearing within ten days of receipt of the statement of the case by the judge. The case and a copy of the judgment or decision of the Crown Court must be lodged in the Crown Office at the High Court, failing which the Crown Court may proceed as if no case had been stated. Failure to meet the time limits must be explained to the satisfaction of the Divisional Court; an application to extend the time limit for entry of the appeal must be served on the respondent to the appeal.

(f) Judicial review

Section 29(3) of the Supreme Court Act 1981 provides:

> "In relation to the jurisdiction of the Crown Court, other than its jurisdiction in matters relating to trial on indictment, the High Court shall have all such jurisdiction to make orders of mandamus, prohibition or certiorari as the High Court possesses in relation to the jurisdiction of an inferior court".

Since the decision of the Crown Court on appeal from the magistrates' court is not part of its jurisdiction on indictment, its decisions in the course of an appeal are amenable to judicial review.

The procedure of judicial review is governed by Order 53 of the Rules of the Supreme Court. Essentially, the High Court will intervene if the Crown Court has acted in excess of its jurisdiction, if its decision reveals an error of law on the face of the record (which can include the reasons given for the decision), or if the decision of the Crown Court is so unreasonable as to be irrational or a decision that no reasonable court would make. There is a time limit of three months.

Judicial review would cover the actual decision on the appeal, the refusal to state a case after the appeal, decisions in relation to time limits on appeals and so on.

(g) Appeals directly from the magistrates to the High Court

If the substance of the appeal from the magistrates' court is a point of law, the appeal can be taken either directly to the High Court by way of case stated or to the Crown Court for rehearing; if one appeals to the Crown Court and the conviction is confirmed, it is possible thereafter to appeal the decision of the Crown Court by way of the case stated procedure. Taking the matter to the Crown Court on a point of law therefore allows "two bites of the cherry". If, however, the appellant received an acceptable sentence in the magistrates' court, and there is a risk that the Crown Court might increase the sentence to the disadvantage of the appellant, then that might outweigh the advantage of having two bites. If the appeal is against sentence only, the usual course will be an appeal to the Crown Court, since the basis of the appeal will rarely be a point of law; see *Tucker* v *DPP* [1992] 4 All ER 901.

6. Appeals against refusal to grant bail

(a) Introduction

If in the course of proceedings relating to summary-only offences or the preliminary stages of cases which will be dealt with on indictment in the Crown Court, the magistrates remand the defendant in custody, there are two avenues of appeal. The Crown Court or the High Court may grant bail. The High Court also has jurisdiction to vary the conditions of someone remanded on conditional bail by magistrates. The question of bail might also arise if a defendant is sentenced to a term of immediate imprisonment and wishes to appeal against that sentence.

(b) Defendant may not wish bail

An unconvicted defendant may not wish to be granted bail. Unconvicted prisoners are entitled to various privileges not accorded to those who have entered pleas of guilty. Consequently, if the defendant is eventually to plead guilty and the likely outcome is immediate custody, it might be preferable not to have bail. It may also be the case that a defendant on a case which merits a custodial sentence is more likely to receive a suspended sentence of imprisonment or a community order if he has had a "taste of custody". This is particularly so if the defendant is under 21 and therefore cannot receive a suspended sentence.

(c) Time for appeal

If bail is refused by the magistrates and the defendant wishes to be released on bail, an application to the Crown Court can be made after the first application in the lower court; however, because of the relatively short time before the second appearance in the magistrates' court (within eight days), it is usual to use the defendant's right under the Bail Act 1976 (as amended) to make two applications in the lower court and then apply to the Crown Court.

(d) Procedure

A bail application to the Crown Court must comply with rule 19 of the Crown Court Rules 1982. At least 24 hours' written notice must be given to the prosecution and the court. Schedule 4 to the rules contains the appropriate form for the application: details of previous applications must be given, as must the grounds of the application; objections previously raised must be answered and details of any proposed sureties must be given. The prosecution then indicates to the court and the applicant whether or not it opposes the application; if it does oppose the application, it either sends to the court and the applicant written objections to bail or it indicates that it intends to be represented at the hearing. The latter course of action is the most usual.

The defendant will not be present at the application unless leave is given by the court; this will only happen in most unusual circumstances. The hearing will be in chambers: rule 27 of the Crown Court Rules. Whether this is in the judge's private room or in the courtroom (with a notice on the outside preventing entry) depends on the practice of the individual judge. Being in chambers the procedure is not set and is dependent on the judge. The advocates should therefore be able and willing to present a fully argued bail application (or outline fully the objections to bail), or to answer the judge's specific questions.

(e) Prosecution applications

It is worth noting that the prosecution may apply to the court to vary conditions of bail, or add conditions to unconditional bail, pursuant to s 3(8) of the Bail Act. The application must be made to the court which has granted unconditional bail or bail with conditions, although the application may be made to the Crown Court in respect of bail imposed by the magistrates when they commit the defendant to the Crown Court.

If an application is made to the Crown Court, 24 hours' notice in writing is served on the court and the defendant; the defendant then responds in much the same way as the prosecution in an appeal by a defendant. Naturally, the defendant is entitled to be present at the hearing of the application by the prosecution.

7. Appeals in custody time limit cases

(a) Time limits

Appeals lie to the Crown Court in respect of the decision of a magistrates' court to allow an extension of the custody time limits; the prosecution may appeal against a refusal to extend the limits. The basic rule in the Prosecution of Offences (Custody Time Limits) Regulations 1987 (SI 1987 No 299)—as amended—is that an accused may be retained in custody for 70 days between first appearance and the commencement of committal proceedings; if an either-way offence is to be tried summarily, the maximum time before the trial begins is 56 days. The trial begins when the court commences to hear evidence.

(b) Grounds for extension

Under s 22(3) of the Prosecution of Offences Act 1985 the magistrates' court may extend the time limit (and further extend it) if there is "good and sufficient cause" and the "the prosecution has acted with all due expedition". This can be done at any time before the expiry of a time limit: there is no provision for extension of the time limit after it has expired. Under s 22(7) and (8) of the same Act, the prosecution and defence may appeal to the Crown Court against the decision of the magistrates' court.

(c) Procedure

Rule 27A of the Crown Court Rules governs the procedure on appeal. Essentially, the procedure is the same as for appeals in bail decisions: a written notice is to be served on the clerk to the magistrates, the Crown Court, and the prosecutor or accused, as appropriate. The appropriate officer in the Crown Court will enter the appeal and give notice to the appellant, prosecutor and clerk to the magistrates of the time and place of the hearing.

Pursuant to rule 27 of the Crown Court Rules 1982, applications relating to the custody time limits are heard in chambers rather than open court.

8. Appeals in respect of bind-overs

There is a specific statute allowing an appeal against a decision to bind over an individual—whether a defendant or other person in front of the court, for example a witness—to be of good behaviour: the Magistrates' Courts (Appeal from Binding Over Orders) Act 1956. Rule 6 of the Crown Court Rules—which covers appeals against conviction and sentence—is expressed to apply to "every appeal ... under any enactment" and so governs the procedure in respect of bind-over appeals.

9. Legal aid

Legal aid for an application to the High Court is dealt with under the civil legal aid scheme, and is treated as if it was an ordinary civil case. If the appeal is to the Crown Court, legal aid is dealt with under the criminal scheme. Appeals in bail decisions are covered under the grant of aid for proceedings in the magistrates' court: s 19(2) of the Legal Aid Act 1988. In respect of appeals against conviction or sentence, if criminal legal aid has been granted in the magistrates' court, it is most likely that it will be granted in the Crown Court. Section 22 of the Legal Aid Act 1988, which sets out the factors to be taken into account in deciding whether it is in the interests of justice to grant legal aid, applies equally to trial in either the magistrates' court or the Crown Court or on appeal to the Crown Court.

PART III:
TRIAL ON INDICTMENT

Chapter 3

Pre-trial matters

1. Introduction

When a case is committed to the Crown Court, the defendant will be bailed to attend the Crown Court at a date and time to be notified to the parties by the Crown Court, or remanded in custody to be produced at the Crown Court at the appropriate date. The bill of indictment will be prepared, presented and signed, and preparations will be made for the trial or the entering of the plea of guilty. Various matters have to be dealt with before this can happen.

2. Venue of trial and classification of offences

(a) Administrative transfer from committal venue

Examining justices commit a case to a particular location of the Crown Court; a notice of transfer will also specify a location. There are, however, provisions for transfer of a case, pursuant to s 76(1) of the Supreme Court Act 1981. An official of the court—usually the listing officer—may give the appropriate direction. This decision is an administrative decision based usually on the workload of the various locations of the Crown Court.

An important factor in this decision is the type of offence charged: offences are split into four categories, some of which require a more senior judge. The listing officer has to place the case in front of an appropriate judge. If the case is an appeal from the magistrates' court, the availability of magistrates will also be taken into account.

(b) Classes of judge

The judges who sit in the Crown Court are either High Court judges, circuit judges or recorders. Around 20 High Court judges sit, at the request of the Lord Chancellor, to hear criminal cases. Circuit judges are appointed by the Crown on a full-time basis to sit in the Crown Court and/or county courts. Recorders are appointed by the Crown to sit part-time as judges of the Crown Court. The Courts Act 1971 also allows the Lord Chancellor to appoint deputy circuit judges (who are retired full-time judges) or assistant recorders, who can perform all the functions of a circuit judge or recorder.

Individual courts come within one of six geographical circuits. Within each circuit the courts are classified into three tiers, categorised according to the regularity with which High Court judges sit there. At first-tier courts, High Court judges regularly sit; at second-tier courts, High Court judges may sit, and at third-tier courts High Court judges do not normally sit.

(c) Classification of offences

Offences triable on indictment are classified into four categories, pursuant to a Practice Direction of 2 November 1987 *(Practice Direction (Crown Court Business: Classification)* [1987] 1 WLR 1671).

(i)   Class 1 offences—including murder and spying—must be tried by a High Court judge, although murder cases may be released to a circuit judge approved by the Lord Chief Justice.

(ii)   High Court judges must also hear Class 2 offences, which include manslaughter and rape, though they may also be released to a circuit judge; only circuit judges approved by the Lord Chief Justice may try cases of rape and serious sexual assaults against children.

(iii)   All other indictable-only offences (except wounding or causing grievous bodily harm with intent, robbery and conspiracy—unless it is a conspiracy to commit a Class 1 or 2 offence) are in Class 3 and may be tried by a High Court judge, a circuit judge or a recorder.

(iv)   Class 4 covers all either-way offences and wounding or causing grievous bodily harm with intent, robbery and conspiracy; such cases may be heard by assistant recorders as well. Such cases are not to be heard by a High Court judge without his consent.

The Practice Direction also authorises the giving of further directions by the senior High Court judge for a particular geographical circuit as to the types of case to be allocated to a particular level of judge, and the various other factors to be taken into account in deciding which judge should hear which particular case. Naturally, the more serious and more complex a case, the more senior the judge should be; similarly, if a case has given rise to widespread public concern, or raises difficult or novel points of law, this will justify a more senior judge being assigned to preside over the case.

If the case is an appeal from a magistrates' court, then pursuant to s 74 of the Supreme Court Act 1981, the Crown Court must consist of a High Court or circuit judge or a recorder sitting with two to four lay justices; an assistant recorder may sit in such a case. The availability of justices will also play a part in the listing decision.

(d) Application by the parties to change venue

The parties—defence or prosecution—may also apply for the venue to be changed (either the venue set initially or as changed by the Crown Court); the application is heard in open court by a High Court judge. The relevant statute—s 76 of the Supreme Court Act 1981—gives the judge a general discretion as to the location. Typical grounds for making an application would be that the notoriety of the case in a particular locality might make it difficult to find an unbiased jury.

The application might be based on administrative factors: for example, if a defendant has other matters proceeding in one particular court, it might be appropriate for all cases to be heard in that court. In such circumstances, the listing officer can be asked to use his powers. If necessary, the request can be made in open court in front of a judge other than a High Court judge; although such a judge cannot direct that the case be transferred, it would be unusual for a listing officer to go against the view of the judge that it was appropriate to make use of administrative powers. Of course, if the issue is contested by the parties and has to be decided on the merits, it should be listed in front of a High Court judge so that a direction can be given.

(e) The circuits and transfer between the circuits

Since the Crown Court is a single entity, an indictable offence committed anywhere in England and Wales can be dealt with by any of the various locations of the court. Each court comes within one of the six circuits—Midland and Oxford, North-Eastern, Northern, Wales and Chester, Western, and South-Eastern. Each circuit has a presiding judge, who is a High Court judge. If an application is made to transfer a case from one circuit to another, a judge who proposes to grant the application must be satisfied that the presiding judges of the circuits approve (either on the individual case or under general arrangements approved by the presiding judges): see paragraph 9 of the Practice Direction of 2 November 1987.

3. Preparation by the defence solicitors

The Law Society has produced a booklet entitled *The Crown Court—A guide to good practice* under the auspices of the Lord Chancellor's Standing Commission on Efficiency. Most of the guidelines cover what in any event are sensible working practices in a solicitor's office. The following points are worth particular notice.

(i) Full instructions should be obtained, together with witness statements, at an early stage, and counsel should be briefed as soon as possible after the matter is committed to the Crown Court. The *Guide to Proceedings in the Court of Appeal Criminal Division*, published by the Registrar of Criminal Appeals, the 1983 version of which is printed at (1983) 77 Cr App R 138 and [1983] Crim LR 415, reminds solicitors to include in the brief for trial instructions to advise on appeal after conviction or sentence and prepare appropriate grounds of appeal within 14 days of the conviction and/or sentence.

(ii) If there is any unusual preparation or expenditure, it might be prudent to seek the advice and support of counsel to justify any application to the Legal Aid Board; this covers such matters as expert witnesses, additional counsel, preparing transcripts of interviews, or other actions involving unusually large expenditure.

(iii) Consideration should be given to visiting the scene of the alleged crime, and any necessary maps and photographs should be prepared (if the prosecution is not planning to provide them).

(iv) The prosecution should be asked to supply various items of information if it has not done so already: the antecedents of the defendant, details of convictions recorded against co-defendants and prosecution witnesses, details of all unused material, names and addresses and copies of statements from witnesses interviewed by the prosecution who will not be called to give evidence, copies of custody records, copies of crime reference entries (crime reports), medical reports prepared by the police surgeon, and details of any offences to be taken into consideration.

(v) Although it is permissible to interview prosecution witnesses—there being no property in a witness—the prosecution should be notified and its consent sought; if the prosecution does not give its consent, consideration should be given to listing the matter so that a judge can give directions as to the issue. Naturally, care should be taken to avoid any conduct which might amount to attempting to pervert the course of justice.

(vi) The court should be advised of difficulties in obtaining instructions from the client—though the duty of confidentiality otherwise applies.

(vii) Conferences with counsel should be held in most cases. The solicitor should take an active part, not merely taking notes; a list of action to be taken should be prepared.

4. Preparation by the defence advocate

There are specific standards applicable to barristers in criminal cases, contained in Annex H to the Bar Code of Conduct. These standards set out what amount to the sensible steps which should be taken in any event. On receiving a brief to appear, the barrister should attend to the following.

(i) If the brief relates to more than one defendant, check that there is no conflict of interest which requires separate representation. For example, if any of the defendants has previous convictions and there is in prospect an attack on the character of one of the prosecution witnesses, then the defendants ought to be separately represented. The Criminal Evidence Act 1898 prevents a defendant's previous convictions from being placed in evidence before the jury unless he puts his character in issue or attacks the character of a prosecution witness. If all the co-accused are represented by one counsel, then an attack on the character of a witness will delete the character shield of all the defendants.

If the conflict between the defendants is such that they may blame each other for the criminal behaviour alleged, then the advice should be that the defendants should see separate firms of solicitors as well.

(ii)   Arrange a conference with the client.

(iii) Advise in writing as to any enquiries which are necessary.

(iv)   Consider whether any witnesses for the defence are required, including expert witnesses.

(v)   Consider whether any notice of alibi is required, and draft any appropriate notice (see below).

(vi)   Ensure that there are sufficient instructions for cross-examination of prosecution witnesses, and ensure that witnesses who will not be cross-examined are conditionally bound. This is a standard of dubious merit in some cases, since there might be good tactical reasons for allowing certain witnesses to give evidence from the witness box without cross-examination.

(vii) Consider admissions which can be made by the defence and which can be requested of the prosecution.

(viii) Consider a view of such exhibits as cannot be copied and supplied.

(ix)   Advise on the appropriate plea and whether or not the client should give evidence.

(x)   Review the record of any interview supplied as part of the prosecution case and, if it is not agreed, within 21 days from the date of committal serve a notice specifying the part of the record to which objection is taken or the omitted part which the defence wishes to have included; in the event of a failure to reach agreement as to the record of the interview, or, if there is a challenge to the integrity of the master tape, then the court should be informed so that directions can be given by the court (or a pre-trial review ordered). The full details of this are contained in the *Practice Direction (Crime: Tape Recording of Police Interviews)* of 26 May 1989 [1989] 1 WLR 631.

5. Defence disclosure to the prosecution

The defence is entitled to keep its case secret until the trial, subject to three exceptions: alibi evidence, expert evidence and in serious fraud cases.

(a) Alibi evidence

Section 11 of the Criminal Justice Act 1967 requires the defendant to supply a notice of particulars of any alibi on which he will rely, provided that he was warned at committal of the need to supply details. The notice is in the form of a letter to the prosecuting solicitor indicating what the defendant will state in evidence (or what the alibi witnesses will state), and giving the names and addresses (if known) of any witnesses who may be called in support of the alibi. The prosecution may then arrange for the alibi witnesses to be interviewed by the police.

The notice of alibi should be served within seven days of committal; failure to do this means that alibi evidence can only be given with the leave of the court. It is unlikely that the defendant will be refused the chance to call alibi evidence if the notice has not been served; however, if the notice is served so late in the day that the prosecution requires and is granted an adjournment to investigate the alibi, the defence may be subject to an order to pay the costs thrown away.

(b) Expert evidence

Expert evidence (of opinion or fact) is to be disclosed in writing as soon as practicable after committal, along with copies of records of any tests on which the opinion is based (or access to the materials must be allowed). This is governed by the Crown Court (Advance Notice of Expert Evidence) Rules 1987, SI 1987 No 716, made pursuant to s 81 of the Police and Criminal Evidence Act 1984. The rules apply to both defence and prosecution; however, in the case of the prosecution, much of the material will be disclosed in any event as part of the committal evidence or the unused material (see below).

The evidence need not be disclosed if there are reasonable grounds for believing that there would be interference with the course of justice or intimidation of witnesses; however, in such a case the fact that there is such evidence, and the reason for its being withheld, should be disclosed.

Failure to comply with this requirement may result in the evidence being excluded; however, since this would often be unfair, it is more likely that the defence would be made the subject of a costs order in respect of costs wasted. It should be noted that this provision does not apply to a hearing in the Crown Court on appeal from the magistrates' court.

(c) Serious fraud cases

The judge may order the disclosure of a summary of the defence in a serious fraud case (see below).

6. Preparation by the advocate for the prosecution

The advocate in charge of the presentation of the prosecution's case must always act with a view to presenting the case fairly and impartially, not in a partisan fashion. The following steps should be taken.

(i) The indictment should be checked, with the desirability of not overloading the indictment borne in mind.

(ii) Advice in writing should be given as to the need for any additional evidence so that it can be served on the defence as quickly as possible.

(iii) Consideration should be given to the question of compliance with the Attorney-General's guidelines relating to disclosure of unused material (see below).

(iv) Unnecessary material and exhibits should be eliminated, and appropriate admissions should be drafted for service on the defence.

(v) In cases which fall within Class 1 and 2 pursuant to the Practice Direction of 2 November 1987 (see above) and other cases of complexity, a case summary should be drafted for transmission to the court.

(vi) Consideration should also be given to matters of policy, and views conveyed to prosecuting solicitors. The Farquharson Committee, which considered the role of prosecuting counsel and reported in 1986, noted the right of prosecuting solicitors to disagree with their selected advocate on matters of policy—such as dropping a case or accepting a plea to a lesser offence or to part only of the indictment; if necessary, the solicitor may withdraw the brief and seek a second opinion. If it is too late in the day to withdraw the brief, the view of counsel takes precedence.

7. Disclosure of information by the prosecution

(a) Evidence

The statements of the prosecution's witnesses must be disclosed to the defence. If the evidence to be called at trial did not form part of the committal evidence, then a notice of the intention to call further evidence must be served, along with a copy of the statement of the witness (or extra statement of an existing witness). There is no statutory procedure governing this: however, anything which takes the defence by surprise will doubtless lead to an adjournment (and possibly an order for costs), or may be excluded under s 78 of the Police and Criminal Evidence Act 1984 if it has a sufficiently adverse effect on the fairness of the proceedings.

(b) Unused material: the Attorney-General's guidelines

The prosecution must disclose to the defence material in its possession which is relevant to the offence or the surrounding circumstances but which it does not plan to use as part of its case. The prosecution must also disclose any earlier statements of witnesses on whom it proposes to rely. The Attorney-General issued guidelines in December 1981, the main points of which are set out below; the importance of compliance with these rules was emphasised in the *Judith Ward* case [1993] 1 WLR 619.

(i)   Disclosure should be before committal, unless to do so would delay the committal and, in any event, the disclosure is unlikely to influence the committal; if the material might have some influence on the course of the committal proceedings or the charges upon which the justices might commit, disclosure should be before the committal and might even justify delaying the committal.

(ii)   Disclosure will involve serving copies of statements and the like, or allowing a defence solicitor to examine the material if it is longer than 50 pages or unsuitable for copying.

(iii) The duty to disclose can be outweighed by the following factors:

    (a)   if there is the possibility of the witness being called by the defence and his statement is negative or neutral towards the defence, and there are grounds for believing that the witness will be persuaded to change his story in favour of the defence, then the statement can properly be withheld for use in cross-examination as a previous inconsistent statement; in such a case, the name of the witness should be disclosed;

    (b)   if the material is sensitive—for example involving national security, a police informant, the possibility of intimidation, or has been supplied on a confidential basis—and it is not in the public interest to disclose it, then it may be retained by the prosecution; if the sensitive part of the material can be deleted and an amended statement can be served, that should be done, though as an alternative the factual content of the statement can be put into the form of an admission pursuant to s 10 of the Criminal Justice Act 1967.

The issue of public interest immunity was considered in *Davis* [1993] 1 WLR 613. The court is the final arbiter of whether public interest immunity applies. The procedure for the decision is as follows, dependent on the nature of the material. Normally, the prosecution will indicate to the defence that they intend to apply to the court for a ruling as to disclosure and give notice as to the category of material held; the defence will be allowed to make representations to the court. If the prosecution believe that it would breach public interest to reveal even the category of material held, the defence should simply be told that an application is to be made to the court for a ruling as to public interest immunity, and then make the application *ex parte*. In an entirely exceptional case, where to provide notification even of the fact of an application would stultify the application, the prosecution could simply make an *ex parte* application. In the latter two situations, the court is able to order notification to the defence or a full *inter partes* hearing in accordance with the normal procedure.

(c) Previous convictions

The previous convictions of prosecution witnesses must be disclosed: see *Paraskeva* (1982) 76 Cr App R 162, in which the failure of the prosecution to reveal a conviction which was spent under the Rehabilitation of Offenders Act 1974 was held to be a material irregularity in the course of a trial which in the circumstances caused the Court of Appeal to quash the conviction.

(d) Custody records, tapes of interviews

The defence is entitled to copies of the custody record maintained on the defendant whilst in police custody, and tapes of any interview. See para 2.4 of Code C of the Codes of Practice issued pursuant to s 66 of the Police and Criminal Evidence Act 1984 in respect of custody records; tape recordings of interviews are exhibits in the case and as such the defence should have access to copies of the tapes.

8. Legal aid

(a) General

Most defendants in the Crown Court will be represented pursuant to the terms of a legal aid order made under the Legal Aid Act 1988. If the case is indictable-only, the legal aid order made in the magistrates' court will usually have been a "through order" covering proceedings in both the higher and lower courts: s 20(5) of the Act. Otherwise, one of the usual orders made at committal is for legal aid to be extended to cover the proceedings at the Crown Court: s 20(4). This provision applies to committals for trial or sentence, and notices of transfer; the magistrates' court may also grant legal aid for an appeal to the Crown Court.

(b) Power of the Crown Court to grant legal aid

The Crown Court may grant legal aid to those appearing before it: s 20(2) of the Act. Legal aid must be granted, subject to the means of the applicant and the possibility of a contribution being required, to a defendant charged with murder, and where the defendant is kept in custody for pre-sentence reports to be prepared: s 21(3). Otherwise, legal aid may be granted if it is in the interests of justice: s 21(2). Among the factors to be taken into account are the prospects of a custodial sentence or loss of livelihood or serious damage to reputation if convicted, whether the case involves a substantial question of law or expert cross-examination of prosecution witnesses, and whether the defendant will be able to follow the proceedings because of language or other difficulties.

If there is no outstanding legal aid order, the application may be made on a standard form which is considered by an officer of the court; alternatively, an oral application may be made to a judge.

(c) Representation

(i) Solicitor and counsel

Legal aid will usually allow the provision of assistance by counsel and solicitor. However, an emergency grant of legal aid may cover counsel only when the circumstances are such that there is no time to instruct a solicitor: this is the equivalent of the "dock brief".

The defendant may choose any firm of solicitors, though a firm will be assigned by the court if no choice is indicated on the application form. The solicitors may choose any counsel, though they must take account of any wish their client might have as to the counsel to be briefed. The Bar Code of Conduct requires that the barrister selected must do the case unless he would be professionally embarrassed. This can arise, for example, through lack of experience or competence, because other professional commitments prevent proper preparation of the case, or through a possible conflict of interest. It cannot arise if the barrister does not wish to work at legal aid rates, because the legal aid rate is deemed to be a proper professional fee unless the Bar Council determines otherwise. See Part V of the Code of Conduct of the Bar of England and Wales.

(ii) Co-defendants

Two or more co-defendants will usually be represented by the same firm of solicitors, unless the interests of justice require separate solicitors—usually because there is a conflict between the defendants, for example one blaming the other for the act. However, this does not mean that two co-accused have to be represented by the same counsel. When a brief is received to represent more than one defendant, counsel must examine whether the interests of each co-accused require that they be separately represented at trial.

(iii) Two counsel

In a more complex or serious case, the question may arise as to whether more than one barrister should be involved. Regulation 48 of the Legal Aid in Criminal and Care Proceedings (General) Regulations 1989 (SI 1989 No 344) provides that in a trial involving a charge of murder, or where the case is one of exceptional gravity, complexity or difficulty, two counsel may be assigned: the two may be Queen's Counsel and junior, two junior counsel, or Queen's Counsel or junior with a noting junior. The application may be made to an officer of the court or to a judge in open court.

(iv) Exceptional expenditure

Legal aid may also be extended to cover the cost of exceptional items—expert reports, transcripts of tape recordings, and other expensive or unusual steps. Prior authorisation for the expenditure can be obtained from the local area committee of the Legal Aid Board (regulation 54 of the General Regulations). The alternative course of action is to incur the expenditure and hope that it will be approved by the legal aid officer who taxes the solicitor's fees after the hearing; in such a case, a written advice from counsel as to the necessity of the expenditure, or a judicial comment that it was appropriate, will be of assistance.

9. Listing

(a) Introduction

The listing of cases over which the Crown Court has jurisdiction with a view to their disposal is a matter for the listing officer of the particular Crown Court centre, working in combination with the listing officers of the Crown Court centres in the same circuit. The aim of the listing officer is to ensure that available courts and judges are being utilised. This is a considerable logistical exercise, since the availability of defendants, witnesses and lawyers has also to be taken into account. Barristers' clerks and solicitors' firms are well advised to be on good terms with the listing officer, so that the convenience of the clients and their representatives is taken into account.

(b) Information on which listing decisions are based

Most Crown Court centres send out a form to defence solicitors which requests information on such matters as the likely plea, the likely length of the trial if it is to be contested, and any dates which are inconvenient for participants in the trial. On the basis of the information supplied on this form, the case may be listed for plea or for trial.

If the form requesting information is not completed, the court's officials may look at the witness orders made by the magistrates' court and list the trial for plea or trial accordingly: the fact that the prosecution witnesses are conditionally bound indicates that their evidence is not to be challenged, which in turn usually indicates that the plea is to be one of guilty.

(c) Listing for pleas to be entered

A case may be listed for trial without the need for a separate listing for pleas to be entered; this depends on the practice of the individual court centre. In some courts, most cases will be listed initially for plea.

The advantage of the case being listed for pleas from the point of view of the listing office is that a number of defendants will plead guilty once the case is in front of the court. Arrangements can often be made between the prosecution and the defence as to the entering of pleas which are suitable to both sides. Quite often what happens is that the prosecution advocate, having reviewed the papers because the matter has been listed, will decide that the evidence reveals a lesser offence than that on which the defendant was committed, or that in a case of several counts or several indictments the justice of the case is met by pleas to some of the charges. Although "plea bargaining" is not sanctioned in English law, there is often scope for the prosecution to accept a plea of guilty to a lesser offence or to certain counts on the indictment(s).

If a not guilty plea is entered and the case is adjourned for trial, then directions will be given at the pleas hearing which will assist the future listing of the case. The opportunity will be taken to give directions relating to matters which have not been dealt with already. The following orders are typical:

(i)   that witness orders be communicated within 7 or 14 days;

(ii)   that any outstanding notice of alibi be served within 7 days;

(iii) that any unused material be served. The availability of the unused material may have an impact on the witness orders; defence counsel should therefore ask for an order that the witness orders be communicated within a given time after service of the unused material.

(d) Fixed dates

Some cases will be assigned a fixed date for their trial some considerable time in advance. Others, however, may come into court at very short notice. Fixed dates may also be assigned for pleas to be entered.

A wide number of factors may justify giving the case a fixed date for trial: for example, the length of the trial, the seriousness of the allegation, the fact that there are young or frail witnesses, or witnesses who have important commitments elsewhere (which will be useful particularly in the case of professional witnesses); the availability of the advocate chosen by the defendant may also play a part.

The listing officer may fix a case of his own volition. Alternatively, the parties may apply in advance for a case to be given a fixed date: this can be done by listing the case for an application to fix a date, or the application may be made when the case is listed for some other purpose.

(e) Applications to break fixtures

If a fixture becomes inconvenient for one or other of the parties, or it is apparent that the preparations of one side will not be completed before the date, the party should apply to the court to have the fixture broken. A date which has been fixed by the listing officer may sometimes be changed by the listing officer, though more often the question of breaking the fixture will require an application in open court. If the date of the fixture has been set in accordance with the order of a judge, the listing officer will invariably place the matter in front of a judge in order to break the date of the fixture.

Possible reasons for applying to break a fixture are many; the application is one which has to be considered judicially, even if the other party does not object or the application is a joint one. Examples of reasons which should receive favourable consideration are delays in the supply of prosecution evidence and exhibits, or unused material, or late service of such material which means that the defence will not have its case ready for the date of the fixture; or if an essential witness becomes unavailable for the date of the trial after the date has been fixed.

If the party making the application is to some extent to blame for not being ready for the fixture, that may be taken into account against the application. It is always wise to attempt to obtain the consent of the other party to breaking the fixture. Tactical reasons may prevent the other party from consenting. The consent of both parties does not necessarily mean that the fixture will be broken: that remains the decision of the listing officer or the judge who considers the matter.

(f) Warned lists

Cases which do not receive a fixed date will be placed in a "warned list"; the warned list usually covers a two-week period. The effect of being warned is that the case may be called into court on any day during the period of the warned list that court time becomes available. The listing officer will notify in advance the parties and their lawyers that the case is in the warned list for a particular period. The case may be warned for plea or for trial.

Listing for trial is dealt with further in Chapter 6.

10. Pre-trial reviews—general

There are no general provisions for the holding of pre-trial reviews: it is a matter for which each centre of the Crown Court has its own rules. In cases of any complexity, it is right that there be a proper review before the trial date. (See *Thorn* (1977) 66 Cr App R 6.) Any party may request that the case be listed for pre-trial review; in the unusual event that the listing officer does not agree to such a listing, the case should be listed for mention in open court so that a judge can decide whether or not a full pre-trial review is merited.

There are specific rules for pre-trial reviews at the Old Bailey, the Practice Rules (Central Criminal Court) of 21 November 1977. Any party may apply for the matter to be listed, or the court may list it of its own volition; at the hearing, counsel will be expected to inform the court of the pleas to be tendered, the prosecution witnesses required by the defence, facts which can be admitted, points of law and admissibility which may arise at the trial, alibis not yet disclosed, and other significant matters. Other Crown Court centres have adopted similar provisions.

However, in *Hutchinson* (1985) 82 Cr App R 51, the Court of Appeal made it plain that the pre-trial review has no legal status and what happens there does not bind the parties as to their conduct at the trial. So, for example, if an application is made to sever the indictment at a pre-trial review and that application is denied, that decision does not bind the trial judge (who may or may not be the same judge as the one who presided over the pre-trial review).

11. Pre-trial reviews and disclosure—fraud cases

(a) When a preparatory hearing is appropriate

If a judge takes the view that substantial benefits are likely to accrue from a preparatory hearing in a fraud case of seriousness and complexity—whether committed to the court or the subject of a notice of transfer—he may order such a hearing. The judge may make such order on his own motion or following an application by the prosecution or any defendant. The review is designed to identify the likely material issues, assist the jury's comprehension of those issues, expedite the proceedings and assist the judge's management of the trial. See ss 7 ff of the Criminal Justice Act 1987 and the Criminal Justice Act 1987 (Preparatory Hearings) Rules 1988 (SI 1988 No 1699).

(b) Matters which may arise

The defendant will be arraigned at the preparatory hearing (and the trial deemed to begin) and questions of law and the admissibility of evidence may be determined. Decisions on these matters will govern the conduct of the trial once the jury has been sworn (subject to variation in the interests of justice). However, orders and rulings made may be taken on appeal to the Court of Appeal, with the leave of the Crown Court judge or the Court of Appeal; the jury may not be sworn until the appeal has been heard or abandoned. The Court of Appeal has indicated in *In re Case Statements*, The Times, 18 December 1992, that it will not interfere with an order made unless it was plainly wrong because, *inter alia*, it imposed too onerous a burden.

(c) Outline of the case and the defence

The judge may order the prosecution to supply an outline of its case, identifying the principal facts, material witness statements, exhibits, propositions of law and the necessary inferences from these matters. The defence may be ordered to give notice of any objection it has to the prosecution case statement, and to set out in general terms the nature of the defence and the principal matters which are contested, together with any points of law and relevant authorities. The defence need not identify its witnesses (unless they are alibi witnesses or expert witnesses—see above).

Either party may depart from its case statement in front of the jury, but the judge may comment on the departure and allow the jury to draw such inferences as are appropriate, and may give leave for the other party to comment; whether or not leave is granted will depend on the extent of the departure and the reason for it.

12. Mentions, applications and so on

A case will be listed for plea and/or trial. It may be listed for mention in front of a judge for a number of reasons, or for various applications to be made. Examples are:

(i) the defendant has not been in contact with his representative to give instructions, with the consequence that the case will not be ready for trial if it is listed. Since solicitors are officers of the court, there is an obligation to ensure that costs are not thrown away. The case will be listed with the defendant being under an obligation to attend: if he does and is willing to provide instructions, the appropriate application is to have the matter adjourned generally. If the defendant does not attend, the court will usually exercise its power to issue a warrant for the arrest of the defendant. This of course places the solicitor in the strange position of having to inform the court as to matters which might well lead to an order that the defendant be remanded into custody on being located;

(ii) the prosecution has not disclosed materials which it is obliged to disclose. In such a case the prosecution will be asked to attend so that such argument as is necessary about disclosure can be heard and the judge can formulate the appropriate order;

(iii) any other good reason for seeking an order from the court—such as the granting of legal aid or the extension of legal aid to cover two counsel or leading counsel.

13. Bail

Once a case has been committed to the Crown Court, the court has jurisdiction over the question of whether the defendant is or should be on bail or in custody, and if on bail what the conditions should be. This is in contrast to the Crown Court's pre-committal powers, which are limited to hearing an appeal from a decision to withhold bail: s 81(1)(g) of the Supreme Court Act 1981. Consequently, a bail application can be listed at any stage before trial. In practice, there often needs to be a fresh argument to have any real prospect of success. However, in some cases—depending on the charge and the likely sentence—such an argument can be found in the fact that the defendant has already served before trial the equivalent of the sentence he might receive if convicted, thus reducing the likelihood of his absconding.

14. Other matters

The Crown Court Rules deal with various other matters which require the parties to take action before trial.

(a) Witness orders and summonses

If a witness was conditionally bound at the committal, and the party wishes the witness to attend the trial, notice to that effect should be given to the Crown Court which will then give notice in writing to the witness that he should attend to give evidence when the trial is held (rule 22 of the Crown Court Rules). In practice, the responsibility of securing the attendance of witnesses is undertaken by the prosecution; so the defence should inform the prosecution as well as the court of its witness orders.

A witness may be required to attend court pursuant to a witness order made by the magistrates' court; failure to attend carries the sanction of arrest and remand in custody pursuant to s 4 of the Criminal Procedure (Attendance of Witnesses) Act 1965. If the witness was not used at the committal or if the hearing at the Crown Court is an appeal, there can be no witness order; such a witness can, however, be made the subject of a witness summons issued by either the Crown Court or the High Court, pursuant to s 2 of the Act. Such a summons can require the person to produce a document or other item.

If the summons is issued out of the High Court, application is made pursuant to RSC O 79, r 10. There are prescribed forms, precedents of which are contained in Forms 101 and 103 of Appendix A of the Rules of the Supreme Court.

A witness who has been summonsed and who considers that he cannot give any material evidence, or produce any document or item likely to be material evidence, may apply in writing to the Crown Court or the High Court for a direction that the summons shall be of no effect. The application should give reasons. Notice of the application is given to the party who caused the summons to be issued, who shall be given the chance to make representations. The person making the application has the burden of satisfying the court that the summons should not have effect. (See rule 23 of the Crown Court Rules.)

(b) Television link evidence

Section 32 of the Criminal Justice Act 1988 allows evidence to be given through a live television link in certain circumstances. Witnesses outside the United Kingdom may give such evidence in homicide and serious fraud cases. (The Criminal Justice Act 1988 (Commencement No 12) Order 1990 (SI 1990 No 2084).)

If the offence involves assault, injury, threat of injury, a sexual offence or indecency with children, a child witness may give evidence via a television link. A written application must be made pursuant to rule

23A of the Crown Court Rules. A form is prescribed in Schedule 5 to the Crown Court Rules. Although the statute defines a child as one under 14, the rule extends the age limit to 17 in respect of sexual offences (which is consistent with the provisions for the receipt of video-recorded evidence).

The time limit for the application is 28 days from committal or the voluntary bill procedure. This time limit may be extended after it has expired; such an application to extend the time limit must be in writing and is to be determined by a Crown Court judge without a hearing, although the judge may decide to hold a hearing.

If the other side objects to the application, it must do so in writing within 14 days of receiving the notice of application. The reasons must be given, and served on the court and the applicant. The judge considers the application on the papers, although he may decide to hear oral representations. Where the judge gives leave, the notification of the decision will include an indication of the location of the trial (there being certain Crown Courts equipped with the necessary technology) and, where the witness is for the prosecution, there will be an indication of the name of the witness and the name, occupation and relationship to the witness of the person who is to accompany the witness whilst he is giving evidence. Whether the witness is for the prosecution or defence, the witness shall be accompanied by a person approved by the judge. The presence of other people—including camera operators—requires a direction from the judge.

Rule 23B of the Crown Court Rules contains similar provisions for an application with respect to witnesses abroad. The main difference is that the time limit for written objections to the application is 28 days; the judge may determine the application on the papers or at a hearing in chambers with the parties represented.

(c) Video evidence

In the cases in which a child can give evidence through a television link, s 32A of the Criminal Justice Act 1988 (inserted by the Criminal Justice Act 1991) allows a pre-recorded video interview between the child and an adult to be played as part of the evidence of the child witness. The age limits are as follows: children under 14 if the offence involves assault or cruelty, and under 17 if the offence is a sexual offence, may give video-recorded evidence; if the child was under the appropriate age when the video was made and is currently under 15 or 18 respectively, the video may still be played.

The leave of the court is required, and such leave shall be given unless the child is not available for cross-examination (which will be via television link), or rules of court have not been complied with to the satisfaction of the court, or it would not be in the interests of justice; leave can be declined in respect of part of the video, thereby requiring that evidence to be given via normal examination-in-chief.

An application should be made pursuant to rule 23C of the Rules of the Crown Court, and must be on the prescribed form. The application must give various items of information, including details of the place where the video was made, who was present, the timings of the video; a statement that the witness is willing and able to attend for cross-examination is required; the applicant should also indicate when the video was disclosed to the other parties. The application should be made within 28 days of the committal or the giving of a notice of transfer; the time limit may be extended by the Crown Court. The other party has 14 days in which to make any objections, giving reasons why it would not be in the interests of justice to admit the video or a particular part of the video; the objector should also indicate that he wishes to be present and to be represented at the hearing of the application. If there are objections and a request to be represented at any hearing, there shall be a hearing to determine the application.

The Practice Direction (Crime: Child's Video Evidence) [1992] 1 WLR 839 indicates that the applicant should ensure that the video recording is produced by the interviewer or any other person present; that the person adducing the video should make the appropriate arrangements for the operation of the video-playing equipment at the trial; and that if it becomes necessary to adjourn a trial to edit a video, the court should consider whether costs should be awarded.

(d) Application for hearings in camera

The Crown Court may hear evidence in camera in limited circumstances, pursuant to its common law power to control its procedure; this applies only where the presence of the public will genuinely frustrate justice—saving the witness from embarrassment, for example, is not enough. This power is supplemented by statute in respect of trials under the Official Secrets Act (s 8 of the Official Secrets Act 1920) and where children or young people are giving evidence in cases where they are the victims or the offence involves conduct contrary to decency or morality (s 37 of the Children and Young Persons Act 1933). (This is discussed further in Chapter 6.)

If a party intends to apply for the court to hear evidence in camera for reasons of national security or to protect the identity of a witness, it should give notice at least seven days before the trial is due to begin. The notice must be displayed in the precincts of the court. The application will be heard after arraignment but before the jury has been sworn. The decision of the court can be appealed to the Court of Appeal, in which case the trial is adjourned until the Court of Appeal has determined the matter. (See rule 24A of the Crown Court Rules.)

(e) References to the European Court

In certain circumstances, particularly in cases involving the importation of goods, the decision of the Crown Court might turn upon the interpretation of European Community law. Under Article 177 of the Treaty of Rome, the Crown Court may refer a question involving the interpretation of European Community law to the European Court.

Given that it takes some time for a ruling to be obtained from the European Court, that the Crown Court case is invariably adjourned until the ruling has been obtained, and that it would be unwise after a jury has been sworn to adjourn a case for that length of time, the question of a reference to the European Court should be raised before the trial commences. However, this itself presents problems, because it is often difficult to seek a ruling from the European Court until the facts of the alleged offence have been ascertained. A Crown Court judge might therefore take the view that he can rule on the matter of law, direct the jury accordingly and allow the reference to the European Court to be obtained during the appeal process.

Nevertheless, there are provisions in the Crown Court Rules—rule 29—for a reference to be made to the European Court on the court's own motion or on application by a party.

(f) Criminal Justice (International Co-operation) Act 1990

The Criminal Justice (International Co-operation) Act 1990 is designed to enable the UK to participate in the action being taken against transnational crime, particularly drug trafficking. There are provisions to allow evidence from overseas to be used in the UK, and for evidence to be taken in the UK for use in proceedings abroad: ss 3 and 4 of the Act. An application for overseas evidence to be used in the UK can be made by the prosecution or a defendant. Rules 31 and 32 of the Crown Court Rules govern the procedure.

In the case of an application for evidence to be obtained for use in the UK, a written application is required (unless the court allows an oral application in exceptional circumstances). The application may be heard *ex parte*, and may be in camera if the court thinks it necessary in the interests of justice.

If the application is granted, "letters of request" are sent via the Government, though they may be sent direct to the foreign court or tribunal in cases of urgency. The admissibility of evidence received is governed by ss 24 ff of the Criminal Justice Act 1988.

Chapter 4

The indictment

1. Contents

A trial in the Crown Court, being a trial on indictment, can occur only if there is a valid indictment, which sets out the allegation(s) made by the prosecution against the defendant(s). The form of the indictment must follow the model of Schedule 1 to the Indictment Rules 1971. If more than one offence is alleged, each offence will be a separate count in the indictment. Counts in a single indictment must meet the requirements for joinder. Similarly, there must be a link between the defendants who appear on the same indictment. If the links are not established, there will be separate indictments. If the allegations are contested, each indictment is dealt with in a separate trial with a separate jury.

2. Time limits for presenting an indictment

The bill of indictment is usually drafted by the prosecution, though it is possible for an officer of the Crown Court to perform this task. Time limits for the presentation of the bill are set out in rule 5 of the Indictments (Procedure) Rules 1971. The bill is to be delivered to an officer of the Crown Court ("preferred") within 28 days of committal or the date of the notice of transfer. This time limit can be extended by the officer for up to 28 days; if he thinks it inappropriate to extend time, the matter is referred to a judge.

A judge has a general discretion to extend the time limit, taking into account the likelihood of prejudice to the accused. The application should be in writing unless the judge directs otherwise, and must include reasons. If the application is made after the 28-day period has expired, reasons should also be given for the late application. The judge may allow the accused to make representations as to prejudice caused by the delay. Given that most bills of indictment will reflect the draft indictment used at committal, it is only in unusual circumstances that an accused will suffer prejudice (which could arise if, for example, the bill contained a count which caught the defence by surprise and, by virtue of the late preferment of the bill, the search for defence witnesses was hampered). Often the defence will have no grounds for realistic objections, in which case the application will be allowed by the judge.

If the preferment of a late bill is denied, the prosecution may apply for a voluntary bill of indictment or institute fresh committal proceedings.

3. Signature

Although the rules relating to time limits have been held to be directory rather than mandatory, the requirement that the indictment be signed is essential. A conviction on an unsigned bill of indictment is null because there is no indictment until the bill is signed. The signature is that of a proper officer of the court: s 82 of the Supreme Court Act 1981. That will be someone in the employ of the Lord Chancellor's Department, such as a court clerk or other authorised officer. The officer shall sign the indictment if satisfied that the appropriate steps have been taken to give the Crown Court jurisdiction.

4. The contents of a count

(a) General

Each count consists of a statement of the offence and the particulars of the offence. The statement of offence names the offence. If the offence is one created under statute, the section of the statute or subordinate instrument creating the offence shall be referred to in the statement (Indictment Rules 1971, r 6); otherwise the statement will state that the offence is contrary to common law.

Particulars must give reasonable information as to the nature of the charge (Indictment Act 1915, s 3). This will invariably include the names of the defendants, the date of the offence, the criminal *actus reus*, the name of the victim (if known), and the *mens rea*. There is no need to mention the location of the offence unless the location is an essential element of the offence: for example, burglary involves entering a building as a trespasser, so the location of the building must be stated. In offences involving property—theft, for example—the property must be described in general terms, but need not be valued.

(b) Date of offence

The date of the offence will be given if it is known. Of course, in many instances the precise date will not be known, in which case the allegation can be phrased as occurring "on or about" a specified date, "on a day unknown" before a certain date, or "on a day unknown" between two specified dates—which will be the dates immediately before the first possible date of the offence and immediately after the last possible date.

The date may be of particular importance when the substantive offence itself is subject to time limits: for example, the common law definition of the *actus reus* of murder involves death following within a year and a day from the action of the defendant; similarly, the evidential inference of theft and/or handling based on recent possession of stolen goods may also require precision as to the date of the theft of the goods.

(c) Requesting further particulars

The defence can request that further particulars be given: these can be included in the indictment or provided in writing separately. If the offence involves recklessness, for example, or false representations, it might be appropriate to seek to tie down the prosecution by asking for detailed particulars. Whether failure to do this will render a conviction unsafe depends on whether injustice is done to the defence; if the defendant knows what is alleged, there will be no prejudice.

(d) The rule against duplicity

An essential rule is that each count must allege one offence only: counts which do not meet this test should be quashed. The question of whether a number of acts constitute one offence or more than one is a question of fact and degree in the particular circumstances of each case. In other words, duplicity cannot be defined but lawyers are supposed to be able to recognise it when they see it.

A simple example will be that alleging separate acts on separate days will be duplicitous. However, it is possible to have a single offence which continues over a period of time. Conspiracy is an obvious example; there the offence is the agreement, and various acts over a period of time may be proved in order to show the agreement. As a matter of construction a particular statutory provision may define an offence as continuing over a period of time. (See for example *Hodgetts* v *Chiltern District Council* [1983] 2 AC 120, where the offence of contravening the requirements of an enforcement notice served under planning legislation was alleged to have occurred "on and since" a given date; this was held to be acceptable in the context of the offence alleged.)

(e) Alternative methods of committing an offence

A question may also arise as to whether the statute quoted creates one offence (which may be committed in several ways) or several offences. If the prosecution wishes to allege that the defendant acted in one of several ways, each of which would be criminal, the alternatives can be included in one count (Indictment Rules 1971, r 7) provided that the statute creates one offence rather than several offences in the one statutory section. For example, handling stolen goods contrary to s 22 of the Theft Act 1968 can involve receiving, assisting in the retention, removal, disposal or realisation, or making the appropriate arrangements.

(f) Joining defendants in a single count

More than one accused may be named in a single count if they are alleged to have committed a single offence. This will cover a situation where more than one person has committed the offence—a number of people joining together in a violent disorder or conspiracy, for example.

It will also cover a situation where the defendants are principals and secondary parties. The latter may be indicted as a principal; there is no need to have a separate count alleging that the secondary party aided and abetted (or otherwise participated) in the principal offence. The look-out at a burglary may therefore be joined with the person who enters the property, for example.

Although defendants may be properly joined, the court always retains a discretion to order separate trials in respect of the co-defendants if to do so is necessary for justice to be done. This may be particularly important where one of the defendants is of good character and another is not. The person of good character is entitled to have the jury directed that their unblemished record is relevant to their credibility as a witness and also their propensity to commit a crime. If the judge gives such a direction with respect to one defendant only, it is an obvious inference for the jury that the other defendant is not of good character—which is something the jury are rarely allowed to know. The only solution to allow fairness to both defendants may be to order separate trials. See, for example, *Shaw*, The Times, 31 December 1992.

5. Counts in a single indictment

Each trial deals with a single indictment. This may allege one offence only. If there are several offences and therefore several counts, the issue will arise as to whether the counts should appear on one indictment and, if contested, be tried by one jury.

(a) Joinder of counts in an indictment

Rule 9 of the Indictment Rules 1971 provides:

> "Charges for any offences may be joined in the same indictment if those charges are founded on the same facts, or form or are part of a series of offences of the same or a similar character".

(i) Same facts

The first limb of the rule—"same facts"—does not require contemporaneity; it has been interpreted to require simply a common factual origin, which can be satisfied if the later offence would not have occurred but for the earlier offence. In *Barrell* (1979) 69 Cr App R 250, the allegations involved a fight outside a discotheque (affray and assault) and an attempt two months later by one of the defendants to the affray to bribe one of the witnesses (attempting to pervert the course of justice). The Court of Appeal held that "founded on the same facts" required the charges to have a common factual origin; the attempt to pervert the course of justice could not have been alleged but for the earlier offences, and the charges were therefore founded on the same facts. This is difficult to justify.

(ii) Series of offences

The second limb—covering a "series of offences of the same or a similar character"—has been considered by the House of Lords in *Ludlow* v *Metropolitan Police Commissioner* [1971] AC 29. What is required is a "feature of similarity which in all the circumstances of the case enables the offences to be described as a series". This imprecise definition allows a wide discretion as to whether there is a sufficient nexus, derived either from the legal characteristics of the offences or from the facts. Ludlow was charged with an attempted theft on 20 August 1968 and a robbery on 5 September 1968, both occurring at public houses in Acton. The nexus was derived from the facts that the offences involved theft or attempted theft, and occurred within a short period of time and were geographically proximate.

(b) Joinder of defendants

There must be some nexus between two or more defendants joined in a single indictment; this is obviously satisfied if the defendants are alleged to have committed a single offence and therefore appear as co-accused in the same count. It is also possible for defendants charged with separate offences to be joined in one indictment. An indictment may also contain a joint count against two or more defendants and a further count against one of the defendants alone.

If the defendants appear in separate counts, joinder ought to meet the requirements of rule 9 of the Indictment Rules, which is expressed to cover charges (and is not limited to charges against a single defendant). There are, however, *dicta* in *Tizard and Ruxton* (1962) 46 Cr App R 82 to the effect that the forerunner of rule 9 applied only in respect of an indictment against one defendant. Even if this is correct, the Crown Court's power to control its own procedure in the interests of justice would lead to the application of similar principles as are contained in rule 9 in considering the joinder of defendants in separate counts.

(c) Separate trials of properly joined counts

Even if the counts are properly joined, the judge may order separate trials if the defendant "may be prejudiced or embarrassed in his defence by reason of being charged with more than one offence in the same indictment, or that for any other reason it is desirable to direct that the person should be tried separately for any one or more offences charged" (Indictments Act 1915, s 5(3)).

A specific example of this is when the indictment is overloaded and will lead to a long or complicated trial; in such a case, several shorter trials are preferable. Special consideration is required when the indictment contains several counts alleging sexual offences, because of the requirement of corroboration and the issues of similar fact evidence: recent cases include *Cannan* (1991) 92 Cr App R 16 and *DPP* v *P* (1991) 93 Cr App R 267.

(d) Inclusion of summary-only offences

Section 40 of the Criminal Justice Act 1988 allows the drafter of an indictment to include on the indictment certain offences which are classified as summary only. These offences will then be tried by the judge and jury as if they had been committed to the Crown Court for trial, though the sentencing powers remain those of the magistrates' court.

The summary offences which may be included on the indictment are common assault, taking a conveyance without authority (or driving or allowing oneself to be carried in such a conveyance), driving whilst disqualified, and criminal damage to a value within the summary-only limit; the statute allows the list to be extended by statutory instrument, provided the offence is punishable by imprisonment or disqualification from driving.

The summary offence must be revealed in the committal documents, and must meet a test similar to that for joinder of counts—namely, be founded on the same facts or evidence as a count charging an indictable offence, or be part of a series of offences of the same or similar character as an indictable offence which is also charged. It is to be noted that, as a result of this legislation, the offence of common assault is an alternative verdict to assault occasioning actual bodily harm only if there is a count on the indictment charging common assault: see *Mearns* (1990) 91 Cr App R 312.

An example of this section in action is provided by *Callaghan* (1992) 94 Cr App R 226. The appellant was charged with the theft of a van and the destruction by arson of the same van in October 1989 (counts 1 and 2); a further theft of another van later the same month (count 3); an offence of taking a conveyance without authority in November 1989 (count 4); a further offence of taking a conveyance in January of 1990 (count 5) and a final offence of driving whilst disqualified (count 6), which related to the vehicle which was the subject of count 5. Counts 4 and 5 were held properly joined as part of a series of offences, being of a similar nature to the indictable offences in counts 1 and 3; count 6 was, however, not founded on the same facts and was not of the same or a similar character to any of the indictable offences. Its link was with count 5, which was a summary offence rather than an indictable offence. The conviction on count 6 was therefore quashed.

Any summary-only offence can be committed to the Crown Court pursuant to s 41 of the Criminal Justice Act if it arises out of circumstances which are the same as or connected with the either-way offence which is being committed for trial. However, under this section, the offence is not included on the indictment; instead, the charge is put to the defendant at the end of the trial and, if the defendant pleads guilty to it, the judge may sentence for the offence. If the defendant does not admit the s 41 matter, any trial must be in the magistrates' court. The charge is deemed to have been adjourned *sine die* in the magistrates' court following the committal. It should be noted that the power to commit a summary matter to the Crown Court cannot be used if the main offence is indictable only.

(e) Relationship with committal charges

The offence for which the defendant was committed for trial need not appear in the indictment. It may contain counts alleging such indictable offences as are disclosed by the evidence from the committal proceedings. Analogous provisions apply with respect to the notice of transfer system: the indictment may include counts alleging offences revealed in the material served with the notice. With respect to voluntary bills of indictment, the High Court judge must be presented with the bill of indictment which the prosecution seeks leave to prefer. The trial judge cannot quash such an indictment (*Rothfield* (1937) 26 Cr App R 103), and presumably cannot allow it to be amended.

If the committal charge is different from that which appears in the indictment, care should be taken that the offence alleged is disclosed by the committal evidence (or notice bundle). It is not sufficient that the offence is disclosed by evidence made available after the committal in the form of a Notice of Additional Evidence. The relevant provision is s 2 of the Administration of Justice (Miscellaneous Provisions) Act 1933, which states:

"... no bill of indictment ... shall be preferred unless ...

(a)   the person charged has been committed for trial for the offence

Provided that

(i)   where the person charged has been committed for trial, the bill of indictment against him may include, either in substitution for or in addition to counts charging the offence for which he was committed, any counts founded on facts or evidence disclosed [at the committal]".

This has to be read in conjunction with rule 9 of the Indictment Rules, which indicates what can be included on the same indictment (*Lombardi* (1989) 88 Cr App R 179). Although it is possible for there to be more than one indictment from a single committal (if, for example, charges committed together cannot properly be joined in one indictment), the separate indictments must contain either a committal charge or a charge which can properly be joined to a committal charge. Consequently, as in *Lombardi*, if there is no committal in respect of the additional or substituted charge (even if it is revealed in the committal evidence) and it does not meet the requirements for joinder, it cannot be added and then severed into a separate indictment. The separate indictment in such a case must be quashed.

(f) Joining charges from separate committals in a single indictment

As long as the charges meet the requirements for joinder, there is nothing to prevent the joinder of defendants or charges against one defendant which have been the subject of separate committals (*Groom* (1976) 62 Cr App R 242).

(g) Effect of misjoinder

If the indictment contains counts without any nexus, it is invalid and any convictions may be quashed on appeal. The indictment can be saved by amendment deleting the charges not properly joined. Alternatively, the trial judge may grant leave for the preferment of a fresh indictment or indictments and then require the prosecution to elect on which indictment(s) to proceed; naturally, it will elect not to proceed on the invalid indictment. If there is an attempt to prefer a fresh indictment consisting solely of misjoined charges in respect of which there was no committal, this is invalid (see the discussion in (e) above).

6. Amending and quashing the indictment

(a) Amendment

The court has a general discretion to order the amendment of any defective indictment, subject to the amendment being possible without injustice (see Indictments Act 1915, s 5). The power applies to technical defects—wrong dates, mis-spellings and so on—as well as substantive amendments such as adding new counts. The power may be exercised at any stage before the end of the trial.

The later the application to make a substantive amendment, the more likely the defence is subject to the risk of injustice, in which case the amendment might not be allowed. The judge has additional powers which might compensate the defence for any injustice caused by a late amendment. It will be a question of fact in each case whether the risk of injustice can be remedied by, for example, granting the defence an adjournment to prepare for the amended situation. It may also be possible, if the amendment is ordered after the jury has been sworn, to discharge the jury and order a retrial on the amended indictment.

(b) Quashing

The defence or the prosecution may apply to the judge to quash the whole indictment or any count on the indictment. Misjoined counts and counts which do not reveal known offences will be quashed. A motion to quash should also be made when there has been a failure to comply with the requirements of s 2 of the Administration of Justice (Miscellaneous Provisions) Act 1933, discussed above. If there has been no committal (or alternative to committal) with respect to any count on the indictment, the whole indictment must be quashed.

The indictment

If a count on the indictment relates to an offence in respect of which the defendant was not committed for trial, so that the defence has not had an opportunity to submit that the defendant should not be placed on trial for that particular offence, the judge can be asked to consider the committal statements and decide whether there is a case to answer: if there is not, then the count involved should be quashed. This applies equally in respect of a charge on which the prosecution sought committal but which the magistrates declined to commit.

Since a single committal may be used as the basis for more than one indictment, the prosecution can solve the problem of a defective indictment by seeking leave to prefer a further indictment and then electing to proceed only on the technically proper indictment.

A defective indictment amounts to a material irregularity in the course of the trial, though the Court of Appeal will often apply the proviso to s 2(1) of the Criminal Appeal Act 1968 on the basis that no injustice has been done to the defendant. If the advocate representing the defendant has not made a motion to quash, that is an indication that no injustice has been done: this rests on an assumption that advocates will be aware of procedural matters.

The application to quash must be made at the trial; it is not sufficient to raise the point after conviction (proviso (b) to s 2(3) of the Administration of Justice (Miscellaneous Provisions) Act 1933).

Chapter 5

Arraignment

1. Introduction

(a) Listing

After a case has been committed from the magistrates' court, it will in time be listed at the Crown Court. The issue of listing is covered in Chapters 3 and 6. Essentially, the Crown Court will inform the defendant and his solicitors of the date to appear at the Crown Court, though there is a pilot scheme involving committal to a date announced at the time of committal.

(b) Arraignment

Arraignment usually occurs at the time of the defendant's first appearance. The trial begins on arraignment, which involves the clerk of the court reading the counts on the indictment and asking the defendant(s) to plead guilty or not guilty. In most cases, the appropriate plea will then be entered. However, there are a variety of other possibilities, which are considered below.

(c) Time limits for arraignment

There are time limits governing the period between committal (or the giving of a notice of transfer) and arraignment. Rule 24 of the Crown Court Rules provides that the trial shall not begin until the expiration of 14 days from the committal, unless the defendant and prosecution consent; this may be appropriate if the defendant is before the court for sentence on one matter and intends to plead guilty to a further matter which has only just been committed to the Crown Court (so that all matters can be sentenced together). The maximum time limit is 8 weeks "unless the Crown Court has otherwise ordered". This has been held to be directory rather than mandatory, and is of little practical significance: *Urbanowski* [1976] 1 WLR 455.

In any event, since the trial begins on arraignment and the Crown Court has a discretion to adjourn proceedings as it deems fit, the matter can be listed for pleas to be entered and then adjourned for the swearing of the jury and the calling of evidence to begin outside the period.

There are separate rules governing the re-arraignment of a defendant on a fresh indictment following an order by the Court of Appeal that there be a retrial. These are contained in s 8 of the Criminal Appeal Act 1968. Essentially, the arraignment must occur within 2 months unless the Court of Appeal gives leave for a later arraignment; if there has been no arraignment within the time period, the Court of Appeal must direct an acquittal unless the prosecution have acted with due expedition and there is good and sufficient cause for a late retrial. See, for example, *Coleman* (1992) 95 Cr App R 345.

(d) Custody time limits

Of more significance in the case of an arraignment following a committal or transfer in custody are the custody time limits. Under s 22 of the Prosecution of Offences Act 1985, regulations may be made to limit the time for the prosecution to complete a preliminary stage of proceedings or to limit the time a defendant may remain in custody. However, s 22(3) of the Act provides that, as long as the prosecution has acted with all due expedition, the court may extend the time limits (or further extend them). If the time limits are not extended, the basic provisions are that committal proceedings must begin within 70 days of the first appearance of a defendant who is in custody; the period between committal and arraignment is 112 days. If the time limit expires, the accused person is automatically entitled to bail without surety or security, though conditions such as a curfew or residence may be imposed.

2. Fitness to plead

(a) Raising the issue

A defendant may be mentally unfit to be tried. This will usually be apparent on arraignment, but may arise during the course of the trial. The procedure for deciding this question is governed by the Criminal Procedure (Insanity) Act 1964, as amended by the Criminal Procedure (Insanity and Unfitness to Plead) Act 1991. The issue can arise "at the instance of the defence or otherwise" (s 4(1) of the Act); this allows the prosecution or the judge to raise the question.

(b) Time for resolving the issue

The issue need not necessarily be resolved immediately it is raised: if the defendant has already been acquitted, the issue of fitness to be tried shall not be determined (s 4(2)). It is also possible to delay consideration of the issue until the start of the defence case if it is expedient and in the interests of the accused (s 4(3)). This may apply if, for example, the case against the accused is likely to be discharged on a submission of no case to answer at the close of the prosecution case.

(c) Issue to be resolved by jury

The issue of fitness to plead is to be determined by a jury: if the matter was raised at arraignment, a jury is to be sworn to consider this issue alone. This jury will not determine the issue of guilt at the trial. If, however, the issue of fitness to be tried arises after arraignment, the court may empanel a fresh jury to determine the issue or may allow the jury which is considering the substantive charge to make the decision. If the course of the enquiry as to fitness to be tried raises matters which are to the detriment of the accused, then a separate jury should be empanelled.

(d) Test of unfitness

The test for the jury is whether the defendant is of sufficient intellect to comprehend the course of proceedings: *Pritchard* (1836) 7 C & P 303. The jury can only find unfitness if there is evidence from two or more doctors, at least one of whom has special experience in the diagnosis or treatment of mental disorder and is certified as such under s 12 of the Mental Health Act 1983 (s 4(6) of the Criminal Procedure (Insanity) Act 1964). The standard of proof depends on who raises the issue: the defence need only meet the balance of probabilities, whereas the prosecution must prove the matter beyond reasonable doubt.

(e) Proceedings after verdict

If the accused is found fit to be tried, the trial will proceed (or continue). If found not fit, then a jury must consider whether the defendant did the act or made the omission charged. If the jury finds that the *actus reus* was not committed by the defendant, an acquittal shall follow. The jury deciding this finding of fact shall be the jury which determined the question of fitness to plead if that question arose after the trial had begun; if the question of fitness was determined on arraignment, then a separate jury should be sworn to consider whether the accused committed the *actus reus* of the offence (s 4A of the 1964 Act).

If the defendant is found unfit to plead and to have committed the *actus reus*, then the court may make one of several orders: an absolute discharge, a supervision order with a condition of treatment, a Mental Health Act guardianship order, or an order that the accused be admitted to an appropriate hospital.

3. Failure to plead

A defendant may remain silent on arraignment. That may be because of a deliberate choice, in which case the defendant is said to be "mute of malice": such a defendant will be taken as having entered a plea of not guilty, and the trial will continue. The failure to answer may not be a choice: the defendant may have a speech handicap or be suffering from an injury to the throat. Such a defendant is "mute by visitation of God", whereupon the court will adjourn for a sign-language interpreter, or for the illness to heal, etc; if the muteness is permanent and cannot be overcome, the question of fitness to be tried will be raised.

The question of whether the failure to plead amounts to muteness by malice or by visitation of God is a question of fact for a jury to determine; if the prosecution contends that it is malice, it must prove this beyond reasonable doubt.

4. Special pleas in bar: autrefois acquit and autrefois convict

(a) Circumstances in which the pleas are appropriate

The rule against "double jeopardy" means that a person cannot be tried again for an offence in respect of which he has already been convicted or acquitted. According to Lord Morris's judgment in *Connelly* v *DPP* [1964] AC 1254, the plea of autrefois is proper where:

(i) the defendant has been convicted or acquitted by a court with proper jurisdiction of a charge identical in law and on the facts;

(ii) the defendant could have been convicted of the offence on a previous indictment: in other words, where the jury in a previous trial could have found the defendant guilty of a lesser offence (see Chapter 6) but chose to acquit, the defendant cannot be tried subsequently for the lesser offence;

(iii) the previous trial was for a crime which is in effect the same or substantially the same as the current charge. For example, if the defendant has been acquitted on a charge of manslaughter, he cannot then be charged with murder of the same victim.

The quashing of a conviction by the Court of Appeal amounts to autrefois acquit (though the Court has a specific power to order a retrial).

(b) Circumstances which do not amount to autrefois

There are situations in which a case comes to an end which do not amount to an acquittal:

(i) the jury being discharged from giving a verdict (see below);

(ii) withdrawal of a summons before plea, dismissal of an information because of the non-appearance of the prosecutor (under s 15 of the Magistrates' Courts Act 1980) or the service of a notice of discontinuance under s 23 of the Prosecution of Offences Act 1985. These situations are in contrast to the prosecution offering no evidence after a plea of not guilty has been entered. Consequently, if the prosecution is to be brought to an end without a trial, the defence should always seek to have the defendant enter a plea and to force the offering of no evidence, since that will prevent the charge being resurrected;

(iii) discharge at committal, either because the prosecution was not in a position to proceed and its application for an adjournment was denied, or because the matter was considered on the merits and the examining justices declined to commit the defendant for trial. If, in the latter situation, the prosecution disagreed with the decision to discharge, it would usually seek a voluntary bill of indictment rather than find a different set of examining justices. If further evidence came to light, there is no bar to a further attempt to commit;

(iv) allowing counts to lie on the file (see below);

(v) having an offence taken into consideration rather than appearing on an indictment;

(vi) any other situation where the defendant has not been placed in jeopardy. See, for example, *Dabhade* (1993) 96 Cr App R 146: the defendant consented to summary trial on a charge of obtaining property by deception, but at the trial a charge of theft was substituted, in respect of which jurisdiction was declined and the appellant was committed for trial. It was held that the plea of autrefois did not apply because he had never been in jeopardy of conviction on the original charge.

(c) Procedure for raising the pleas in bar

The plea of autrefois ought to be raised in writing: s 28 of the Criminal Procedure Act 1851. This is directory rather than mandatory, and so the plea can be raised orally if the circumstances merit.

(d) Pardon

Historically, the fact of a pardon could also be raised as a special plea in bar; this was when a person could be pardoned before being tried and convicted. Since a pardon now requires a conviction, it cannot be a plea before trial.

5. Demurrer

This is a plea which is entered in writing and which challenges the form or substance of the indictment. This is a plea which effectively mirrors a motion to quash the indictment; the latter is more usual.

6. Plea to the jurisdiction

Objection to the jurisdiction of the Crown Court ought to be made in writing before arraignment. This plea will be appropriate if the offence is summary only and not covered by s 40 of the Criminal Justice Act 1988 (see Chapter 4), if there has not been a proper committal, voluntary bill or notice of transfer, of if the courts of England and Wales do not have territorial jurisdiction (see Chapter 1).

7. Staying proceedings; abuse of process

A further matter which may be raised in order to prevent the proceedings going further is that their continuation amounts to an abuse of the process of the court. The Crown Court has an inherent power to prevent its processes being used in an oppressive manner. This can be the result of a wide variety of factors, and each case must be considered on its particular merits. It may be that the facts mean that the order to stay proceedings applies as against one only of several defendants or as regards part of the indictment: see *Munro*, The Times, 18 December 1992.

A frequently-occurring factor leading to an abuse of process argument is the time that has elapsed between the offence and the criminal proceedings. In *Attorney-General's Reference (No 1 of 1990)* (1992) 95 Cr App R 296, the Court of Appeal held that the power of the trial judge to order a stay on the basis of mere delay should be used only if the defendant could show on the balance of probabilities that the delay caused serious prejudice to his case to the extent that no fair trial could be held.

Another situation which has been held to amount to an abuse is a prosecution in breach of a promise not to prosecute: *R* v *Croydon Justices, ex p Dean* (1993) 1 WLR 198.

8. Plea of not guilty

This is a proper plea if the accused denies the charge or feels that there is not sufficient evidence for the prosecution to prove guilt beyond reasonable doubt. There will then usually be a contested trial. However, there may be no trial for a variety of reasons.

If there are several counts, pleas of guilty to certain counts may be acceptable to the prosecution; similarly, if there are several defendants, the fact that some of them enter pleas acceptable to the prosecution may mean that proceedings against the others are not pursued. (See Mixed pleas, below.)

The prosecution may also decide that there is insufficient reason to continue the prosecution. The following circumstances are typical:

(i)   A review of the evidence indicates that there is no realistic prospect of a conviction. The prosecution is duty bound to consider whether there is sufficient evidence to justify continuing with a case. This assessment may be altered by changes at a late stage, such as the non-availability of a crucial witness, a statement from a victim withdrawing the allegation, and fresh information affecting the credibility of important witnesses.

(ii)   Information indicates insufficient public interest in continuing in the light of the particular circumstances of the accused. Regard can be had to a wide variety of factors, including the staleness of the allegation, the youth, old age, infirmity or mental state of the defendant, and the seriousness of the offence. (See paragraphs

7 and 8 of the Code for Crown Prosecutors, issued pursuant to s 10 of the Prosecution of Offences Act 1985 and reproduced in the annual report of the Crown Prosecution Service.)

(iii) In some cases, wider considerations of public policy may lead the prosecution to withdraw. For example, compliance with the duty of disclosure to the defence might involve revealing in open court information which the Government requires to be kept secret; if the latter is more important than the prosecution, the trial may come to an end.

9. Plea of guilty

(a) Entering the plea

A defendant may enter a plea of guilty at any stage before the jury returns its verdict, though the plea will usually be entered before a jury is sworn. The plea:

(i) must be entered personally by the accused, and cannot be entered by his legal representatives. Where there are language difficulties, an interpreter can inform the court as to what the accused person has said;

(ii) must be unequivocal. If, for example, the accused says "guilty but with an explanation" and the explanation amounts to a defence, then the plea must be entered as one of not guilty;

(iii) must also be voluntary. If the accused was subject to such pressure that he did not genuinely have a free choice, the plea is a nullity. See *Turner* [1970] 2 QB 321, where the guilty plea was entered by a defendant who believed that his counsel had been told that a guilty plea would lead to a non-custodial sentence whereas a finding of guilt would most likely lead to a period of custody.

(b) Plea of guilty to a lesser offence

A particular offence may be an aggravated form of another offence—so the allegation of the former offence necessarily involves an allegation that the accused committed the latter. For example, robbery involves theft; an allegation of violent disorder or affray in a public place involves an allegation of the less serious offence under s 4 of the Public Order Act 1986. A defendant may admit his guilt of the lesser offence when the more serious allegation is put by entering a plea of not guilty to the offence mentioned but guilty of the lesser offence. This is authorised by s 6 of the Criminal Law Act 1967.

The prosecution may accept this plea, weighing the costs of holding a trial against the public interest in seeking a conviction for the more serious allegation. If the prosecution refuses to accept the plea, then it is deemed to be withdrawn and a trial proceeds as if there has been a simple not guilty plea. If in due course the jury acquits the defendant of the more serious charge and does not use its own power to convict of the lesser offence, the defendant cannot be dealt with in respect of his earlier plea to the lesser offence (*Hazeltine* [1967] 2 QB 857).

The same result can often be achieved by amending the indictment to add a count alleging the lesser offence as an alternative. If there is an alternative offence which is not truly a lesser offence, then it will be necessary to have an extra count on the indictment to cover the alternative offence. For example, a defendant charged with violent disorder might admit assault occasioning actual bodily harm; the latter would have to be added to the indictment.

(c) Mixed pleas—one defendant

If there are several counts on the indictment (or there is more than one indictment) and the defendant admits some of the allegations, a decision will have to be taken by the prosecution as to whether or not to proceed with the remaining matters.

(i)   The counts on one indictment may be alternatives (such as theft and handling of the same items); in this case, once the plea has been entered to one count, the defendant will not face a trial on the other.

(ii)   The counts to which guilty pleas have been entered may reflect the majority of the criminality alleged against the defendant. The prosecution will have regard to such matters as the cost of holding a trial and the fact that, when sentencing, the judge must have regard to the totality of the sentence against the defendant.

(d) Mixed pleas—co-defendants

If there are several defendants and some admit their guilt, the question will arise as to proceedings against the others. There may be circumstances in which the case against co-defendants is, in practice, weaker as a result of the absence of other co-defendants; there may also be cases, particularly where the party pleading not guilty played a peripheral role, in which the fact that others have admitted their guilt means that the public need to see the crime punished is satisfied without having recourse to a trial of those who do not admit their guilt.

(e) If mixed pleas are not acceptable

If the pleas entered by a single defendant are not accepted, there will have to be a trial in respect of the outstanding charges. The defendant will not be sentenced for the matters which are admitted until after the trial, since the defendant should be sentenced on one occasion in respect of all outstanding matters. The issue might arise of allowing a defendant to change all pleas to not guilty and putting the prosecution to proof on all matters; see below for a discussion of the discretion to allow a change of plea.

Sentence should be adjourned where guilty pleas are entered by one co-defendant but others contest the case. It is a long-standing principle that co-defendants should be sentenced together: see *Payne* [1950] 1 All ER 102. The reason for this is to ensure that the court is able properly to reflect the different involvement of the co-defendants. This principle is subject to exceptions. For example, if the co-defendant who pleads guilty has other matters outstanding, the desirability of sentencing him on one occasion for all outstanding matters may be more compelling. Or if the co-defendant who has pleaded guilty plays a minor part in the case, and the case will not be completed for a considerable time, it may not be just to keep him in suspense.

(f) If the mixed pleas are acceptable; lying on the file and entering verdicts

If the prosecution accepts the pleas as entered, it may then offer no evidence on the counts to which not guilty pleas have been entered or ask the judge to order that the counts lie on the file. The latter order means that there can be no trial in respect of the counts without the leave of the court (or the Court of Appeal). Leave will usually be sought and granted only if for some reason guilty pleas are overturned on appeal. In the interests of the defendant and finality, it is better to have the prosecution offer no evidence wherever possible.

If the prosecution offers no evidence on the count(s), under s 17 of the Criminal Justice Act 1967 the judge may direct—if he thinks fit—that a verdict of not guilty be recorded. The discretion to refuse to enter the verdict is limited: the prosecution can simply decline to call any evidence when the jury has been sworn, in which case a submission of no case to answer will inevitably be successful. The advocate for the prosecution should remember that the decision on whether or not to prosecute is for the prosecution, not for the judge; indeed, the judge should not be placed in the position of sanctioning a prosecution. In *DPP* v *Humphreys* [1977] AC 1 at p 46C, Lord Salmon noted that "a judge has not and should not appear to have any responsibility for the institution of prosecutions".

(g) Function of the prosecutor when guilty pleas are entered

In the event of a guilty plea on arraignment, the advocate for the prosecution will summarise the relevant facts. In doing so, there must be no attempt to influence sentence; a neutral account of the facts is therefore required. The only exception to this principle is that there is a duty to assist the unrepresented defendant by pointing out matters of mitigation: see Bar Code of Conduct, Annex H, para 1.8.

The prosecution will also present the antecedents of the accused and, if appropriate, present information with respect to ancillary orders. (See Chapter 7.) The court may ask for the assistance of the prosecutor on such matters as the maximum sentence allowed. The prosecutor has a general duty to draw to the attention of the court errors which will lead to an appeal: this includes the handing down of a sentence which is outside the guidelines of the Court of Appeal.

(h) Disputes as to facts; Newton hearings

The most important element in the sentencing decision of the judge is the facts of the offence to which the accused has pleaded guilty. If the version of the facts presented by the prosecution is not accepted by the defence, the defence will put forward the facts upon which the plea is based. If there is a variance between the two accounts—both of which, of course, must involve the defendant being guilty of the offence alleged—and the variance is sufficiently substantial that it will have an impact on the sentence, the judge should follow the guidelines of *Newton* (1982) 77 Cr App R 13.

(i)   It may be possible to add a count to the indictment which deals with the matter in dispute and have a jury decide the issue of guilt on this count: for example, dispute as to whether a mugger was carrying a knife can be resolved by adding a count for possession of an offensive weapon.

(ii)   The judge can hear evidence from both sides, and can decide whether the prosecution version of the facts is accurate beyond a reasonable doubt. If so, the matter proceeds as if it were a trial: consequently, there must be compliance with the rules of evidence (including the admissibility of confessions and the exclusion of unfair evidence — see Police and Criminal Evidence Act 1984 ss 76 and 78), a full opportunity for cross-examination, and proper account taken of circumstances in which a jury would be directed as to the need for caution (evidence from accomplices, for example).

(iii)   Alternatively, the judge can listen to submissions from the advocates, in which case he must accept the defence version as far as is possible: there is no need to accept a defence account which is untenable, or to call evidence before rejecting it as untenable (*Walton* (1987) 9 Cr App R (S) 107).

The judge will then proceed to sentence—see Chapter 7.

10. Change of plea

A defendant who has pleaded not guilty may change that plea to guilty at any stage before the jury has returned its verdict. This may happen if a submission of no case to answer has failed, or where the judge has ruled evidence as admissible which the defence argued ought to be excluded.

The judge has a general discretion to allow a defendant to change a plea of guilty to not guilty before sentence: *Dodd* (1981) 74 Cr App R 50. An example is where a defendant faces two or more matters, and pleads guilty to a less serious allegation and thereafter is remanded into custody pending his trial on the more serious matter; such a defendant, being a convicted but not sentenced prisoner, may lose the normal privileges of a remand prisoner and will regain those privileges if the plea of guilty is vacated.

11. Pleas contrary to instructions

A defendant who admits his guilt is entitled to plead not guilty, since the burden of proof always rests on the prosecution. A client must be advised on the possible disadvantages of a not guilty plea (in terms of costs and loss of mitigation) and advised also as to the strength of the prosecution case. However, the final decision on plea rests with the client. The prosecution case must then be tested, though it is not permissible to put forward a positive defence which is inconsistent with the confession. Similarly, a defendant whose instructions are such that a plea of not guilty is proper may nevertheless plead guilty if that is his wish: the barrister must advise the client as to the consequences of a guilty plea and also that mitigation before sentence will have to be on the basis that the client committed the offence.

Chapter 6

The course of a trial on indictment

1. Listing

Although the trial technically commences on arraignment, the calling of evidence and the legal arguments on which the fate of the defendant rests will not necessarily follow immediately after arraignment. This will happen only if the case is listed for trial. If the case is listed for pleas to be entered, and the plea tendered on arraignment is one of not guilty, then the prosecution will be granted an adjournment to get its witnesses to court. The court in such an event is exercising its general discretion to adjourn.

(a) Fixed dates

A case which is to be contested will eventually be listed for trial. Some cases will be given a definite date on which the trial will commence. A number of factors can justify a fixed date, such as the seriousness or likely length of the case, which in turn may require the availability of a particular category of judge, or the fact that professional witnesses have to be called and that importance is attached to their convenience, or the need to have special facilities in the courtroom (such as video screens for child witnesses, or computers). A fixed date allows for much more certain preparation of cases and is clearly desirable for all parties involved.

(b) Application for a fixed date for trial

This is a standard pre-trial application in an appropriate case. The issue can often be raised through the listing officer, who has the discretion to assign a fixed date. If necessary, either party can request that the matter be decided by a judge in open court, with the parties' representatives allowed to make comments on the desirability or otherwise of assigning a fixed date. The issue can also be raised if the case is listed for any other pre-trial purpose.

(c) Breaking fixed dates

Fixed dates are not, however, cast in tablets of stone, and can be changed: this may be necessary for the administrative convenience of the court, or it may be because witnesses and/or legal representatives are not available. In the latter case, the prosecution or defence should make representations to the listing office as soon as it becomes clear that a date fixed will not be convenient; it may be useful to contact the other parties to see if they have any objection to a fixed date being moved. Some listing officers are more receptive than others to such suggestions. If the listing officer is unwilling to change the fixture, the matter can be listed in front of a judge (as an application to break a fixture) for representations to be made as to the matter and a judicial decision rendered. The judge has a general discretion and can take into account all relevant factors—the age of the case, the danger of injustice if unavailable witnesses cannot be called, the reason why the matter cannot proceed. Some listing officers will, as a matter of course, refer the issue to a judge.

If a trial given a fixed date is not ready to proceed on that date, for whatever reason, an application to stand it out of the list will have to be made. (See below.)

(d) Warned lists

A case which is not given a fixed date in advance will be placed on a "warned list" for a certain period, which means that the case can be listed for trial at any time on overnight notice. A defendant and his solicitors, and the Crown Prosecution Service (or the other prosecuting agencies) will be informed in advance that the case is to be placed on a warned list in a given period (usually lasting two weeks). During that period, the parties are required to review the lists of the Crown Court and ensure, if necessary, that the defendants and witnesses are present if the case comes into the list for trial.

The case can be given a definite date in that warned period, making it a fixture, albeit one with a limited run-up, or it can be listed with no further warning than its appearance on the list published the day before it is due to commence.

(e) Action to be taken if warned list case not ready

If a case is clearly not ready for trial during the period of a warned list, the listing officer should be informed as soon as possible after the warned list is published. If the listing officer does not remove the case from the warned list, then consideration should be given to having the matter listed for mention to record in open court the difficulty being faced; a judge can direct that the case be removed from the list and order that it should not be placed in a warned list until after a given date. Failure to alert the listing officer may result in a case being listed for trial when it cannot proceed: this raises the possibility of an order of costs against persons at fault for causing court and witness time to be wasted. For similar reasons, the listing officer should be kept informed of the unavailability of witnesses (because of holidays, other commitments etc) and of advocates involved in a particular case.

(f) Cases not heard during a warned list

A case which is not reached during the period of a warned list will, at the end of the warned list period, be taken out of the list and placed in another some weeks ahead. Priority will be given to older cases and to cases involving persons remanded in custody.

(g) Listing of warned list cases

If a case is not given a definite date during the period of the warned list, it is necessary for the parties to consult the daily list of the appropriate court. A provisional daily list for the court will be available at some stage on the previous day, usually in the late morning; this will be updated when necessary, as assessments of the progress of existing cases and the availability of court time are made. There is usually some system for the provisional list to be supplied to solicitors' firms and barristers' clerks, who can make representations as to the readiness of a case for trial, and the availability of the advocate selected for the matter, with a view to having the case removed from the list. Some listing officers and court centres are more sympathetic than others to such representations.

A case may be listed in a number of ways. It may be assigned to a courtroom and given a time at which it will commence. The time assigned for the case to commence will depend on whether there are other cases listed in the same courtroom: there may be a number of matters listed for bail applications, for pleas to be entered and so on, or the court may be completing a trial. So the trial may be listed to commence at the start of the day or "not before 12:00" or some other time.

(h) Back-up trials; "floating" trials

In some courts, two cases will be listed to commence at the same time. The justification for this is that cases are often not ready to proceed (leading to an application to stand out), or defendants will sometimes change their pleas and therefore avoid the need for a trial. If two trials are listed, the prospects of using court time are therefore doubled. Of course, there are also occasions when both trials are effective, in which case only one can go ahead; priority will usually be given to the first case listed—though there is a judicial discretion in this regard. The witnesses, defendants and lawyers involved in the other case will have had a wasted day, which not only is frustrating for all concerned, but also means less money for those lawyers who are paid by the Legal Aid Board.

Other courts operate a "floating" system. Floating trials are such that they can be listed for trial in any court in the court complex which becomes available during the course of the day. The lawyers in the case will communicate with the listing officer at the start of the day to indicate whether their floating case is ready to proceed to trial, and pass on other useful information such as a time estimate for the completion of the trial, so that the listing officer can assign a courtroom as one becomes available. If a case is not ready to proceed, a courtroom will be found for an application to stand the case out from the day's list (though some cases will be stood out by the listing officer).

In some court complexes, all the floating cases will be listed in front of a judge at the start of the morning, so that the status of the various cases can be decided at an early stage in the day, necessary applications to stand out can be made, warrants issued in respect of defendants who have not attended, and so on.

If there is simply not enough court time on a particular day, those "floating" cases which are not reached will be stood out either to another warned list or to another day in the current warned list. It is often not possible to make the final decision as to whether a case will be started or not until late in the day. Most listing officers are, however, able to make the decision by lunch-time or before; then, if the case has to be heard by a judge for any reason—a variation of bail, for example—that can be done at the end of the morning court or the start of the afternoon.

(i) Reserve lists

There will be times when all the matters fixed for trial have been completed, and all the cases in the current warned list have been listed or removed from the list for whatever reason. Since a premium is placed on court time, cases which were not on the warned list may be brought into the list for trial. It is good practice for listing officers who have run short of warned list cases to contact solicitors, the prosecution and barristers' clerks to seek cases which are ready for trial. However, some courts operate a reserve list of cases which may be brought into the warned list or the actual list at any moment. Again, representations can usually be made as to whether or not a case brought into the actual list at short notice should be removed from that list.

2. Applications to stand-out

(a) General

If the matter is listed for trial and either side is not ready for trial, an application will have to be made to have the case stood out to be relisted on another day. The court has a discretion in this regard, as part of its general discretion to allow an adjournment during a trial. Innumerable factors can be taken into account in deciding what is in the interests of justice in the circumstances of the particular case.

There are many reasons why an application to stand a matter out may have to be made. The main reasons will be that witnesses are not available to give evidence (through illness, or simply because they are known to be away from their homes on the day) or that investigations into potential sources of evidence have not been completed. Other matters might be that the defendant is ill and not in a position to follow the trial properly or to give evidence as forcefully as when well.

(b) Prosecution decision if its application is refused

If the prosecution is not in a position to proceed and the judge declines to grant an adjournment, then the prosecutor will be forced to choose whether to proceed on the available evidence or, if an essential witness is absent, to offer no evidence and allow the defendant to be acquitted. The prosecutor, in making this decision, should act in the role of "minister of justice", weighing the interests of the defendant as well as those of the prosecution. So, for example, among the factors to be taken into account are whether the defendant is in custody, how old the matter is, and whether the missing witness is suspected of being an unreliable witness. If the prosecution can proceed on the available witnesses, consideration should be given to whether the missing witness will give assistance to the defence.

(c) Approach to defence application

If the defence is not in a position to proceed, the judge must consider whether there will be injustice to the defendant if the trial proceeds. The judge should not give undue weight to the question of the costs thrown away by the inability of the defence to proceed: that does not have much impact on the question of whether it is unjust to proceed, and can be dealt with, where appropriate, by an order for the payment of costs. If the judge requires the case to proceed when the defence is not ready, there may be grounds for challenging any conviction.

(d) Non-attendance of defendant

The defence may not be in a position to proceed by virtue of the fact that a defendant does not attend. This applies equally to cases listed for plea, trial, or for any other reason when the defendant is required to attend. If the defendant does not attend at the time the case is listed to begin, the case will often be put back to commence at a later stage during the day, so that attempts can be made to locate the defendant.

If the defendant does not attend and there is no information to indicate that he is *en route* to the court, the case will be stood out and, unless the defence can provide an explanation for the non-attendance of the missing defendant, a warrant will be issued for the arrest of the defendant. The warrant may be "backed for bail", in which case the defendant will be arrested by the police and released on bail to attend court. More often, the warrant will be "not backed for bail". In such a case the defendant, when arrested on the warrant, will be brought to the court and a decision made as to whether he should be remanded in custody or on bail.

Often, the defendant's failure to attend is due to not knowing about the listing of the case or being unavoidably detained elsewhere (and failing to notify his solicitors or the court so that the explanation can be put forward to the court as a reason for not issuing the warrant). In these circumstances the defendant may often attend at court voluntarily rather than under arrest. In these circumstances, the defence will seek the withdrawal of the warrant for the arrest of the defendant and request that he be released on bail until proceedings can continue.

3. Surrendering to the dock; bail during the course of the trial

When the trial is ready to commence, a jury will have to be sworn. Prior to that, a defendant who is on bail will surrender to the custody of the court by entering the dock. A defendant who has been remanded in custody will be brought into the dock from the cells. Whenever the court is adjourned, the question of bail will arise; this includes adjournments at lunch-time and at the end of each day, as well as other breaks in the sitting of the court.

If the defendant is on bail (unconditional or with conditions), it is usual practice to deal with the issue of bail at the start of proceedings and for the defence to request that bail be allowed during adjournments on the same or similar terms as those applicable before the defendant's surrender to the dock. It may be possible to argue that some conditions are otiose once the trial has begun—such as a condition of weekly signing at a police station.

Care should be taken in respect of bail on condition of the provision of a surety: if the surety was taken at committal, it will be to secure the attendance of the defendant on the first day of the trial, and will therefore have to be taken again. The judge may allow that the surety be continuous to the end of the trial, or may require that it be taken at the end of every day.

The judge has a discretion in matters of bail during the course of the trial. The general right to bail recognised in s 4 of the Bail Act 1976 applies to a person who appears before the Crown Court in the course of proceedings for the offence. If the judge does not act judicially, the only solution is for application to be made to a High Court judge. Events may occur during the course of the trial which cause the judge to impose fresh conditions or withhold bail altogether: for example, if a defendant is late to court, or if there is evidence of interference with witnesses. Equally, a defendant who has been in custody may be granted bail during the course of the trial (though in practice that would be unusual). If, for example, a number of charges are dropped, that will give a fresh argument in favour of the right to bail being upheld, namely that the case against the defendant is less serious.

4. Presence of defendant

The defendant must plead personally on arraignment, and must be present throughout the trial except in limited circumstances.

(a) Voluntary absence

If the defendant absconds at some stage after the jury has been sworn, the judge may allow the trial to continue and (if convicted) sentence the defendant; naturally, a warrant for the arrest of the defendant will be issued. Alternatively, the judge may discharge the jury from giving a verdict and issue a warrant for the arrest of the defendant; a new trial will commence when the defendant is found.

This judicial discretion applies also if a defendant does not attend but consents to the trial continuing in his absence. This may be useful in a lengthy trial involving several defendants. A defendant might seek the permission of the trial judge to be absent when the evidence does not concern him. If the trial judge does not consent, the defendant will be in breach of his bail if he does not attend.

A defendant in custody may indicate that he does not wish to be present in court; a defendant who is on bail and refuses to surrender to the dock will doubtless be held to be in breach of bail and arrested, and will have to continue to not recognise the court from the cells. A defendant who refuses to come into the court from the cells cannot be compelled.

(b) Involuntary absence through illness, duress etc

The trial of a defendant who is absent through no fault of his own may continue, but the discretion of the judge to allow such a trial to continue should be exercised sparingly; the trial should not be allowed to continue if the accused's defence could be prejudiced by his absence (*Howson* (1981) 74 Cr App R 172). Similarly, the trial of a defendant who is physically present but too ill to follow the proceedings or to give instructions cannot be allowed to continue if his defence will be prejudiced.

(c) Disruption of the trial

A defendant who disrupts the trial may be barred from the court, or may be held guilty of contempt of court (and receive a separate penalty for that). Naturally, a judge should warn a defendant about his conduct before exercising the power to remove the defendant.

(d) Death of defendant

If a defendant dies during the course of proceedings, evidence should be given to the court that the defendant has died. The indictment will then be declared to be of no legal effect and the file closed. The indictment should then be endorsed to that effect.

5. Points of law arising before evidence is called

(a) Matters relating to the indictment

It may be necessary to deal with certain points of law before evidence can be called. The judge's function in the trial is to make rulings on points of law which arise. If there are any points relating to the indictment—an application to quash the indictment, or to split counts on the indictment into separate indictments—these should be dealt with before the jury is sworn.

(b) Judicial view on whether there is a case to answer

It might be appropriate in some cases to invite the judge to indicate his view on a potential submission of no case to answer. If the prosecution does not accept that the case will go no further than the end of its evidence, it might be appropriate to invite the judge to indicate his view as to whether the papers reveal a case to answer (resting on the assumption that the witnesses for the prosecution come up to proof). Some judges are more robust than others in this regard and are willing to give an indication; others will decline to make a ruling until the end of the prosecution case, which is said to be the appropriate time for the issue to be resolved.

(c) Other questions of admissibility of evidence and points of law

The usual time for determining the admissibility of evidence is when the time comes for the evidence to be adduced before the jury. However, the parties may seek to ask the judge to rule on such questions before the jury is sworn. Other points of law may arise, such as whether a particular item is an offensive weapon. Again, some judges are more willing than others to consider such questions before the jury is sworn rather than at the appropriate time during the trial when the point arises. In some circumstances, the point in question might have a considerable impact on the evidence which is called and the necessary cross-examination, in which case an early judicial ruling is sensible. (See below.)

6. Selecting the jury; jury vetting and other matters relating to juries

(a) Composition of the jury panel

The jury panel is comprised of persons summoned for jury service by the Lord Chancellor's department. The jury for any particular location of the Crown Court may be from anywhere in England and Wales, but will usually be persons who live within a reasonable daily travelling distance. If for some reason there are insufficient summoned jurors for the business of the court, the court may require persons in the geographical vicinity of the court to join the jury panel—a procedure called "praying a tales".

The panel must be published, and the parties to the case are entitled to reasonable facilities to inspect the panel at any time until the end of the trial: s 5 of the Juries Act 1974. In practice, the defence will not have the resources to investigate individual jurors, whereas the prosecution (except in the case of a private prosecution) has the resources of the police.

(b) Selecting jurors for each case

Whenever a trial is ready to commence, 15 or so of the available panel of jurors are brought into court. The clerk of the court selects a random 12 from the panel (from cards containing the names). The 12 will step into the jury box in order to take, individually, the jury oath or affirmation, which will occur unless:

(i)   they are challenged for cause by either side;

(ii)   they are asked to stand-by by the prosecution;

(iii) they are excused by the judge.

This may often depend on the result of investigations into the jury panel by the prosecution.

(c) Checks on the jury

Challenging a juror or asking that the juror stand-by is a difficult task without information on the jurors. The prosecution has the resources of the police, and following *Mason* [1981] QB 881 may properly check criminal records of potential jurors with a view to informing prosecuting counsel of reasons to challenge or stand-by a juror. It is said that the main reason for this is to prevent disqualified persons committing an offence by sitting on a jury.

(d) Eligibility for jury service

Individual jurors may be challenged on the grounds that they are not eligible for jury service but have nevertheless been summoned. The basic rule of eligibility involves being aged between 18 and 70, being on the electoral roll, and having been ordinarily resident in the UK for a total of 5 or more years since the age of 13.

Certain groups are ineligible: the clergy, those being treated for mental disorder, and those involved in the administration of justice (judges, magistrates, lawyers, court staff, police, probation officers and so on).

Persons who have been convicted of a criminal offence may be disqualified, depending on their sentence:

(i)   anyone sentenced to more than 5 years' custody is permanently disqualified;

(ii) anyone who has served any period of custody, or received a suspended sentence of imprisonment or an order to perform community service is disqualified for 10 years from the date of the sentence;

(iii) anyone placed on probation is disqualified for 5 years from the date of the order.

It is an offence for a disqualified person to sit on a jury.

Other people may be excused from service if they wish; this group includes MPs, medical professionals, those over 65 and those who have been summoned to serve on a jury within the previous 2 years. Individuals may also be excused on grounds of hardship or conscientious objection to jury service.

(e) Attorney-General's guidelines on jury checks

The check on a potential juror's criminal record is not the sole ground for investigation into the background of jurors. The Attorney-General has issued guidelines for the occasions when it is thought to be proper for jury panels to be investigated further than checks on criminal records ((1989) 88 Cr App R 123). The Attorney-General must authorise any such checks personally, and the prosecution should be under the direct control of the Director of Public Prosecutions.

(i) In cases involving national security, where some of the evidence is likely to be in camera, checks can be made on Special Branch and security service records with a view to discovering whether a potential juror's political views are "extremist", such that the juror may be biased or may seek to exert improper pressure on other jurors; or whether improper use might be made of sensitive material heard in camera. This latter consideration includes the possibility of the juror revealing information under pressure.

(ii) In terrorist cases, the investigation will be to find "extremist" or sectarian views; the guidelines refer only to searching Special Branch records, but will no doubt include security service records now that these services are taking over counter-terrorist activities.

Where a jury check reveals information which indicates potential bias against the defendant, the gist of the information should be passed on to the defence. In addition, the Attorney-General may authorise that checks be done on potential jurors at the request of the defence.

(f) Challenging jurors for cause

Jurors can be challenged for cause by either the prosecution or defence. The challenge can be to individuals (known as a challenge to the polls) or "to the array" (s 12(6) of the Juries Act 1974), which amounts to an allegation that the person summoning the panel has acted improperly or in a biased fashion. The cause may be that the juror is ineligible for jury service, or is biased in some fashion.

(g) Procedure for challenging jurors

The procedure for challenging a juror is to raise the challenge before the juror starts to take the oath or affirmation. The challenging party must produce *prima facie* evidence of the grounds for the challenge, after which questions may be asked of the juror. The hearing can be in open court or in camera. The challenging party bears the burden of proof, and it is a question of fact for the judge whether the cause has been proved.

If the challenge is to the entire jury panel (the array), the challenge ought to be placed in writing in advance of the trial so that the other party has the opportunity to challenge it. Reasons for the objection should be given.

(h) The prosecution's request to stand-by

The prosecution may ask a juror to stand-by; no reason need be given. The juror involved will wait until the available jury panel has been exhausted. The available panel includes that in the building; it is not clear whether it includes any jurors added to the panel by "praying a tales". If there are spaces in the sworn jury, the juror who has been stood-by must be accepted unless cause for challenge can be made out.

The Attorney-General has issued guidelines ((1989) 88 Cr App R 123) on when the prosecution should exercise this right. It should be exercised only sparingly, giving due recognition to the principle of random selection of juries. The prosecution should use its powers only in two circumstances:

(i)   where an authorised jury check has revealed that the the juror involved might be a security risk or susceptible to improper approaches or be influenced in reaching a verdict—there is no duty to disclose the information on which this is based; and

(ii)   where the person is manifestly unsuitable and the defence agrees—such as where a juror selected to try a complex case with documentary evidence is illiterate.

(i) The discretion of the judge to exclude jurors

The trial judge has a residual discretion to exclude a juror who is not competent to sit for such reasons as infirmity, difficulty of hearing or reading (when the case involves documents). This power cannot be used to assist racial or religious balance on a jury (*Ford* [1989] QB 868). The judge has a similar discretion to excuse jurors on grounds of personal hardship, which will be considered particularly in relation to a lengthy trial, or conscientious objection to jury service.

(j) Swearing the jury

The members of the jury take an oath or affirmation to faithfully try the defendant and give a true verdict according to the evidence. Since there is no way of knowing what happens in the jury room, it cannot be known whether the jurors have acted in accordance with their oath. The jury may be invited on behalf of a defendant to ignore their oath and do what they consider to be the justice of the case requires (in a situation where the offence is made out but it is wrong that the defendant have the conviction against his name).

7. Putting the accused in the charge of the jury

Once the jury is sworn, the accused is put in the charge of the jury. The clerk will indicate the contents of the indictment and inform the jury that its obligation is to listen to the evidence and decide whether the accused is guilty or not. The judge may then give the jurors some general information—such as the fact that they ought not to discuss the case with people other than their colleagues on the jury, since it is supposed to be the decision of the jury: if this warning is not given at the outset, it will be given on the first occasion when the jury leave the courtroom and reminders may be given at appropriate times.

Once the accused is in the charge of the jury, any verdict must be given by the jury. Consequently, if the judge directs that a not guilty verdict be entered, that must be done by the jury.

Unless there is to be a *voir dire* first, the next stage in proceedings will be the prosecution's opening speech. However, before that is discussed, it is convenient to deal with the situations in which a jury or jurors may be discharged during the course of the trial.

8. Discharge of jurors in the course of the trial

The twelve jurors who are sworn before evidence is called are usually the same individuals who go on to consider the case and return the verdict. However, there are circumstances in which jurors can be discharged by the judge.

When a juror dies or becomes incapacitated, or for some other good reason is unable to continue, he can be discharged; this can include being unable to rearrange a holiday when a trial has become much longer than was expected: s 16 of the Juries Act 1974; *Hamberry* [1977] QB 924. It may also be proper to discharge a juror when it becomes apparent that he or she knows the accused or one of the witnesses. The decision is one for the judge, though most judges would ask for representations from the parties. In *Gough* [1993] 2 All ER 724 the House of Lords has indicated that that test to be applied is whether there is a real danger of bias. Up to three jurors may be discharged without the case stopping.

The alternative to discharging individual jurors is to discharge the entire jury. This can occur when the jury is unable to agree on a verdict (see below), but also in the course of evidence:

(i)   When the jury is informed accidentally of the bad character of the accused or hears other prejudicial information which is not properly evidence in the case. The trial judge has a discretion in respect of discharging the jury; this turns on whether the jury can properly consider the case against the accused. Defence counsel should take the initiative to apply for the jury to be discharged.

(ii) Misconduct by a juror—such as talking to a prosecution witness—will also lead to the discharge of the jury if there is a real danger of prejudice to the accused: *Spencer* [1987] AC 128. The judge may hear evidence as to whether, for example, the conversation was about the case or something innocent.

(iii) When it comes to light that a juror knows the accused (or knows that the accused has a bad character) or knows a witness in the case, this may lead to discharge of the individual juror or of the entire jury. Jurors are given instructions that facts such as this should be brought to the attention of the judge via a note. In *Bliss* (1987) 84 Cr App R 1, the Court of Appeal held that there must be evidence pointing directly to the fact, or evidence from which it might properly be inferred, that the defendant might have been prejudiced or might not have received a fair trial.

(iv) When it becomes apparent that there is friction among the jury so that they might not be able to reach a verdict according to the evidence; in such a case, the entire jury should be questioned as to their ability to continue as a body, after which the judge will decide how to proceed: *Orgles*, The Times, 9 June 1993.

9. The prosecution case

(a) Opening speech

Once the jury has been sworn and the defendant put in its charge, counsel for the prosecution will outline the evidence to be called as part of the case, outline the legal elements of the offence and explain the burden and standard of proof. Emotive language should be avoided. Reference should not be made to evidence to which the defence has indicated objection will be taken on the grounds that it is inadmissible.

(b) Prosecution evidence

Having opened the case, the prosecutor will call the evidence used at the committal or in respect of which a notice of additional evidence has been served (subject to a discretion not to call certain witnesses: see below). Prosecution evidence will usually be given by the witness live from the witness box; there are provisions allowing evidence to be read even though the other party objects (see below in this section), and further provisions allowing evidence to be read if all agree (discussed below). Witnesses who give live evidence will take the oath or affirm to tell the truth, be examined in chief by the prosecution, cross-examined by the defence, then re-examined by the prosecution, after which the judge may ask questions. The judge will usually allow either side to ask questions relating to matters he has raised.

The prosecution will also produce any exhibits which form part of its case. As exhibits are produced, they are given a number and retained by the court; they may be used by the jury in the course of its deliberations. The exhibits will often include interviews of the defendant by the police. The usual practice is to give the jury a transcript of the admissible questions and answers in the interview and have it read to the court by the prosecutor and a police officer, the officer reading the questions and the prosecutor playing the accused.

(c) Discretion not to call available witnesses

There is a discretion not to call a witness whose credibility has been undermined since the committal: see *Oliva* (1965) 49 Cr App R 298. There is also a discretion not to call a witness whose evidence will undermine the Crown's case or cause confusion: see *Nugent* (1977) 65 Cr App R 40. Witnesses in the latter category should be released to the defence. Similarly, if the witness is someone whose evidence never formed part of the case and whose statement had been served as unused material, there is no duty to call that witness simply because the defence request: see *Richardson*, The Times, 9 June 1993.

In making the decision, the prosecutor should take into account his duty to present the case fairly, which may involve revealing evidence to the jury which casts some doubt on the case. Consideration should be given to the fact that the defence will not usually be able to cross-examine a witness it has called, which may impose constraints; it may be possible for the prosecution to call the witness and merely tender the witness for cross-examination. If the judge believes that the prosecutor's discretion is being exercised wrongly, the judge may call the witness.

(d) Inconsistent statements of prosecution witnesses

It should be noted that the prosecution is under a specific duty to draw to the attention of the defence any statement made by a prosecution witness which is inconsistent with the evidence given on oath by the witness.

(e) Written evidence—s 13 of the Criminal Justice Act 1925

The normal rules of cross-examination cannot apply to evidence which is read by the prosecution pursuant to s 13 of the Criminal Justice Act 1925, which allows the reading of statements used in the course of a paper committal or the depositions given at an old-style committal.

(i) The evidence of witnesses who are the subject of conditional witness orders will usually be read. It may be that the defence advocate on the day of the trial wishes to have the witness to give live evidence: it is within the discretion of the judge to require the witness to give live evidence and to be subject to cross-examination. If an adjournment is required (because it is not possible to arrange for the witness to attend at short notice), the question of costs thrown away will arise.

It is important for the defence, when reviewing a brief, to check the witness orders and ensure that those witnesses who should give live evidence, and who were conditionally bound at the committal, are notified of the need to attend court. The onus to do this is on the defence, although the usual practice is to notify the Crown and the court of the change in the witness order and rely on the Crown to arrange the attendance of the witness. Indeed, now that the addresses of witnesses are not revealed to the defence in advance of the trial, it is difficult for the defence to serve the appropriate notice on the conditionally bound witnesses to make them fully bound.

(ii) The statements of witnesses who are dead, ill or insane may be read, subject to the discretion of the trial judge. The judge should consider whether it is fair to the defendant to be tried on the basis of evidence which is not tested by cross-examination. It is unusual for this to be fair.

(iii) The statements of witnesses who are "kept out of the way by means of the procurement of the accused or on his behalf" may also be read if this is proved by the oath of a credible witness. The judge retains a discretion as to whether it would be fair to allow a trial without cross-examination of the witnesses, though this discretion is less likely to be used if the accused is shown to have kept the witness out of the way.

(f) Written evidence—Criminal Justice Act 1988

There is an overlap between the provisions of the Criminal Justice Act 1925 and Part II of the Criminal Justice Act 1988. The latter provides for the admissibility of written statements in certain circumstances, despite defence objections, thereby depriving the defence of the opportunity of cross-examination. Section 23 of the 1988 Act allows a statement to be read to the jury if the statement was made to a police officer by a person who is now being intimidated or kept out of the way, or the person is dead or too ill to attend, or the person is abroad and it is not practicable for him to attend, or the maker of the statement cannot be found after all reasonable steps have been taken. The final ground is the one most often invoked: defence advocates should be careful to elicit what steps have been taken to locate the witness, since it is often the practice of the prosecution—through the police—to warn witnesses the night before they are required to give evidence: it is a question of fact whether all reasonable steps have been taken.

Section 25 of the 1988 Act gives the court a discretion to refuse leave for the prosecution to read a document if it is in the interests of justice that it should not be admitted. This discretion is general, but regard must be had to the likely authenticity of the document, the extent to which the evidence in the document is otherwise not readily available, the relevance of the document to an issue in the trial and the risk of unfairness to the accused. It should be remembered that the English system of criminal justice accords great importance to the testing of evidence via cross-examination, and the loss of that right by the defence without its consent amounts to a loss of something regarded as having great intrinsic value.

(g) Some common evidential matters

An exposition of the law of evidence is beyond the scope of this book. However, the following matters arise with some frequency, more often during the course of the prosecution case.

(i) Refreshing memory

Outside court, a witness may refresh his memory from a statement made after the event. If the statement was made some considerable time after the event and is likely to be clouded and inaccurate because of the passage of time, the advocate should be cautious about allowing the witness to read the statement outside court because there is a danger that the evidence in court will merely repeat inaccuracies which were in the statement. Although the advocate for the other party can attempt to undermine the evidence given on the basis that it involves the regurgitation of the statement, it is fairer if the witness is simply asked to recall the events rather than his statement.

There are circumstances in which witnesses will be allowed to refresh their memories in the witness box from notes they made at the time of the incident in respect of which they are giving evidence. Typically, they will be police officers. The document which the witness wishes to use must have been made or verified by the witness soon after the event and while the facts were fresh in his mind; the document must also be produced for the other side to inspect and, if necessary, cross-examine on its contents.

The question of whether to allow the use of a memory-refreshing document in the witness box is one for the judge. Usually, the prosecutor will establish from the witness the basic information as to when the note was compiled, whether it was while events were fresh in the mind of the witness, and whether it was at the first available opportunity. Most judges will invite the opposing counsel to ask any questions and raise any objections before deciding whether to grant leave.

(ii) Expert opinions

The basic rule that witnesses can give factual evidence rather than their opinions does not apply when an expert is asked to give evidence as to his opinion on a matter on which a lay person could not be expected to decide without listening to expert evidence. When such a witness is called, the first task is to establish that the expert has the qualifications or expertise necessary to allow his opinion to be received by the jury.

(iii) Children

There are many cases in which children give evidence. Those under 14 do not give evidence on oath: s 33A of the Criminal Justice Act 1988, as inserted by s 52 of the Criminal Justice Act 1991. However, the court has to determine whether or not the child is competent to give evidence. This requires the court to decide whether the child is able to communicate intelligibly and coherently; the same test applies to adults, particularly those who may be of unsound mind.

(iv) Hostile witnesses

Witnesses often give evidence which does not accord with what they are expected to say, the expectation being based on what was in their statement. If the evidence they give is more favourable to the prosecution, the defence will usually cross-examine on the basis of what is in the statement. If, however, the evidence is less favourable to the prosecution, the prosecutor may seek to have the witness declared hostile. The general rule is that one cannot cross-examine (which can include attacking the credibility and putting previous inconsistent statements) one's own witness. If, however, the witness demonstrates hostility towards the prosecution (rather than merely being forgetful or modifying his recollection), the judge may give leave to the prosecution to cross-examine its own witness. Any questions asked in order to allow the judge to decide whether or not the witness is hostile should be asked in the presence of the jury since it is important that the jury should form an opinion as to the credibility of the witness. A previous statement made by a hostile witness which contradicts what the witness has said from the witness box can then be put to the witness.

(h) Objecting to prosecution evidence; *voir dire*

(i) Rulings on questions of law

One of the judge's functions in a trial is to rule on questions of law, which includes the admissibility of evidence, such as whether a confession complies with s 76 of the Police and Criminal Evidence Act 1984, whether the probative value of evidence outweighs its prejudicial effect and so on. If the advocates cannot agree in advance whether the evidence is admissible, the issue will have to be argued and the judge asked to make a decision. It may be necessary to call witnesses to establish facts to assist the judge in making such a ruling: the process of establishing such facts involves a trial within a trial, commonly known as a *voir dire*. It is only when the necessary facts cannot be agreed or are not evident from the depositions that a *voir dire* should be held.

(ii) Disputed evidence and the opening speech

Evidence whose admissibility is in question should not be mentioned in the prosecution's opening speech. Then, during the trial, at the point when the disputed evidence is to be given, the issue of admissibility will be decided. It may be that the prosecution cannot sensibly make an opening speech without referring to disputed evidence, in which case it will be proper to have the question of admissibility determined before the opening speech. In this situation, it is the usual practice for the jury to be sworn first (even though a ruling that the evidence is not admissible may lead to the case being dismissed); this rests on the basis that the trial has not commenced until the defendant is put in the charge of the jury, and any ruling made by the judge would be open to challenge once the trial has begun. However, there is no apparent reason why the question of admissibility should not be decided before the jury is sworn if all parties consent and undertake that they will not try to argue subsequently that the trial had not commenced and that they therefore will argue the point again.

(iii) Absence of the jury during arguments concerning admissibility of evidence

Since the usual reason for disputing the admissibility of evidence is that it will prejudice the defence case, steps have to be taken to ensure that the jury—if it has already been sworn—does not hear the evidence. Consequently, the jury will usually be told that a question of law has arisen which is a matter for the judge and not for them, and that they therefore should retire. Since the jury may be prejudiced against the defendant if it sees defence counsel rising to object to the admissibility of evidence, the prosecutor should draw the attention of the judge to the fact that the question of admissibility has arisen.

In some cases, the defence may for some tactical reason wish the jury to hear the legal argument or the cross-examination of the witnesses called during the *voir dire*; the defence must consent to the jury being asked to retire: *Ajodha* v *The State* [1982] AC 204. This will, of course, be unusual.

(iv) After the ruling

Once the question of admissibility has been decided, the trial progresses as normal. If disputed evidence is ruled admissible, the defence may still attempt to undermine its weight (for example, repeating some of the questioning used in the course of a *voir dire*). It is always possible, if evidence has been ruled admissible and further evidence comes to light in the course of the trial which supports the argument for ruling the evidence inadmissible, to ask the judge to reconsider a decision: the judge always has the power to do what is necessary to prevent injustice, which may include directing the jury to ignore evidence which it has heard but which is inadmissible, or indeed discharging the jury and ordering a retrial in front of a fresh jury.

If the disputed evidence is crucial to the case and is ruled inadmissible, the prosecution will have to decide whether it has sufficient evidence to proceed. If there is not sufficient evidence, and the jury has not yet been sworn, the prosecution will offer no evidence and the judge will direct that a not guilty verdict be entered. If the jury has been sworn, the prosecution will indicate that there is not sufficient evidence to prove the guilt of the defendant, whereupon the judge will order the jury to return verdicts of not guilty.

10. Submission of no case to answer

(a) General

At the end of the prosecution case, the defence may request the judge to order an acquittal on some or all of the counts because the evidence is such that there is no case for the defendant to answer. The procedure is that the jury is invited to leave the court whilst the submission is made. The defence makes the submission and the prosecution is given a chance to respond; the judge may choose to conduct the submission in a less formal manner, inviting counsel to address points which are of concern to the judge.

(b) Basic principles

The leading authority on the approach to a submission of no case to answer, *Galbraith* (1981) 73 Cr App R 124, identifies the following situations.

(i)   There is no evidence of an essential element of the case: the judge has a duty to stop the case.

(ii) There is tenuous evidence (weak, vague, inconsistent with other evidence) which is such that a jury properly directed could not properly convict on it: the judge has a duty to stop the case.

(iii) There is limited evidence but its strength relies on the jury's assessment of the reliability of the witness, or other matters of fact traditionally left to the jury: the case should proceed.

The line between the second and third categories is sometimes difficult to draw. For example, if the issue is whether a witness is or is not lying, that is a matter for the jury; only if the evidence of the witness is so improbable or inconsistent that the witness must be lying (rather than "may be lying") is it within the second category.

(c) Identification evidence

Special care is required in cases which turn on identification evidence. It is recognised that there is a special need to protect a defendant in cases which rely on identification evidence because an honest witness can be mistaken and yet appear convincing. The guideline case for this situation is *Turnbull* [1977] QB 224. If the only evidence in the case is identification evidence which is of poor quality, then the judge should accede to a submission of no case to answer.

(d) Confession evidence of mentally handicapped defendants

Special care is also needed in respect of confession evidence: in *McKenzie* [1993] 1 WLR 453, the Court of Appeal indicated that where the prosecution case depends wholly on the confessions of a defendant who suffers from a significant degree of mental handicap, and the confessions are unconvincing to a point that the properly directed jury could not properly convict upon them, then the judge should withdraw the case from the jury. The court gave examples of when the confessions may be regarded as unconvincing: lack of the incriminating details to be expected of a guilty party, inconsistency with other evidence, or being otherwise inherently improbable.

(e) Proceedings after submission

If the submission of no case to answer is not upheld, the defence will put its case. If the submission is upheld, the jury will return and the judge will direct it to enter a verdict of not guilty. The judge will usually explain to the jury the reasons for the decision. Then the clerk of the court will ask a representative of the jury to stand and formally enter the verdict.

If the submission is upheld with respect to some but not all counts, the judge will indicate to the jury that he will in due course direct it to return verdicts of not guilty on the appropriate counts and that it need not consider those counts any longer.

A submission can also be made with a view to having the jury directed that it should consider only a lesser included offence: for example, if the charge is robbery and there is no evidence of violence, then the judge can be asked to rule that the case should be left to the jury as one of theft only.

(f) Failure of the defence counsel to make a submission

If the defence counsel fails to make a submission at the end of the prosecution case when it is appropriate, the judge should invite a submission.

11. The jury's right to acquit after the prosecution case

A jury has a right to acquit at any time after the close of the prosecution case (though it must wait until the end of the defence case before convicting); a judge who finds that the prosecution case is weak but not such as to warrant upholding a submission of no case to answer (because, for example, the weakness depends on a question of reliability of a witness) may be invited to remind the jury of this power.

12. The defence case

(a) Opening speech

The defence may make an opening speech if it is going to call witnesses of fact other than the defendant; character witnesses are not sufficient for this purpose. The speech may outline the defence case and/or criticise the prosecution evidence.

(b) Defence witnesses

Of course, the defence need not give evidence. If the accused person is to give evidence, that should be done before other evidence is given on his behalf; the court has a discretion under s 79 of the Police and Criminal Evidence Act 1984 to allow defence evidence to be given out of order. This may be appropriate for the convenience of a professional witness or another witness who has an urgent need to be elsewhere.

Defence witnesses are examined in chief by defence counsel, cross-examined, re-examined and then open to questions from the judge. They may produce exhibits, just as may prosecution witnesses. The same rules apply with respect to hostile witnesses, expert witnesses etc as to prosecution witnesses. The provisions of Part II of the Criminal Justice Act 1988 (relating to written evidence) also apply, as do the provisions relating to the Criminal Justice Act 1967 mentioned below.

The Court of Appeal in *Bevan*, The Times, 30 March 1993 indicated that it was good practice that the decision of the defendant not to go into the witness box be recorded in writing and signed by the defendant. This is particularly the case if the defendant is not called to give evidence when reason and good sense mandate it, since that might be a reason for overturning a conviction, as in *Clinton*, The Times, 11 March 1993.

(c) Revealing the defence case in advance

The court will not necessarily know in advance what the defence case is. In serious fraud cases, the court may order a summary of the defence case to be revealed: see Chapter 3. Otherwise, only alibi and expert evidence need be disclosed in advance. These requirements are contained in s 11 of the Criminal Justice Act 1967 (in respect of alibi evidence) and the Crown Court (Advance Notice of Expert Evidence) Rules 1987 (SI 1987 No 716) made pursuant to s 81 of the Police and Criminal Evidence Act 1984.

(i) Alibi evidence

At committal, a defendant should be warned of the need to give a notice of alibi within seven days of the committal. The alibi notice provisions can only apply if the prosecution case identifies the time of the alleged offence. The notice states where the accused was at the time of the offence, and gives the names and addresses of any supporting witnesses (or any information which might assist in locating such a witness), so that the police can, if they wish, interview the witnesses. If these details are not supplied in the notice and come to the attention of the defence subsequently, they should be served then. If the witnesses do not attend for police interview, this is a fact which can be proved to undermine their credibility.

If a notice has not been given, the leave of the court is required before the alibi evidence can be given. Leave cannot be refused if the defendant was not given the alibi warning at the committal. The court should exercise its discretion judicially. It may be possible, for example, to grant the prosecution time to investigate and call evidence in rebuttal.

The alibi notice is deemed to be given with the authority of the defendant and may therefore be used as a previous inconsistent statement if that is what it turns out to be.

(ii) Expert evidence

Expert evidence must be revealed in advance. The prosecution must do this pursuant to its general obligation to reveal its case; the defence must do this pursuant to Crown Court Rules (see Chapter 3). The judge may refuse to allow expert evidence to be given if there has been a failure to comply with these rules.

13. Reopening the prosecution case

Before the defence case opens, the prosecutor will indicate that he has closed the case for the prosecution. There are certain instances in which the prosecution can reopen its case and call further evidence. This may include formal evidence of an indisputable nature which has been inadvertently omitted; it may also include more contentious matters.

(a) Evidence to rebut an alibi

If a notice of alibi has been given, the prosecution should be in a position to disprove the alibi before it has been given in evidence by the defendant. However, s 11(4) of the Criminal Justice Act 1967 indicates that evidence tendered to disprove an alibi may be given before or after evidence in support of the alibi, subject to the discretion of the court. This discretion should be exercised judicially, having regard to any unfairness to the accused if the prosecution is allowed to reopen its case when it had the opportunity to rebut the alibi in advance. Naturally, if the defence is given leave to produce alibi evidence of which no proper notice has been given, such that the rebuttal could not be part of the prosecution's case, the prosecution will be allowed to reopen its case.

(b) Evidence to rebut surprise defence points arising *ex improviso*

The fact that the defence is not required generally to reveal its case allows it to raise evidence in its defence of which the prosecution has no notice. The prosecution is supposed to ensure that it has the guilty party before bringing or continuing the case. To fulfil this duty, it should investigate the obvious lines that the defence might take, and call evidence to counter this. If, however, the defence raises issues or calls evidence which could not reasonably have been anticipated, the judge has a discretion to allow the prosecution to call rebuttal evidence.

(c) Evidence to undermine the credit of defence witnesses

As a general rule, a witness's answers on matters which go to the credibility of the witness cannot be rebutted—in order to avoid the trial becoming involved in issues of limited relevance to the main issues. There are exceptions to this rule, as set out below. The rules of evidence apply equally to the defence's desire to undermine the credit of prosecution witnesses; the defence will be able to do this as part of its case.

(i)   Previous convictions which are denied may be proved.

(ii) If a defence witness has a reputation for being untruthful, that may be proved.

(iii) Medical evidence that a witness's mental state is such that he is unreliable may be called (if it is available).

(iv) Previous statements made by a witness may be proved in evidence if the witness denies making them: Criminal Procedure Act 1865, ss 4 and 5.

(v)   Evidence that a witness is biased or partial may be called if the witness denies any bias or partiality.

(d) Evidence previously unavailable

If evidence becomes available for the first time after the prosecution has closed its case, leave may be given for it to be called. The judge must weigh the issue of justice to the parties, remembering always that the protection of defendants from injustice requires notice of the prosecution's case in advance. The judge should also remember that the prosecution has the resources of the police and should seek all available evidence long before the case comes to trial. Consequently, it will be unusual for fresh prosecution evidence to be allowed at a late stage.

14. Reopening the defence case

The judge has a discretion to allow the defence to call further evidence at any time before the jury retires to consider its verdict: see *Sanderson* (1953) 37 Cr App R 32, where a witness did not arrive until the summing-up was almost complete.

15. Witnesses called by the judge

The judge has a discretion to call a witness not called by either of the parties. However, in the light of the adversarial nature of the proceedings, the judge should not be keen to enter the arena. In *Roberts* (1984) 80 Cr App R 89, it was noted that the power should be exercised with caution. Consistent with the general duty of the judge to ensure that the defendant is fairly treated, the power to call witnesses can be exercised more freely if the defence agrees. An example of a circumstance in which it would be proper for the judge to call a witness is where the prosecution decides not to call a witness who might prove adverse to its case, particularly under cross-examination: if such a witness was called by the defence, there would be no possibility of cross-examination, whereas it would be possible if the judge calls the witness.

16. Evidence read by agreement

The parties may agree to read certain statements or admit certain facts. This is permitted by ss 9 and 10 of the Criminal Justice Act 1967. A statement may be read if:

(i)   it is signed;

(ii)   it contains a declaration as to its truth to the best of the witness's knowledge and belief, and that the witness realises that he may be prosecuted for wilfully stating what is not believed to be true;

(iii)   a copy is served on the other parties; and

(iv)   none of the parties objects within seven days of receiving the copy of the statement.

The parties can agree to ignore the time limit. Equally, the court can require the person to attend even though the section has been complied with; this can be done on the court's own motion or on the application of a party.

An admission of facts may be made under s 10 of the 1967 Act. It may be made orally by the advocate in court; it may also be reduced to writing. The procedure under s 10 may be useful if the original of a s 9 statement is not available.

The judge should remind a jury that evidence which is read to them is just as much evidence as that which is given from the witness box.

These provisions are used in respect of evidence which cannot usefully be subjected to cross-examination because it is peripheral to the case. For example, the evidence of police officers who transport exhibits between stations or to forensic laboratories, and which merely shows the continuity of possession of the exhibits, will often be read.

However, consideration should also be given to allowing the reading of evidence which is relevant to a central fact in the case. The defence should always remember that the witness in the witness box might give evidence which is more useful to the prosecution than that which is contained in the statement. If the evidence is not to be contradicted, but merely to be the subject of comment as to its inadequacy, it might be tactically better to allow the statement to be read.

17. Views

The court may have to view an item which cannot be brought into court, or may have to inspect the place where an incident is alleged to have occurred (if, for example, the parties cannot agree that photographs are sufficient). The view should be attended by all the parties (unless they refuse to attend), their representatives, the judge, the jury and the shorthand writer; if necessary, a witness may be present and may be asked questions by the parties.

18. Closing speeches

After evidence has been called, the advocates have a right to make closing speeches, commenting on the law and evidence in the case. The prosecution will speak first, though it loses the right to make a speech if the accused is not represented and calls no witnesses other than himself and character witnesses. If the defendant is represented, but no defence evidence is called, the prosecution has a right to make a closing speech, but should rarely do so except in long and complex cases, and should make only a short speech (*Bryant and Oxley* (1978) 67 Cr App R 157). The prosecution may also decide not to make a speech where the case has been short.

The advocate for the prosecution should always remember that he is not to make an impassioned speech in favour of a conviction. It is wrong, for example, to bolster the credibility of prosecution witnesses who are police officers by commenting on the potentially serious consequences for their professional career if their evidence is disbelieved: *Gale*, The Times, 2 June 1993. It is also improper for the prosecution to comment on a defendant's failure to give evidence: Criminal Evidence Act 1898, s 1(b). A similar rule applies to a failure to call a spouse, since the latter cannot be compelled to give evidence except in limited circumstances: Police and Criminal Evidence Act 1984, s 80(8). This prohibition on commenting on such a failure to give evidence does not apply to the advocate for a co-defendant.

19. The judge's summing-up

The judge's functions are to rule on matters of law and procedure which arise in the course of the trial, and to sum up the case to the jury. The latter is an important function, and mistakes in the course of a summing-up are a main cause of appeals against conviction to the Court of Appeal. Before summing up, the judge may ask for the assistance of counsel (in the absence of the jury if the defence agrees) in relation to aspects of the summing-up, including the appropriate direction on a point of law. The judge will have had the prosecution papers in advance and so will be aware of the prosecution's case; he may need some assistance in how the defence case fits the evidence, since that case will usually not have been revealed before the trial.

(a) Reminder of functions

The judge should remind the jury that it makes the final decision on matters of fact, but that the judge rules on law and the jury must abide by the judge's ruling on points of law. This does not mean that the jury must find a defendant guilty when technically he is guilty but it would be unjust to find guilt. Since the basis for the jury's decision to acquit is not known, it will never be known whether the jury has exercised its residual power to ignore the law and do what is just.

The judge is entitled to comment on the evidence, but should remind the jury that his comments are merely his views and are not binding on the jury.

(b) The burden and standard of proof

The jury should be reminded that the prosecution must prove the case against the defendant, and must do so beyond a reasonable doubt so that the jury is satisfied that it is sure that the defendant is guilty. The jury should be reminded that it is to convict on the basis of evidence rather than suspicions, and that care should be taken in respect of circumstantial evidence.

There may be a burden on the defence—the evidential burden of raising an issue such as self-defence, or the burden of proving certain defences on the balance of probabilities. If so, the jury should be reminded of this burden and of the standard of proof required of the defence.

(c) The ingredients of the offence

A full direction should be given as to the elements of the offence with which the defendant is charged—both the *actus reus* and the *mens rea* of the offence.

(d) Separate consideration of separate counts and co-defendants

The judge should explain that the fact that the jury finds the defendant guilty of one offence does not mean that he is guilty of another count on the indictment: the evidence on each count should be considered separately. Similarly, there is no guilt by association, and so the jury should be reminded to consider the evidence against co-defendants separately.

(e) Specific directions on issues of law

The facts of a case may require a specific direction on a point of law or evidence, such as the need to be cautious about the uncorroborated evidence of an accomplice, or the right of the defendant to refuse to answer questions put in a police interview, or the right not to give or call evidence in the trial, or the significance of character.

There are standard directions on the elements of offences and issues of law, which are distributed to all judges and which are based largely on model directions given by the Court of Appeal. Reference to these in trials is perhaps becoming more widespread as more use is made of part-time judges, many of whom have limited experience of criminal law. The standard directions are not, as yet, generally available.

(f) Alternative verdicts

The indictment may contain counts which allege alternative offences. However, even without the presence of such a count, there are circumstances in which the jury can return a verdict of not guilty of the offence charged but guilty of a lesser, alternative offence. This is permissible under specific statutory provisions, and as a general rule if the latter offence is expressly or impliedly part of the more serious offence: s 6(3) of the Criminal Law Act 1967. The judge should give appropriate directions to the jury on this point, subject to it being in the interests of justice.

If certain particulars of the alleged offence can be crossed out with the effect of leaving another offence, the latter is expressly included. So, theft is robbery without the violence; it is also burglary without the entry as a trespasser. Express statutory provisions include the following. An allegation of any offence includes an allegation of an attempt to commit the offence: s 6(4) of the Criminal Law Act 1967. Allegations of violent disorder and affray which occur in public include an allegation of threatening behaviour: s 7 of the Public Order Act 1986. An allegation of theft of a motor vehicle allows a verdict of taking without the owner's consent: s 12(4) of the Theft Act 1968. An allegation of murder allows the jury to return verdicts of manslaughter, causing grievous bodily harm with intent, attempted murder, infanticide or child destruction.

The question of one offence being impliedly part of another is more complicated. The leading case is *Metropolitan Police Commissioner* v *Wilson* [1984] AC 242, the precise *ratio* of which is difficult to discern. The case was decided at the time that the Court of Appeal had decided that "impliedly" meant that the lesser offence was necessarily a step towards committing the more serious offence. The House of Lords rejected this test and seemed to indicate that where in many cases (though not necessarily all) the more serious offence will involve the less serious, the latter is impliedly an alternative offence for the purposes of s 6(3) of the 1967 statute. This, of course, means that there is much scope for argument and reference to decided cases.

(g) Summarising the evidence

The judge will invariably summarise the evidence that has been given. Comments may be made, provided that the judge reminds the jury that the final decision on fact is for the jury. In commenting, the judge should remember that the defence case must be presented fairly to the jury. This part of the summing-up is of vital importance, and a failure to be fair to a defendant may provide a ground of appeal. Of course, some jurors will become well disposed to a defendant in response to obvious prosecution bias by the judge in the course of summing-up.

(h) Duties of advocates in relation to the summing-up

The prosecution's advocate is under a duty to draw to the attention of the judge mistakes made in the summing-up, whether they are misdirections on the law or incorrect summaries of the evidence. The defence advocate may advise the judge of a mistake, or may raise it as a ground of appeal in the event of a conviction.

20. Retirement of the jury

(a) Direction

At the end of the summing-up, the judge will advise the jury that they are to retire to consider their verdict. He will remind them of the advantage of electing a foreman to organise their proceedings. There will also be a reminder of the need for a verdict to be unanimous; the jury may be told that the time for accepting majority verdicts is something on which they will receive direction at the appropriate time. What the appropriate time is should not be revealed.

(b) Jury bailiff

The jury bailiff—the court usher—will swear an oath to take the jury to their room to consider their verdict, and ensure that no one can communicate with them. The jury will then retire, taking with them the exhibits in the case and whatever notes they have made on the evidence.

(c) Jury to stay together after retiring

The jury must stay together until they have reached their verdict; if necessary, they will be kept together overnight in a hotel booked by the court. They may be brought food at appropriate times.

(d) Questions

The jury may have questions to ask, or they may wish to see exhibits (such as video films) which they have not taken to their retiring room. To do this, they will pass a note to the judge (via the jury bailiff). The judge should bring the note to the attention of the advocates, and seek their assistance on how to deal with it if, for example, it asks for a further direction on law or a reminder of the evidence. The jury will then return to the court-room, and their question will be answered. If the note asks for further evidence, the jury should be told that they have to consider the case on the basis of the evidence which has been called.

21. Majority verdicts

(a) General

The jury verdict ought to be unanimous. However, after a certain amount of time, if the jury have failed to reach a unanimous verdict, the judge will give a majority direction—that is, he will instruct them that a verdict of a majority of people is acceptable.

(b) Time

The time for accepting a majority verdict is expressed in s 17 of the Juries Act 1974 as such time as is reasonable in light of the nature and complexity of the case, subject to a minimum of two hours. *The Practice Direction (Crime: Majority Verdict)* of 11 May 1970 [1970] 1 WLR 916 requires that the jury be given ten minutes to settle down before the two-hour period begins to run. The nature and complexity of the case obviously depend on the facts of each case.

(c) Acceptable majorities

A full jury may return verdicts of 11−1 or 10−2. If during the course of the trial one or two jurors have been discharged, only one dissenting voice is allowed: hence majority verdicts of 10−1 or 9−1 are acceptable. It is possible for a trial to continue with 9 jurors; however, their verdict must be unanimous. If the verdict is "guilty" the number in the majority must be disclosed: s 17(3) of the Juries Act 1974. This is a mandatory provision; non-compliance renders the conviction invalid.

(d) Procedure

The procedure for majority verdicts is set out in the Practice Direction of 31 July 1967 (*Practice Direction (Crime: Majority Verdicts)* [1967] 1 WLR 1198).

If the jury return to court in less than the appropriate time for a majority direction, the clerk asks if they have reached a verdict on which they are all agreed. If so, the verdict is taken; if not, the judge will direct the jury to continue to try to reach a unanimous verdict.

After the time considered by the court to be appropriate for a majority verdict, the clerk will again ask if their verdict is unanimous. If it is not, the judge will indicate that he is able to accept a majority verdict and will state the minimum acceptable number. The jury should nevertheless be invited to retire and seek to reach a unanimous verdict.

When the jury return after a majority direction, they will be asked if they have reached a verdict on which at least ten of them are agreed (if there are eleven or twelve jurors) or at least nine are agreed (if there are ten jurors). If the answer is yes, the verdict is taken. If no, the jury will be asked to retire again and seek to reach a verdict unless and until it is clear that they are not able to reach a verdict.

22. The verdict

The jury may return verdicts of guilty or not guilty in relation to any count on the indictment; or they may fail to reach a verdict. If they reach a verdict of guilty by a majority, they will be asked what the figures were.

(a) Failure to reach a verdict

The jury will be given a reasonable time to reach a verdict. If they fail, they will be discharged from giving a verdict. That is the end of the trial, but not necessarily the end of the case as far as the defendant is concerned. There may be a further trial with a different jury. The decision whether or not to proceed further is one for the prosecution, and will depend on the particular circumstances of the case.

There is thought to be a rule that when the jury are unable to agree, a retrial should be held, but if the second jury fail to agree, the prosecution will then offer no evidence. Whether the second trial is worthwhile will depend on such factors as the cost of the trial and the seriousness of the crime alleged, the length of time since the alleged offence and the effect on the witnesses of giving evidence: a simple theft by way of shoplifting may not justify a second trial, whereas a robbery at knifepoint almost certainly will.

(b) Failure to reach a verdict on some counts

If the indictment contains several counts and the accused is convicted of some counts but the jury cannot reach a verdict on others, or certain defendants are convicted but not others, the prosecution will have to decide whether the convictions reflect the criminality alleged. If they do, the prosecution may ask the court to allow the remaining counts to lie on the file and proceed to sentence on the counts on which a verdict was returned. Otherwise, a retrial will be necessary on the outstanding counts; the danger of this leading to inconsistent verdicts is a factor the prosecution should take into account in deciding whether to proceed.

(c) Alternative offences

If the indictment contains counts in the alternative, and the jury can agree on the lesser count but not the more serious, the judge should invite the jury to return the verdict on the lesser count and discharge them from returning a verdict on the more serious alternative.

If the jury have been directed as to alternative verdicts on a count, where the alternative is not on the indictment, the language of ss 4 and 6 of the Criminal Law Act 1967 requires a not guilty verdict on the count on the indictment before they may convict of the lesser offence. If the jury cannot agree on the required not guilty verdict, the only proper solution is to add a count for the lesser offence, take a verdict on that count and discharge the jury from returning a verdict on the more serious count. (See *Collison* (1980) 71 Cr App R 249.)

(d) After a not guilty verdict—defendant's costs order

(i) Discharge

These provisions apply equally to an appellant whose appeal to the Crown Court from the magistrates is successful. Following a verdict of not guilty, applications will be made by the defence to discharge the defendant/appellant. Obviously, if there were other offences of which the defendant was convicted or to which he pleaded guilty, the defendant will be sentenced for those matters.

(ii) Costs—General

There may also be an application for the award of costs. Section 16 of the Prosecution of Offences Act 1985 empowers the Crown Court to make an order that the costs of the defendant be met from central funds in the following circumstances:

(i)   where an accused is not tried;

(ii)   where an accused is tried and acquitted;

(iii)   where a person convicted by the magistrates' court appeals to the Crown Court and the court sets aside the verdict or reduces the punishment.

(iii) Approach to an application for costs

The Practice Direction (Crime: Costs) of 3 May 1991 [1991] 1 WLR 498 indicates that an order should normally be made unless there are positive reasons for not doing so: these include where the defendant's conduct has brought suspicion on himself and misled the prosecution into thinking that the case is stronger than it in fact is, or where the acquittal is on a technicality.

(iv) Amount payable under a costs order

Under s 16 of the Act, the defendant's costs order shall be for the payment of the amount which the court thinks reasonably sufficient to compensate for expenses properly incurred in the proceedings (which includes whatever occurred in the magistrates' court, or on a previous trial in the event of a retrial). This need not be the full amount of the costs if the court is of the opinion that there are circumstances which make an award of the full amount inappropriate; the court shall then assess the amount which it deems to be reasonably sufficient. The amount may be fixed in court or taxed by an officer of the Crown Court. It may include an allowance for travel and subsistence.

(v) Legally aided defendant

The order for costs will not include expenses incurred on behalf of the accused under a legal aid order: s 21(4A)(a) of the Prosecution of Offences Act 1985. Consequently, if a defendant has been legally aided throughout proceedings, the order for costs will only cover travel and subsistence. Expenses incurred before the grant of legal aid can be recovered. If legal aid was granted with a contribution order, the judge should be asked to order that the order be revoked and that any sums already paid be returned.

(e) After a guilty verdict

The judge will then commence the sentencing procedure, which is dealt with in Chapter 7.

(f) Wasted costs orders

A power which seems to be becoming more frequent is the wasted costs order, pursuant to which the court may order the payment by a party or legal representative of costs incurred as the result of an unnecessary act or omission. Similarly, the court may order that payment for such an act not be met through the legal aid fund. See ss 19 and 19A of the Prosecution of Offences Act 1985 and Parts II and IIA of the Costs in Criminal Cases (General) Regulations 1986 (SI 1986 No 1335).

23. Payment of witnesses

Witnesses required by the accused, or by a private prosecutor or the court, and interpreters and medical practitioners are all entitled to the expenses they incurred in attending court, unless the court directs otherwise. Expenses include compensation for loss of time and out-of-pocket expenses. Professional and expert witnesses—including interpreters—are allowed an appropriate fee for their preparation and attendance. (See the Costs in Criminal Cases (General) Regulations 1986 (SI 1986 No 1355).) Character witnesses are not entitled to any payment unless the court certifies that it is in the interests of justice that they attend. Arrangements for the payment of prosecution witnesses in cases brought by one of the normal prosecuting agencies will be made by the prosecuting solicitor.

24. Reporting of proceedings; public justice

(a) Business in chambers

The criminal process is usually public, though the provision of a public gallery is limited in some courts. Some business is conducted in the judge's chambers (which may be in the actual courtroom but with the public excluded). Rule 27 of the Crown Court Rules indicates that the following business may be conducted in chambers: bail applications, the issuing of summonses and warrants, legal aid, procedural matters, extending time limits for appeals from the magistrates' court, setting aside witness summonses, excusal from jury service, applications to state a case, and applications relating to custody time limits. Such cases are not open to the public or the press. The reference to procedural matters in the rules includes such matters as applications to fix a case or to break a fixture. The jurisdiction to hold hearings in chambers is, of course, permissive rather than mandatory.

(b) Hearings in camera; information to the court only

There are limited provisions for hearings in camera, where evidence will be heard by the jury but not in public. Applications for such hearings are governed by rule 24A of the Crown Court Rules, discussed in Chapter 3. The Crown Court has further limited powers pursuant to its inherent jurisdiction to control its own procedure to clear the public gallery if necessary to prevent disorder in court. There are also established practices of allowing some evidence to be written down and communicated to the court only: for example, the name and address of a victim of blackmail, or the identity of an official connected with the security services.

(c) Young persons

Other information may be revealed in court but not reported in the press. Section 39 of the Children and Young Persons Act 1933 allows the court to prevent the publication of information which may reveal the identity of a person under 18 who is a defendant or witness. In *R* v *Leicester Crown Court, Ex p S (A Minor)* (1992) 94 Cr App R 153, the Divisional Court indicated that there were limited circumstances in which it would not be appropriate to impose a reporting restriction, because there was little benefit to anyone on reporting the information whereas the report would have potentially serious consequences for the child or young person. In *Lee* [1993] 2 All ER 170, the Court of Appeal indicated, albeit in *obiter dicta*, that the discretion to allow reporting was not so restricted. In *Lee*, the Court of Appeal referred to the deter rent effect on the contemporaries of the defendant; this is unsatisfactory because the involvement of children and young persons in the criminal justice system should not be used for purposes of general deterrence except in exceptional circumstances.

(d) Sexual offences

The Sexual Offences (Amendment) Act 1992 provides for the anonymity of complainants in a wide variety of sexual offences, extending the protection available to the complainant in rape cases by virtue of the Sexual Offences (Amendment) Act 1986. The court may allow reporting of the identity of the complainant if it is necessary to assist the search for witnesses, if the restriction would unreasonably prevent reporting, or it is otherwise in the public interest.

(e) Contempt of Court Act 1981

The court has a general power under s 4 of the Contempt of Court Act 1981 to order that a report of proceedings or any part of proceedings be postponed where necessary to avoid a substantial risk of prejudice to the administration of justice in those proceedings or other pending or imminent proceedings. Any order should be put in writing by the judge or court clerk and identify its scope, purpose and the time for which the restriction continues: Practice Direction of 6 December 1982 [1982] 1 WLR 1475. It is usual to ask for a restriction where a defendant is to stand trial on a number of indictments; the jury considering the first should not be aware that the defendant has other allegations outstanding.

A person aggrieved by a reporting restriction may appeal to the Court of Appeal under s 159 of the Criminal Justice Act 1988. In *R v Beck and Others, ex p Daily Telegraph and Others* [1993] 2 All ER 177, the Court of Appeal indicated that the court has to balance the need for a fair trial with the requirement of open justice and the legitimate public interest in the subject-matter of the trial. On the facts, the defendants faced three indictments; a reporting restriction was made to prevent reports of the trial on the first indictment—which contained a number of horrific allegations—on the basis that they would prejudice any trials on the further indictments. The Court of Appeal accepted that there was a substantial risk of prejudice, but found that to be outweighed by the public interest in the case.

Reporting of proceedings should, of course, be proper. Sensational and misleading reports can create a risk of prejudice against a defendant such that a conviction will be rendered unsafe: *R v Taylor*, The Times, 15 June 1993.

25. Contempt

Contempt of the court can be committed in a number of ways, from refusing to give evidence, refusing to be sworn as a juror, abusing the judge, disrupting proceedings, retaliating against witnesses, publishing an article which attempts to influence a jury, and so on. Some contempts also amount to distinct offences (such as attempting to pervert the course of justice).

The court may invoke its own summary procedures for dealing with contempt of its own motion and commit the contemnor to prison, or may act pursuant to the procedure of Order 52 of the Rules of the Supreme Court. A court should be cautious about acting summarily, because so to act involves drastic action which is contrary to natural justice: see *Balogh* v *St Albans Crown Court* [1975] QB 73. If the court is being disrupted, then summary action will be justified. When the court does act summarily, it should follow certain procedures before imprisoning someone for contempt: time for consideration should be allowed, and it might be appropriate to allow legal advice to be given to the person risking imprisonment (which will invariably be to apologise to the judge).

PART IV:
SENTENCING

Chapter 7

Sentencing

1. Factual basis

(a) Establishing the facts of the offence

The first task in sentencing—whether following a guilty plea on indictment, a committal for sentence, a trial on indictment or an appeal—is to ascertain the facts of the offence. After a guilty verdict, the judge will form a view based on the evidence called, but should give the benefit of the doubt to the defendant as far as possible: *Stosiek* (1982) 4 Cr App R (S) 205. In the event of a guilty plea, the guidelines in *Newton* (1982) 77 Cr App R 13 should be followed (see Chapter 5).

(b) Outstanding offences

A defendant should usually be sentenced on one occasion in respect of all outstanding matters; this allows the sentencing court to ensure that the totality of the sentence is not excessive. This principle is statutorily recognised in s 28(2)(b) of the Criminal Justice Act 1991.

It might be necessary to adjourn sentencing to allow the completion of outstanding trials, the transfer of cases currently listed in other Crown Court centres or the committal of cases currently pending in a magistrates' court. Whether this is done depends on the circumstances, including the nature of the other cases and the length of time before they can be joined together.

(c) Offences to be taken into consideration

The offender might have admitted a number of offences with which he has not yet been charged. The offender might wish to clear up all outstanding matters by asking that they be taken into consideration by the judge in sentencing. This in practice (though not as a matter of law) means that the offender will not be prosecuted for these offences.

There is no statutory provision for having offences taken into consideration. The usual practice is for a list to be drawn up by the police

119

giving the basic details of these offences, which will be signed by the offender; the judge will ask the offender in open court if he wishes them to be taken into account, and if the offender does so wish, the judge will indicate in open court that he has taken into consideration these other matters.

2. Role of the prosecution

The prosecution must be available to assist the court, in addition to establishing the facts, with questions as to the character and antecedents of the defendant, including details of age, education and employment, and any previous convictions to the extent that they are relevant to the sentencing procedure. If previous convictions are disputed, they must be proved or ignored; a conviction is proved by a certificate which has been signed by a court clerk and which contains the relevant information.

If the accused is in breach of any order—from conditional discharge to suspended sentence of imprisonment—by virtue of his conviction, details should be made available of the offences which led to the imposition of the order, since the court may have to sentence for the previous offence as well as the new offence.

The prosecution may have a more active role to play if there are proceedings for any of the ancillary orders discussed below.

3. Pre-sentence reports

(a) Requirement to obtain reports

Reports from the probation service (or the social services in the case of juveniles) about the offence are a precondition to the imposition of a custodial sentence, unless the offence is indictable-only and the court considers it unnecessary to obtain a report (s 3 of the Criminal Justice Act 1991). A report is not necessary in a murder case because the sentence is fixed by law.

Reports are also necessary before the following community orders can be made: probation or supervision orders with extra conditions, community service orders and combination orders (s 7 of the 1991 Act). It is usual also to obtain a report before making a straightforward probation or supervision order.

(b) Medical reports

If the offender appears to be mentally disordered, the court is required to obtain medical reports before imposing a custodial sentence (unless it considers it unnecessary in the circumstances). The court has to consider the effect of a custodial sentence on the condition from which the offender suffers and on the treatment available for it (s 4 of the 1991 Act).

(c) Bail pending reports

If a report is required but is not available upon the entering of the guilty plea or the verdict, the case should be adjourned for the preparation of the report. The question of bail pending the preparation of the report will arise.

Following conviction, there is an extra ground on which a court can refuse to grant bail. Paragraph 7 of Part 1 of Schedule 1 to the Bail Act 1976 provides that a defendant whose case has been adjourned for the preparation of a report or for inquiries to be made need not be granted bail "if it appears to the court that it would be impracticable to complete the inquiries or make the report without keeping the defendant in custody". This power should not be used except where necessary, such as where the defendant has clearly refused to co-operate voluntarily with the preparation of the report; a suspicion that the defendant will not co-operate can be countered by imposing a bail condition that he meet the appropriate officer when offered an appointment.

If a defendant is to be assessed for a community sentence, the probation service will usually prefer that the defendant be seen whilst on bail so that a proper assessment can be made of the likelihood of co-operation with the sentence: someone who is in custody may present a false impression of their willingness to co-operate.

(d) Failure to obtain reports

The appropriate sections of the Criminal Justice Act 1991 indicate that a sentence is not invalidated by the failure of the court to obtain reports. However, if there is an appeal, the court hearing the appeal is required to obtain a report.

4. Adjournment prior to sentence

(a) Listing and release of prosecution

If there are no reports available in a case where there has been a plea of guilty, and the matter is adjourned for the preparation of the reports, there may be little sense in the prosecution explaining the facts of the offence alleged. This depends on whether the judge in front of whom the plea is entered will be the judge in front of whom the case will be listed when the reports are available. It will usually take four weeks to prepare reports on a defendant on bail, and three weeks if the defendant is in custody. If it is likely to be a different judge, the matter will simply be adjourned. If arrangements can be made so that it will be the same judge, the prosecution can open the case and deal with the matters it wishes to raise; the case can then be adjourned and the prosecution excused attendance on the next occasion. Of course, it may be that the prosecution or the defence do not have all the reports and information they require when the matter is listed for sentence. The court has a general discretion to allow adjournments in such circumstances.

(b) Comments to the defendant on adjournment

In adjourning the case for the preparation of reports, if the court conveys to the defendant the impression that a non-custodial sentence will be given if the reports indicate that that is a feasible option, then the defendant ought not to be given a custodial sentence at the end of the day: *Gillam* (1980) 2 Cr App R (S) 267. Consequently, most judges expressly point out to the defendant that the adjournment of the case for the preparation of reports does not amount to an indication of what will happen when sentence is passed.

5. Speech in mitigation

Once the defence is in a position to mitigate, the advocate for the defendant will make a plea in mitigation. This may involve calling character witnesses, or witnesses to support other facts put forward, such as a person who is willing to offer a home to a defendant who is said to have no fixed address. If there is a pre-sentence report, the advocate may make reference to the relevant parts of that report; sometimes, the person who prepared the report may be available to answer further questions. This might be important if the offender is on the border between a custodial and community sentence. Reference may properly be made to statutory restrictions on sentencing powers, or guidelines of the Court of Appeal.

Different judges may take vastly different courses of action with respect to the same set of facts. There is a wide discretion available, subject only to the limited powers of intervention of the Court of Appeal (or High Court if the sentence followed an appeal from the magistrates). Similarly, some judges are more influenced than other judges by certain lines of mitigation; some can be persuaded by lengthy speeches in mitigation, whereas others become more intransigent the longer the speech continues. Since the aim of a speech in mitigation is to obtain the best possible sentence for the defendant, the art of the advocate is to be aware of the foibles of a particular judge and act accordingly.

6. Limitations on custodial sentences

(a) General rule

Section 1 of the Criminal Justice Act 1991 indicates that where an offence is punishable with a custodial sentence, such a sentence is proper only if:

(i) the "so serious" test is met;

(ii) the protection of the public from a violent offender or a sex offender requires it; or

(iii) the defendant refuses to consent to a community sentence.

(b) Reasons to be given

The court must give reasons for finding that either of the first two grounds apply, and must in all three cases explain to the offender in ordinary language why a custodial sentence is being passed.

(c) Offence "so serious"

Custody is justified where "the offence, or the combination of the offence and one or more offences associated with it, was so serious" that only a custodial sentence can be justified. (This is the language of s 1(2)(a) of the Criminal Justice Act 1991, as modified by s 66 of the Criminal Justice Act 1993.)

(i) Associated offences

An associated offence is one of which the defendant is convicted at the same time, or for which he is to be sentenced at the same time (there being a general rule that a defendant should be sentenced on one occasion for all outstanding matters), which includes offences not on the indictment but which the defendant admits and which he has asked to be taken into consideration. In other words, the judge looks at the offences for which the defendant is to be sentenced and decides whether they necessitate a custodial sentence.

(ii) Definition of "so serious"

There is no definition of "so serious" in the Act. However, s 1(4A)(c) of the Criminal Justice Act 1982, which allowed a custodial sentence on a person under 21 if the offence was "so serious that a non-custodial sentence for it cannot be justified", was interpreted in *Bradbourn* (1985) 7 Cr App R (S) 180. It was said that an offence is "so serious" if it is "the kind of offence which when committed by a young person would make right-thinking members of the public, knowing all the facts, feel that justice had not been done by the passing of any sentence other than a custodial one". In the context of the 1991 Act this definition was approved in *Cox* [1993] 1 WLR 188.

(iii) Previous convictions

Section 29(1) of the 1991 Act (as amended by s 66 of the 1993 Criminal Justice Act) allows the court to take account of previous convictions and failures to respond to previous sentences (including probation orders and conditional discharges) in assessing the seriousness of the offence to be sentenced. Of course, the simple fact that a defendant has offended before will not necessarily mean that the current offence is more serious. That will be a question on the facts of each case. For example, a defendant being sentenced for offences of burglary should not have his offence regarded as more serious on account of a previous conviction for a public order offence.

(iv) Offences committed whilst on bail

The practice of the courts in treating as more serious an offence committed whilst on bail has been given statutory force by s 29(2) of the 1991 Act, as inserted by the 1993 Act. The courts are now required to treat such an offence as aggravated.

(v) Relevance of mitigating factors

Mitigating factors are still to be taken into account: s 28 of the 1991 Act. The fact that an offence is "so serious" does not mean that custody is inevitable if the mitigating factors of the offender are such as to make custody an inappropriate course.

(d) Sexual and violent offences

Under s 1(2)(b) of the 1991 Act, a custodial sentence can be passed if "the offence is a violent or sexual offence" and only custody "would be adequate to protect the public from serious harm" from the offender.

(i) Sexual offence

"Sexual offence" is defined in s 31 of the Act by reference to specific statutory provisions. Certain offences are expressly excluded, including living off the earnings of prostitution or running a brothel. Although attempts—being contrary to the Criminal Attempts Act 1981—are not included in the list of offences, attempted rape is a sexual offence under the 1991 Act: *Robinson* [1993] 1 WLR 168.

(ii) Violent offence

The definition of "violent offence" may cause some problems. It is an offence which "leads, or is intended or likely to lead, to a person's death or to physical injury to a person"; there is a specific provision to include arson. This definition is wide enough to include such offences as dangerous driving and the supplying of certain drugs.

(iii) If sexual or violent offences are "so serious"

The court is not required to look only to this subsection when considering an offence which involves sex or violence. If the offence (or combination with other offences, including previous convictions) is so serious that only a custodial sentence is required, then that head can be used to justify a custodial sentence.

(e) Refusal to consent to a community sentence

If the offence does not meet either of the above tests, but is sufficiently serious to justify a community sentence (see below), and if the community sentence requires the consent of the offender but he refuses to consent, the court may use a custodial sentence. This provision may be useful in the following situation: where an offender has been in custody pending trial, and so will receive credit towards any custodial sentence which he receives (on which see below), but a custodial sentence cannot be imposed under the first two criteria of the 1991 Act, the offender's refusal to accept a community sentence will allow the court to pass a custodial sentence (which perhaps will be of a length to allow the offender's immediate or early release).

It is important to note that under Schedule 2 to the Act (which is given force by s 14) those who fail to comply with a community order may be brought before the magistrates' court: if the order was originally made by the Crown Court, the offender may be committed to the Crown Court. If it is found by the court (not by a jury) that the offender has failed to meet any of the requirements of the order, this is a separate offence which may lead to a fine or a community service order (or an attendance centre order in respect of those aged under 21). Alternatively, the court may revoke the order and impose a fresh sentence for the original offence, giving credit for the amount of the community order completed. In deciding on the fresh sentence, the court may assume that an offender who has persistently and wilfully refused to comply with the requirements of an order has refused to give his consent to the order.

(f) Length of sentence

(i) Where "so serious" or no consent to community sentence

Having decided that the threshold of custody has been passed, the court must fix the length of sentence. If the "so serious" criteria are used to justify custody, or the offender refuses to consent to a community sentence, the length of custody should be "commensurate with the seriousness of the offence, or the combination of the offence and one or more offences associated with it". The seriousness can be affected by the previous convictions of the defendant.

However, s 28 of the Act makes it plain that the court is still allowed to take into account such matters as might mitigate sentence: matters such as youth or old age, loss of good character and the civil disabilities as flow from having a finding of guilt recorded, and please of guilty remain valid factors in mitigation.

(ii) Taking account of early release

(a) Impact of the 1991 Act on early release

The 1991 Act also has an impact on the system of parole and remission. Part II of the Act introduces a system of early release but subjects those released to what is effectively a suspended sentence of imprisonment for the remainder of the term of custody which they were ordered to serve.

With respect to early release, a distinction is drawn between short-term and long-term prisoners: the latter are people sentenced to four years or longer, and the former are those sentenced to less than four years. Short-term prisoners are to be released from prison once they have served one half of their sentence. If the sentence was for twelve months or more, the release is on licence; if the sentence was for less than twelve months, the release is unconditional. Long-term prisoners are released on licence after two-thirds of their sentence; they may be released on licence after serving one half of their sentence, if the Parole Board so recommends. This licence period expires when three-quarters of the time of the original sentence has passed. Section 36 of the Act gives the Home Secretary power to release a prisoner on licence on compassionate grounds at any time.

The old system of remission and parole was more generous to prisoners who did not lose remission or who were granted parole earlier rather than later into their term. Basically, remission was one-half of sentences of twelve months or less, and one-third of longer sentences; however, parole was available to prisoners serving more than twelve months after they had served one-third of the sentence, subject to their having served a minimum of six months.

(b) Effect of the new system

The net effect of the new provisions is that most prisoners sentenced to periods in custody of longer than twelve months will actually spend longer in prison under the provisions of the Criminal Justice Act 1991 than under the old system.

(c) Taking this into account

A Practice Direction issued on 1 October 1992 (1992) 95 Cr App R 456 requires that sentencers should now take account of likely release dates—something they were previously not supposed to do—and modify their sentences accordingly. Although it is not expressed, the clear aim of the Practice Direction is that previous guideline sentences be reduced. Advocates should therefore be in a position to assist the court with the question of when a prisoner would have been likely to have been granted parole under the old system.

(d) Effect of release on licence

If a prisoner is released on licence, he must comply with any conditions attached to the release (which may include supervision by the Probation Service). Failure to do so by a short-term prisoner is a summary offence punishable by fine; the magistrates may also suspend the licence for up to six months and order that the person be recalled to prison: s 38 of the Act. In the case of a long-term prisoner, the Home Secretary may recall the prisoner: s 39.

Section 40 of the Act imposes a suspended sentence on all prisoners, even those short-term prisoners who received sentences of less than twelve months and so were unconditionally released rather than being released on licence. A person who commits an offence punishable with imprisonment before the date on which his sentence would have ended had it been served in full may be ordered to be returned to prison. The order to return can be made only if there has been a conviction: it does not matter if the conviction is after the expiry of the full term, so long as the offence was committed before.

The maximum length of time to be served under the order to return is that between the date of the fresh offence and the end of the full term of custody initially ordered. It may be for a lesser period. It may be concurrent or consecutive. If the fresh conviction is by a magistrates' court, the order to return to prison may not be for more than six months; however, the defendant may be committed to the Crown Court (on bail or in custody) under s 42 of the Powers of Criminal Courts Act 1973. The principles governing whether a suspended sentence of imprisonment should be activated are of obvious value in this situation.

(iii) Deterrence

It has been decided in *Cunningham* [1993] 1 WLR 183 that the principle that the sentence should be commensurate with the seriousness of the offence means commensurate with the punishment and deterrence required. If an offence is prevalent, it may be more serious, because each offence affects not only the immediate victim but all those in the area who are potential victims of that type of offence and are thereby placed in fear and have their freedom of movement limited.

(iv) Sexual or violent offence

The statute provides a separate test for offences of sex and violence in order to allow for sentences for a longer term than is required to meet the seriousness of the offence: s 2(2)(b) provides that the sentence shall be "where the offence is a violent or sexual offence, for such longer term as in the opinion of the court is necessary to protect the public from serious harm from the offender". The word "longer" is a reference to the provisions of s 2(2)(a), which provides that the sentence should be commensurate with the seriousness of the offence.

It is to be noted that the protection of the public must be from the particular offender, rather than from other offenders: in other words, this section cannot be used to justify a longer sentence for the purposes of deterring people other than the offender.

The plain interpretation of s 2(2)(b) is that offences of sex and violence should be met with longer prison sentences than the seriousness of the offence warrants. Defence advocates dealing with offences of sex and violence should therefore encourage a sentence under the first ground for imposing custody rather than the second ground.

Where the sentence is longer than the seriousness of the offence(s) require, the court shall give reasons, and explain in open court and in ordinary language why the sentence is for such a term. Careful note should therefore be taken of the reasons given by the judge for the imposition of the particular sentence.

The Practice Direction of 1 October 1992 applies to sentences passed under this head, though since the aim of sentencing here is expressed to be the protection of the public rather than punishment it cannot apply with equal force. If the offence is a sexual offence, regard should also be had to s 44 of the Criminal Justice Act 1991. As was noted above, the provisions for release on licence of prisoners are that the licence expires after three-quarters of their original term. However, in the case of an offender who was sentenced wholly or in part for a sexual offence, the court has powers under s 44 of the Act to order that the licence shall run until the end of the full term rather than three-quarters. Before making such an order the court should have regard to the matters set out in s 32(6) of the Act, namely the need to protect the public from serious harm from offenders and the desirability of preventing offenders from committing further offences and securing the rehabilitation of offenders.

(g) Maximum sentences

(i) Mandatory life imprisonment; death sentence

The sentence for a person convicted of murder is life imprisonment in the case of a defendant aged 21 or over, custody for life in the case of a defendant aged 18 to 21, and detention during Her Majesty's pleasure in the case of a defendant aged under 18. The question of the time served in custody by a person subject to a custodial term of "life" is determined by the Home Secretary, who will determine when the individual is to be released on parole licence (which means that the person is subject to recall to prison should that prove necessary). The judge in passing sentence may recommend the minimum period to be served before the question of release arises, such a recommendation being in no sense binding on the Home Secretary. High treason retains the death penalty (though it will be commuted to life imprisonment).

(ii) Discovering the maximum sentences

Other than in cases of murder or treason (where the sentence is fixed by law) the judge may impose any sentence up to the maximum allowed; this discretion is, of course, guided by the judgments of the Court of Appeal and limited by the requirements of the Criminal Justice Act 1991.

The maximum sentence may be laid down in a statute; if the offence has been created or modified by legislation, that statute will usually lay down the maximum penalty. Such a maximum might be modified by subsequent action of the legislature. If there has been no statutory intervention in the definition of the offence, such that it remains governed by the common law, the maximum sentence is life imprisonment—unless there has been statutory intervention to limit the maximum sentence.

(iii) Use of the maximum sentence

The maximum sentence should be reserved for the most serious examples of the offence, and generally should not be used where there are substantial mitigating factors (including a guilty plea).

(iv) Discretionary life imprisonment

Certain offences retain a maximum sentence of life imprisonment. It seems that discretionary life sentences will be passed invariably under the "sex and violence" head of the Criminal Justice Act 1991 rather than under the "so serious" head. Section 2(4) of the Act indicates that a custodial sentence for an indeterminate term is to be regarded as being longer than for any determinate term: as such, it is difficult to imagine any offence which is so serious that it requires the imposition of a term of imprisonment longer than any possible fixed term. In addition, s 34 of the Act (discussed below) defines a "discretionary life prisoner" as one whose sentence was imposed for a violent or sexual offence.

This is consistent with the practice approved by cases under the previous sentencing regime, namely that the offence itself be sufficiently grave to justify a long sentence, that the offender be one who appears to be someone who is mentally unstable and who would probably reoffend and present a grave danger to the public, and that the potential danger would be for a long or uncertain period of time.

There are special provisions relating to the release on licence of those who received discretionary life sentences. The sentencing judge may, in handing down a life sentence, specify a term of imprisonment which marks the seriousness of the offence (taking account of the provisions for the release on licence of short-term and long-term prisoners). Once that determinate length of time has been served, the Parole Board may recommend that the prisoner be released if it is satisfied that the protection of the public no longer requires the imprisonment of the offender (s 34 of the 1991 Act).

A Practice Direction issued on 8 February 1993 (1993) 96 Cr App R 398 encourages judges to make use of their powers under s 34 except in the very exceptional case where the seriousness of the offence justifies an indeterminate term; defence counsel should be allowed to make representations as to the length of the determinate part of the sentence.

A person who has received a life sentence and is released on licence remains on licence for the rest of his life. Such a licence may be revoked by the Secretary of State. There are no provisions allowing a court to order the return to prison of one who received a life sentence following a conviction for an imprisonable offence.

(h) Suspended sentences

With respect to custodial sentences, it should be noted that the power to suspend a sentence requires (i) that an immediate custodial sentence is appropriate and (ii) that there are exceptional circumstances justifying the suspension of the sentence. The first requirement is well-known, but the second requirement is new.

The sentencing court has power under s 23 of the Powers of Criminal Courts Act 1973 to bring the suspended sentence into effect (either the full term or a reduced term), impose a fresh period of suspension of the term of imprisonment, or make no order. The court is to bring the full term into effect unless of the opinion that it would be unjust to do so in the circumstances. However, where the fresh offence does not justify custody, it is usually inappropriate to activate a suspended sentence, particularly where the earlier offence was of a different nature: see *McElhorne* (1983) 5 Cr App R (S) 53.

(i) Custodial sentences for juvenile and young offenders

As has been noted, there is a general policy of keeping people under the age of 18 out of the Crown Court; there are also special considerations relating to young adults. Persons under 21 cannot be sentenced to imprisonment; if a custodial sentence is warranted, it is one of detention in a young offenders' institution. A person aged less than 15 cannot be sentenced to detention. Those aged 15 to 17 can be sentenced to between 2 months and 12 months, subject, of course, to the offence being one which carries a custodial sentence of that length; those aged 18 to 20 can be sentenced to between 21 days and the maximum sentence for the offence.

If the offence is one which carries a mandatory life sentence if committed by an adult, a person aged under 21 will be sentenced to detention for life under s 8(1) of the Criminal Justice Act 1982, with the proviso that if the offence is murder, a person under 18 will be sentenced to detention during Her Majesty's pleasure under s 53(1) of the Children and Young Persons Act 1933. In the latter case, there is no power to recommend a minimum period to be served.

Discretionary life sentences can also be imposed, governed by the same principles as apply to adult defendants. The sentences are under different provisions dependent on the age of the defendant. In the case of a young adult, aged 18 to 20, the sentence is under s 8(2) of the Criminal Justice Act 1982. A person aged 14 to 17 is to be sentenced to detention under s 53(2) of the Children and Young Persons Act 1933.

The latter section is also to be used where it is desired to impose a sentence of longer than 12 months on a young person (that being the maximum term of detention in a young offenders' institution for people aged 15 to 17). It can only be used in the following circumstances:

(i) the trial was on indictment (so it cannot be used on a committal for sentence);

(ii) the offence is one which in the case of an adult carries a maximum sentence of 14 years' imprisonment; or

(iii) the offence is causing death by dangerous driving or careless driving whilst intoxicated; or

(iv) in addition in the case of a 16 or 17 year-old offender the offence was one of indecent assault.

The Court of Appeal has made it plain that s 53(2) is to be used as a last resort for crimes of exceptional gravity, and the courts should reflect the desirability of avoiding long sentences for young offenders.

(j) Effect of time in custody awaiting trial

One important provision which can have an impact on the sentence is s 67 of the Criminal Justice Act 1967. This provides that time spent:

(i) in police detention;

(ii) in custody, bail having been withheld; and

(iii) if a juvenile, in local authority care and in secure accommodation,

shall count towards the sentence imposed. The delays which are an inevitable part of the criminal justice process mean that many defendants will come to be sentenced after having served on remand the equivalent of what the offence merits, or more than it merits. In such circumstances, an offence which in fact deserves a community sentence may often lead to a custodial sentence of a length which will allow the immediate or early release of the defendant.

7. Community sentences

(a) Sentences available

Community sentences comprise the following orders: probation, community service, combination (both probation and community service), curfew, supervision, attendance centre. The orders may be combined with other sentences which do not lead to immediate incarceration, save that probation and community service cannot be joined because of the specific provision for a separate combination order.

Probation orders are available for those aged 16 or over; they are to be used to secure the rehabilitation of the offender, prevent further offences or protect the public from harm. They can last for up to 3 years, and may be combined with additional requirements as to participation in specified activities, seeking treatment for drug or alcohol dependency or treatment of a mental condition. The minimum length of an order is 6 months. Supervision orders are of a similar nature and are available for those aged 10 to 17.

Community service orders require a person aged 16 or over to perform between 40 and 240 hours of unpaid work in the community, under the supervision of a community service officer. A combination order requires probation of between 12 months and 3 years and community service of between 40 and 100 hours.

Curfew orders will be available for those aged 16 and over, and will require a person to remain at a specified place for between 2 and 12 hours for up to 6 months. There are provisions for electronic monitoring to regulate compliance with the order. These provisions were not in force at the time of writing (August 1993).

An attendance centre order is available for persons aged under 21, provided that appropriate facilities are reasonably accessible to the offender. They are usually open on Saturdays. The maximum number of hours is 24 for people under 16, and 36 for those aged under 21. However, the normal period is 12 hours unless the court finds that 12 hours would be inadequate. In the case of one aged under 14, the court may find that 12 hours would be excessive and may impose a smaller number of hours.

(b) Criteria for imposition

A community sentence may not be imposed unless "the offence, or the combination of the offence and one or more offences associated with it, was serious enough to warrant such a sentence": s 6 of the Criminal Justice Act 1991 (as amended). The court shall consider which order or orders are both most suitable for the offender and also involve restrictions on liberty commensurate with the seriousness of the offence.

The court shall look to the information it has concerning (i) the circumstances of the offence and (ii) the offender. A pre-sentence report is required in respect of community service orders, combination orders, probation orders with additional requirements or supervision orders with additional requirements. No report is required in respect of simple probation or supervision orders, or curfew or attendance centre orders. However, in the case of probation orders in particular, it is sensible to require a report to assess whether a defendant can work with the probation service.

(c) Supervision of community orders

Compliance with community orders is supervised initially by the magistrates' courts, though failure to comply or other circumstances may eventually lead to the order being revoked and the offender resentenced for the original offence. This may involve an offender who has been given a community sentence by the Crown Court being committed to the Crown Court (see Chapter 1).

8. Fines

(a) General powers

The Crown Court has unlimited powers to fine those convicted on indictment or committed for sentence pursuant to s 38 of the Magistrates' Courts Act 1980. If the person is committed for sentence pursuant to s 56 of the 1980 Act or falls to be sentenced following an appeal from the magistrates' court, the powers of fine are limited to those available in the lower court. These limits are contained in the "standard scale" which was set by s 17 of the Criminal Justice Act 1991 as follows: level 1, £200; level 2, £500; level 3, £1,000; level 4, £2,500; level 5, £5,000. Reference should be made to individual statutes to discover what level of fine is applicable to each given offence.

(b) Combination with other orders

A fine may be combined with other sentences and ancillary orders if the circumstances of the offence so require. It should not be combined with a discharge, since the latter is not a punishment whereas a fine is. It may be proper in exceptional circumstances to combine a fine with a term of custody in order to remove the profit from offending, though this is also possible through a confiscation order. Of course, if the offender will have a substantial debt on being released from custody, this may only encourage a return to crime.

(c) Fixing the level of the fine

The court should take into account the means of the offender when fixing the level of the fine, and should indicate the time allowed for payment. Of course, the fine is designed to be a punishment, and there is nothing wrong in principle with imposing a fine which requires payments for several months—up to two years is acceptable, and up to three years in exceptional cases: *Olliver* (1989) 11 Cr App R (S) 10. The level of the fine must be commensurate with the gravity of the offence, and in imposing fines for several offences at the same time regard must be had to the totality principle (see *R* v *Chelmsford Crown Court, ex parte Birchall* (1989) 11 Cr App R (S) 510).

(d) Custody in default of payment

The sanction for failing to pay a fine is that the offender aged 17 or over will be sent to custody. The court may, under s 31 of the Powers of Criminal Courts Act 1973, allow time for the payment of the fine or direct that it be paid in instalments. The same section requires the court to set a term of imprisonment in default of payment. The maximum terms are as follows: not exceeding £200, 7 days; not exceeding £500, 14 days; not exceeding £1,000, 28 days; not exceeding £2,500, 45 days; not exceeding £5,000, 3 months; not exceeding £10,000, 6 months; not exceeding £20,000, 12 months; not exceeding £50,000, 18 months; not exceeding £100,000, 2 years; not exceeding £250,000, 3 years; not exceeding £1,000,000, 5 years; over £1,000,000, 10 years.

The periods ordered to be served in default may be ordered to run concurrently or consecutively to one another; regard must be had to the totality principle. If part of the fine has been paid at the time the offender comes to be dealt with, the term ordered to be served for default will be reduced accordingly.

(e) Enforcement

The enforcement of fines is the task of the magistrates' court, which may allow extra time to pay, make an attachment of earnings order, reduce the amount of the fine (remit part of it) if the offender's financial circumstances have changed, and ultimately commit the offender to prison if the default in payment is due to wilful refusal to pay or culpable neglect and no other method of enforcement will work. The Crown Court must consent to the remission of any part of a fine which it imposed.

9. Discharges

If the court is of the opinion that the infliction of punishment is inexpedient—looking at the type of offence and the character of the offender—it may discharge the offender. The discharge may be absolute: this is effectively no punishment and is appropriate where a technical offence has been committed, but there is no blame attached. Alternatively, the discharge may be conditional on the offender committing no further offences for a specified period (of up to three years); breach of the terms of the conditional discharge will render the offender liable to be sentenced for the original offence as well as the fresh offence.

10. Mentally disordered offenders

It is unfortunate that a number of people who are mentally unwell become caught up in the criminal justice system. There are a range of sentences available for their circumstances.

(a) Hospital orders: Mental Health Act 1983, s 37

A person convicted of an imprisonable offence may be compulsorily admitted to hospital if the court is satisfied that he is suffering from mental illness, psychopathic disorder, severe mental impairment or mental impairment, that it is appropriate for the offender to be so detained and that that is the most suitable method of disposing of the case. With respect to psychopathic disorder or mental impairment, the court must also be satisfied that treatment is likely to alleviate or prevent a deterioration in the condition.

The evidence must come from two registered medical practitioners—orally or in writing—who agree on the diagnosis; one of the doctors must be approved by the Secretary of State under s 12 of the Act as having special experience in the treatment or diagnosis of mental disorder: s 54 of the Act.

The order must specify the hospital. The offender will be held in prison until it is possible to place him in the hospital. Arrangements must also have been made for the offender to be admitted to hospital within 28 days. The order expires after 6 months, but may be extended by the supervising doctor if necessary for the protection of the public or the interests of the patient's health or safety. If these arrangements have not been made, the judge may be compelled to impose a custodial sentence.

There are powers under s 38 of the Act to impose interim hospital orders for up to 12 weeks (renewable for 4-week periods up to a maximum of 6 months); during this period, the offender must be under the supervision of one of the doctors giving evidence. This allows an assessment of the offender.

(b) Hospital orders with a restriction order

A hospital order may be combined with a restriction order under s 43 of the Act if the antecedents of the offender and the risk of further offences are such that a restriction order is required to protect the public from serious harm. Medical evidence is required; at least one doctor must give live evidence. An offender subject to a restriction order is to be released only on the decision of the Home Secretary or a Mental Health Review Tribunal.

(c) Guardianship orders

These are available in the same circumstances as a hospital order when the court is of the opinion that the mental disorder is of a nature or degree which warrants reception into guardianship. The order will name a social services department or an individual, who will have power to supervise aspects of the offender's life and require attendance for treatment and such like. This order is appropriate where there is no need to detain the offender.

(d) Probation orders with a condition of psychiatric treatment

Where a probation order of at least six months is given in respect of an offence in circumstances where a hospital order is not warranted, but the mental condition of the offender warrants treatment, the court may add a condition of treatment to the probation order. The period of treatment may be for the whole or part of the duration of the probation order; the treatment may be as an in-patient. In respect of those not old enough to be placed on probation, there are provisions for supervision orders with conditions: s 12B of the Children and Young Persons Act 1969.

11. Binding over

(a) General

Section 1 of the Justice of the Peace Act 1968 declares that any court of record with criminal jurisdiction—which includes the Crown Court—has the power to bind over a person who is before the court. Persons before the court include defendants (whether convicted or acquitted) and witnesses who are actually called to give evidence.

The power allows the court to require the person to enter into a recognizance or find sureties in a certain sum to guarantee that the person will be of good behaviour during the specified period of the bind-over. The court should give the individual a chance to make representations as to the use of the power, and it ought to seek information as to the means of the person if the sum is to be anything other than a trivial amount. Once the court has decided to make use of the power, the failure of the person to enter into the recognizance or find sureties can lead to imprisonment, that being the sanction available to the court.

(b) Effect

The effect of a bind-over is analogous to a suspended fine: if the person is shown, on the civil standard of proof, to have breached the bind-over, the forfeiture of all or part of the recognizance or surety may be ordered. A term of imprisonment will be fixed as the sanction for failure to forfeit. Section 1 of the Powers of Criminal Courts Act 1973 allows the court to direct payment by instalments.

(c) Binding over parents of offenders

The use of the power of bind-over extends to the parents of offenders under the age of 16. Under s 58 of the Criminal Justice Act 1991, the court is under a duty to bind over the parent or guardian of the minor to enter into a recognizance of up to £1,000 for a period of up to 3 years or until the minor reaches 18 (whichever is shorter) to take proper care and exercise proper control. The level of the recognizance must take account of the means of the adult—and those means may justify an increase in the amount.

The court must exercise the power if it is satisfied that in the circumstances of the case the exercise of the power would be desirable from the point of view of preventing further offences by the minor. If it does not exercise the power, it must give reasons.

Unreasonable refusal by the parent or guardian to enter into a recognizance is an offence which can be met by a fine on level 3 of the standard scale. The adult may appeal to the Crown Court if the order is by the magistrates, and to the Court of Appeal if the order is by the Crown Court. The adult may also apply to have the order varied or revoked if that is in the interests of justice in the light of changed circumstances.

(d) Binding over to come up for judgment

The Crown Court also has a common law power to bind over a convicted defendant on specified conditions to come up for judgment after a certain period. If he breaches any of the conditions, the defendant will be brought back for sentence for the offence and may be required to forfeit the recognizance entered into on being so bound. If the offender abides by the conditions, either he will not be punished or receive a nominal punishment.

12. Deferring sentence

(a) Power

The power to bind over to come up for sentence has to a large extent been superseded by the power to defer sentence pursuant to s 1 of the Powers of Criminal Courts Act 1973 (which expressly preserves the power to bind over to come up for sentence). The sentence may be deferred for up to six months, if the offender consents and it is in the interests of justice. This will be appropriate when there are signs that the conduct of the offender is changing for the better. The court may also wish to give the offender the chance to make reparation for the offence.

(b) Expectations

The court should set out the expectations it has of the offender: examples are in making attempts to find secure accommodation or employment, to save money for a possible compensation order, or to seek assistance with a drinking problem. A note should be made of what is said to the offender. Substantial compliance with the expectations set out will mean that a non-custodial sentence will be imposed on the offender when he is sentenced at the end of the period of deferment (*George* (1984) 79 Cr App R 26). Failure to attend on the date set for the deferment will lead to a summons or a warrant to attend.

(c) Further conviction during the period of deferment

Section 1(4) of the 1973 Act allows the court which defers sentence to bring forward sentencing if the offender is convicted of another offence before the date set for return for sentencing at the end of the period of deferment. The offender may be summonsed to appear, or a warrant may be issued. Alternatively, under s 1(4A), the court in front of whom the offender is convicted of the subsequent offence may deal with the deferred sentence. The Crown Court may deal with a magistrates' court's deferment of sentence (but may not exceed the maximum sentencing powers of the lower court); the reverse is not true.

If there is an allegation of a further offence which as yet is untried, this should be disregarded by the court at the end of the period of deferment. However, given the desirability of all outstanding matters being sentenced together, it will usually be appropriate for the court to adjourn sentencing until the outstanding matter has been dealt with. This is part of the court's general discretion to adjourn where appropriate.

13. Ancillary matters

There are a wide range of ancillary orders available to the court. The prosecution should be in a position to request the court to make an appropriate ancillary order.

(a) Compensation and restitution

(i) Power and duty to order compensation

Under s 35 of the Powers of Criminal Courts Act 1973, the court may require an offender to pay compensation for personal injury (which includes distress and anxiety: *Bond* v *Chief Constable of Kent* (1983) 76 Cr App R 56) or other loss or damage resulting from the offence. Indeed, the court must give reasons for not ordering compensation. The court need not have an application for compensation, though the prosecution should be prepared to make an application and assist the court in this regard.

(ii) Taking account of the means of the offender

The court should take into account the means of the offender, which may include assets which can be sold. An order may require payments of instalments for two years and, in some cases, three years: *Olliver* (1989) 11 Cr App R (S) 10.

(iii) Fixing the amount

The amount of compensation shall be of such amount as the court considers appropriate in the light of evidence and representations made by the parties: s 35(1A) of the 1973 Act. This does not require the court to embark on complicated enquiries which are best left to actions in the civil courts. The criminal court is to exercise its powers only in clear cases.

The Magistrates' Association has issued guidelines for compensation for personal injury. These range from £30 to £50 for a graze, £100 for a black eye, £300 to £500 for the loss of a tooth (depending on the position of the tooth and the age of the victim), and £550 for a small, uncomplicated fracture.

(iv) Combination with other orders

The order may be combined with other sentences. When a suspended sentence of imprisonment is the main sentence of the court, it is required to consider whether to combine such a sentence with a fine or a compensation order: s 5(1) of the Criminal Justice Act 1991, modifying s 22 of the Powers of Criminal Courts Act 1973.

In appropriate circumstances, the compensation order may be the only order made. Certainly, if the court feels that a fine and a compensation order are appropriate but the offender cannot afford to pay both, priority is to be given to the compensation order: s 35(4A) of the 1973 Act.

(v) Restitution order

A similar power is that of making a restitution order under s 28 of the Theft Act 1968 in relation to goods which are the subject of a Theft Act charge—including theft, burglary, robbery, blackmail, obtaining by deception, handling. The powers of the court are:

(i)   to order that a person having possession or control of the goods restore them to any person entitled to recover them;

(ii)   to order the person convicted to transfer to the victim of the Theft Act offence the proceeds of sale of the goods stolen;

(iii)   to order that the value of the goods which were the subject of the charge be paid out of any money the person convicted had in his possession on being apprehended.

It should be noted that the first order can be made against someone who is not the offender. However, as with compensation orders, the criminal court should not embark on a complicated investigation of entitlement to property which is best left to the civil courts: *Calcutt and Varty* (1985) 7 Cr App R (S) 385. It should also be noted that the second order requires an application to be made by the person entitled; the other two orders do not. Finally, the requirement under the third order that the property be in the possession of the defendant on apprehension includes property subsequently seized and which was under his control at the time of arrest: *Ferguson* (1970) 54 Cr App R 410.

(b) Forfeiture

(i) General power

If the offence consists of the possession of an item or substance which it is unlawful to possess, the court may order the forfeiture of the property.

139

Similarly, any property lawfully seized from an offender (or which was in his possession or control at the time of arrest) which (i) has been used to commit or facilitate any offence, or (ii) was intended to be so used, may be ordered to be forfeited: Powers of Criminal Courts Act 1973, s 43. There must be adequate evidence if the application is to succeed: *Pemberton* (1982) 4 Cr App R (S) 328.

(ii) Totality principle

A forfeiture order is part of the punishment of the court, and must therefore be taken into account in assessing the totality of the sentence imposed.

(iii) Further specific powers

There are specific statutory provisions relating to the forfeiture and disposal of drugs, firearms, offensive weapons, obscene publications, boats and planes used to carry illegal immigrants, and documents used to incite disaffection from the monarch.

(iv) What happens to the property?

The property is taken into the possession of the police and is then subject to the provisions of the Police (Property) Act 1897. This Act allows a magistrates' court to make an order that the property be delivered to the owner or to make such other order as the court thinks fit; such an order may be made on the application of the police or of the person claiming to be the owner of the property. The Police (Disposal of Property) Regulations 1975 (SI 1975 No 1474) allow the police to sell property if there has been no claim within six months of the forfeiture order, or to destroy it if it would not be in the public interest to sell it. The Act allows perishable items to be sold at any time; similarly, items the custody of which would involve unreasonable expense or inconvenience may be sold at any time. Any claim will then be with respect to the proceeds of sale.

Under s 43A of the Powers of Criminal Courts Act 1973, the proceeds (up to a specified amount) of property ordered to be forfeited may be paid to a person who has suffered personal injury, loss or damage as a result of the offender's offence.

(c) Confiscation orders—Drug Trafficking Offences Act 1986 ('DTOA')

(i) Assessment of benefit

When a person is convicted of a drug trafficking offence, the court must determine whether the person has benefited from drug trafficking, if the prosecution ask the court to do so or the court of its own motion decides to do so: s 1 of the Act as amended by s 7 of the Criminal Justice Act 1993. "Drug trafficking" is defined in s 38 of the Act as producing, supplying, possessing with intent to supply, transporting, importing or exporting controlled drugs, together with conspiracy, incitement and participation. "Benefited" involves the receipt of any payment or reward.

(ii) Assumptions that the court is required to make

Section 2 of the Act, as amended by s 9 of the Criminal Justice Act 1993, requires the court to make certain assumptions in assessing the amount of benefit:

(i)   that property received by the defendant in the six years before the proceedings were commenced is the proceeds of drug trafficking;

(ii)   that any expenditures he has made in that period have been funded from drug trafficking; and

(iii)   that property received from drug trafficking is free of any other interest.

The defendant may prove that the assumptions are untrue.

(iii) Section 3 statement from the prosecution

The prosecution will invariably serve a statement assessing the benefit it alleges the defendant has gained from the offence charged on the indictment and other alleged dealings in drugs. Most police forces have officers trained to investigate the financial affairs of drug traffickers. Such a statement is authorised by s 3 of the Act. Rule 25A of the Crown Court Rules provides that any statement shall identify the name of the defendant, the author of the statement, the date and place of conviction if the statement is prepared after the conviction, the relevant information known to the prosecutor and an indication of the dates and amounts of rewards so far as is known. Under the Crown Court Rules, the statement must be served on the court and the defendant.

It is not expressed in the statute that the prosecution must give advance notice of its investigations. However, given the saving in court time of having the statement in advance, and bearing in mind that a defendant upon whom a statement is served at the last minute will almost inevitably be granted an adjournment in order to provide a response, the prosecution should always serve its s 3 statement in advance of the hearing. If they have not done so, the court is authorised by the Act as amended by the 1993 Criminal Justice Act to specify the time for service of the statement.

(iv) Defendant's statement

The defendant may accept any of the allegations, either orally or in writing. The court may require the defendant to indicate the extent to which he accepts the allegations made and to indicate any matters on which he proposes to rely in contesting the allegations. The failure of the defendant to comply with such an order may be treated as an acceptance of the matters contained in the prosecution statement (save the conclusion that he has benefited from drug trafficking or that any payment or other reward was received in connection with drug trafficking). The statement of the defendant is to be served on the prosecution and the court. The prosecution may accept any of the allegations made by the defendant. Acceptance by the prosecution or defendant of allegations made by the other may be treated as conclusive by the court, without the need for further investigation by the court.

(v) Confiscation order

Having assessed the benefit obtained from drug trafficking (including offences not alleged on the indictment, if there is sufficient evidence), the court must make a confiscation order. The amount of the order will be the value of the proceeds obtained by the defendant, or, if that amount cannot be realised, such amount as might be realised. Section 5 of the Act provides detailed rules for determining what is realisable, and the value of the property; it may include gifts from the defendant or property sold at an undervalue. Effectively, a court may strip a drug trafficker of all assets in his name. In determining whether a person has benefited from drug trafficking and the amount to be recovered, the court applies the civil burden of proof: s1(7A) of the Act, as inserted by the 1993 Criminal Justice Act.

(vi) Enforcement

Confiscation orders are enforced in much the same manner as fines; the court may fix a period of custody to be served in default of payment. The Act also authorises High Court proceedings to restrain any dealing with realisable property and to impose charging orders on land and securities, and to appoint receivers: see ss 7 ff of the Act and Order 115 of the Rules of the Supreme Court. There are provisions for the enforcement in England of foreign confiscation orders.

(vii) Postponing the DTOA enquiry; reopening the enquiry

The 1993 Criminal Justice Act introduces specific powers—by amendments to the main Act—to allow the Crown Court to postpone its determination in order to obtain further information; the period should not exceed six months unless there are exceptional circumstances. This does not prevent the court proceeding to sentence (s 1A of the DTOA 1986).

Further, if the prosecution receive fresh evidence which was not available when the defendant was dealt with but which they believe would have had an impact on the decision whether to conduct an enquiry, the assessment of whether the defendant has benefited and the extent of the benefit, the court can be asked to reopen the DTOA enquiry: ss 5A, 5B and 5C of the Act.

(d) Confiscation orders—Criminal Justice Act 1988

Part VI of the Criminal Justice Act 1988—ss 71 ff—introduced a general power of confiscation in respect of any indictable offence, provided that the offender has benefited from the offences for which he falls to be sentenced in the amount of at least £10,000 and has realisable assets of at least that amount. So, if the benefit is less than £10,000, the issue of confiscation orders does not arise; equally, if the amount of benefit is more than £10,000 but the realisable assets of the offender are less than £10,000, no order will be made.

The prosecution must give a written notice to the court that there is benefit and that there are realisable assets of at least £10,000 (s 72). If the notice is given, the court has to determine whether or not to make a confiscation order; it has a discretion, and may consider whether there are pending or likely civil proceedings from the victim of the crime. The procedural provisions—tendering of statements and the like—are similar to the provisions of the Drug Trafficking Offences Act 1986. Rule 25AA of the Crown Court Rules applies. The standard of proof in assessing the question of benefit and the amount to be recovered is the civil standard, and, as with drug trafficking offences, the court may postpone its determination: these provisions were introduced by ss 27 and 28 of the Criminal Justice Act 1993.

(e) Disqualification from driving

(i) General scheme of disqualification and penalty points

Most driving offences carry with them powers or duties to disqualify the offender from driving, or requirements that the fact of the commission of the offence be endorsed on the licence of the offender, sometimes with penalty points. The penalty points may, when combined with points already on the licence, make the offender liable to disqualification as a "totter"—one who has more than twelve points, rendering him liable to obligatory disqualification for six months unless to do so would cause exceptional hardship. There are also provisions requiring an offender to pass a fresh driving test. These provisions are lengthy and detailed, and specialist texts should be consulted; the advocates—particularly the prosecutor—should be in a position to assist the judge as to his powers.

(ii) Causing death

For example, causing death by dangerous driving carries with it—along with any other penalty—disqualification for at least two years (unless there are closely defined "special reasons" for leniency), between three and eleven penalty points and also a mandatory extended driving test. A similar penalty applies to causing death by careless driving when under the influence of alcohol or drugs. Where an offence of manslaughter has been committed by the use of a motor vehicle, the defendant must be disqualified for twelve months, and must pass an extended driving test before being allowed to have his licence returned.

(iii) Other indictable offences

Dangerous driving carries an automatic disqualification of twelve months and a mandatory extended driving test. Driving whilst disqualified gives the judge a discretion to disqualify; the offence must be endorsed on the licence of the offender and six penalty points imposed. Those who take motor vehicles without the consent of the owner (or allow themselves to be carried) have their licences endorsed with eight points, and may find themselves disqualified at the discretion of the court. If the offence is one of aggravated vehicle taking (under s 12A of the Theft Act 1968, as inserted by the Aggravated Vehicle Taking Act 1992), disqualification is mandatory, as is the endorsement of the licence with three to eleven points.

(iv) Where a vehicle is used in a crime

There is a general provision under s 44 of the Powers of Criminal Courts Act 1973, which applies when a person is convicted of an offence punishable with two years' imprisonment and the court is satisfied that a vehicle was used (by the person convicted or anyone else) to commit or facilitate the offence. The court may order disqualification for the period it thinks fit.

(v) Summary offences (s 41 of the Criminal Justice Act 1988)

Various other summary offences may be dealt with in the Crown Court pursuant to s 41 of the 1988 Act if, after the trial of the offences on the indictment, the offender admits his guilt of the s 41 offences. These may include such offences as driving with excess alcohol, where disqualification is obligatory in the absence of special reasons; the minimum period is twelve months, or three years if the offender has committed the second offence within ten years. Refusal to provide a specimen in a police station carries obligatory disqualification if the offender was driving the motor vehicle, and discretionary disqualification if he was merely in charge of the vehicle. All the above offences must be endorsed on the licence of the offender and carry points.

(f) Disqualification from being a company director

An offender convicted of an indictable offence connected with the promotion, formation, management or liquidation of a company or the management of a company's property may be disqualified from being so involved with another company: Company Directors (Disqualification) Act 1986. The maximum period of disqualification is 15 years; breach of the disqualification is a separate offence. In *Re Dawson Print Group Ltd* [1987] BCLC 601, Hoffmann J—exercising the High Court's separate jurisdiction under the Act—indicated that disqualification required conduct which is (a) in breach of commercial reality, or (b) gross incompetence which means that it would be a danger to the public if the person were to be allowed to continue in the management of companies.

(g) Other disqualifications

There are also disqualifications from holding alcohol and gaming licences under the appropriate legislation. A person who has committed an offence involving violence or the threat of it in licensed premises may be excluded from entering the premises and other specified premises without the consent of the licensee: Licensed Premises (Exclusion of Certain Persons) Act 1980.

A person may also be disqualified for a minimum of three months from attending a football match if to do so would help to prevent violence or disorder and the person was convicted of an offence of violence or threats of violence towards people or property at or on the way to a football match (Public Order Act 1986 ss 30 ff). Various other provisions are made by the Football Spectators Act 1989.

(h) Deportation

Under s 6 of the Immigration Act 1971, a court may recommend the deportation of any person aged over 17 who has been convicted of an offence punishable with imprisonment, and who is not a British citizen. The Home Secretary makes the final decision, and may act irrespective of whether there has been a recommendation. The issue for the court is whether the presence of the offender is to the detriment of the country; this will not be so if the offences are minor or if there is little prospect of recurrence. Account can be taken of the likely impact on third parties. The Court of Appeal in *Omojudi* (1992) 94 Cr App R 224 indicated the importance of following the required procedure of serving on the defendant at least 7 days in advance of the recommendation a notice that British citizens are not liable to deportation. The sentencing court will no doubt be able to adjourn the sentencing hearing for a suitable period to comply with this.

14. Costs

Under s 18 of the Prosecution of Offences Act 1985, the court may order that a person who is convicted on indictment, or who unsuccessfully appeals against sentence or conviction in the magistrates' court, should pay an amount which is "just and reasonable" in respect of prosecution costs. The order must specify the costs, and so the prosecutor must be in a position to indicate the amount of the costs. The court may order any amount up to the actual costs incurred by the prosecution.

The Practice Direction (Crime: Costs) of 3 May 1991, [1991] 1 WLR 498, indicates that an order should be made where the court is satisfied that the offender or appellant has the means and ability to pay. An offender sentenced to immediate custody will usually be adjudged not to have the ability to pay. The court has a judicial discretion in fixing the amount, and will take account of such factors as whether, in an either way offence, the defendant elected the expense of jury trial; or whether, in respect of a guilty plea to an offence committed to the Crown Court following a decision to decline jurisdiction, the sentence was one which the magistrates' court could impose, meaning that the committal was unnecessary. Costs will also be apportioned between co-defendants.

The Practice Direction also notes the power of the court to order against a party the payment of costs incurred as a result of an unnecessary or improper act or omission, and to make a "wasted costs" order against a legal representative in respect of costs arising from any improper, unreasonable or negligent act or omission.

15. Power of the court to change its mind

The court has up to 28 days to vary a sentence, pursuant to s 47(2) of the Supreme Court Act 1981. This will be done when the court has mistakenly passed a sentence it could not pass: for example, if a person aged 15 is ordered to undertake community service and the court then realises that the minimum age of the offender for such an order is 16, the sentence may be rescinded and varied by the court within 28 days.

After that period, the matter will have to be taken to the Court of Appeal, which will inevitably quash a sentence which is outside the jurisdiction of the Crown Court. Since the time limit for appealing a sentence is 28 days, the proper course of action if it is discovered that a court has acted without jurisdiction is to have the matter relisted in the Crown Court. The 28-day limit for appeals may be extended by the Court of Appeal; consequently, a failure to discover the mistake within the time limit means that the matter will have to be taken to the Court of Appeal, and the application must include an application for leave to appeal out of time.

The power to vary sentence may be used where the judge on reflection believes the sentence was too harsh. The announcement will be made in open court and recorded by the shorthand writer. This power to vary includes a decision to increase sentence. This should not be done unless both the accused and his advocate are present and have an opportunity to address the court. This general principle is subject to exception if the accused has absconded or refuses to appear: see *McLean* (1988) 10 Cr App R (S) 18. Of course, it will only be in exceptional circumstances that it is proper to increase a sentence: for example, where it becomes apparent that mitigating factors put forward were false.

There is also an inherent jurisdiction to correct errors on the record of the court: see *Saville* [1981] QB 12.

PART V:

APPEALS FROM THE CROWN COURT TO THE COURT OF APPEAL

Chapter 8

Appeals to the Court of Appeal

One result of many trials on indictment is that consideration is given to the possibility of an appeal to the Court of Appeal. The preliminary steps of the appeals procedure are considered in this chapter. The procedure on the actual appeal hearing is outside the scope of this work.

1. Jurisdiction

The Court of Appeal (Criminal Division) has jurisdiction pursuant to a number of statutory provisions. The main statute is the Criminal Appeal Act 1968, which gives jurisdiction to determine appeals against conviction on indictment, findings of insanity or unfitness to plead, sentence following conviction on indictment, sentence following a committal for sentence, and also appeals following a reference from the Home Secretary.

In addition, s 36 of the Criminal Justice Act 1982 allows the Court of Appeal jurisdiction to render an opinion on a point of law at the request of the Attorney-General following an acquittal in a trial on indictment. Section 9 of the Criminal Justice Act 1987 provides for the hearing of appeals against rulings at preliminary hearings in fraud cases, and ss 35 and 36 of the Criminal Justice Act 1988 empower the Court of Appeal to increase lenient sentences following a trial of an indictable-only offence. There is also jurisdiction pursuant to s 13 of the Administration of Justice Act 1960 and s 53 of the Supreme Court Act 1981 in respect of decisions of the Crown Court to punish someone for contempt of court.

There is also an inherent jurisdiction to quash convictions resting on invalid proceedings in the Crown Court and, if appropriate, order that there be a retrial. This is pursuant to the writ of *venire de novo*.

2. Initial steps following conviction or sentence

The Guide to Proceedings in the Court of Appeal Criminal Division, published by the Registrar of Criminal Appeals (the 1983 version of which is reproduced at (1983) 77 Cr App R 138 and [1983] Crim LR 415), indicates that the following steps should be followed.

(i) Solicitors should include with the brief for trial instructions that, in the event of conviction and/or sentence, counsel should settle an advice on appeal and grounds (where appropriate) and forward the same to the solicitors within 14 days of the conviction and/or sentence.

(ii) A convicted or sentenced defendant should be seen immediately after the event and any view as to the prospects of a successful appeal should be conveyed. If only a provisional view can be given, that should be done; if time to consider the matter is required, the client should be informed. If counsel believes there are good grounds for appeal, consideration should be given to requesting the trial judge to certify that the case is fit for appeal (see below).

(iii) Advice on appeal and, where appropriate, signed grounds of appeal should be sent by counsel to solicitors within 14 days and sent by solicitors to the client. Grounds should not be settled unless they have some real prospect of success; counsel should be willing to argue the grounds before the court.

Naturally, the various procedural requirements of the statutes and rules should be met.

3. Appeal against conviction: ss 1 and 2 of the Criminal Appeal Act 1968

(a) Introduction

A person convicted following a trial on indictment has a right to appeal against that conviction on a ground which raises a point of law. If the point of appeal is one of fact or one of mixed fact and law, the leave of the Court of Appeal must be sought. If there are several grounds of appeal, some of which require leave, and others of which do not, leave must be sought in respect of the former; the appellant cannot assume that all grounds will be heard because of the existence of grounds resting on points of law. There is no definition of what constitutes a point of law for the purposes of a right to appeal.

(b) Certificate of the trial judge

The requirement for leave is avoided if the trial judge certifies that the case is fit for an appeal on a point of fact or mixed fact and law: s 1(2)(b) of the Criminal Appeal Act 1968. Consequently, an advocate who believes that there is a clear point of appeal should consider applying for a certificate from the trial judge; the latter may grant a certificate on his own initiative. If the person convicted is in custody, the Crown Court's jurisdiction to grant bail pending appeal is dependent on the granting of a certificate that the case is fit for appeal. *The Practice Direction (Crown Court: Bail Pending Appeal)* of 10

November 1983, [1983] 1 WLR 1292, requires that there be a particular and cogent ground of appeal. A certificate should not be granted where the judge considers that the chance of a successful appeal is not substantial.

(c) Procedure

The following is the procedure to be observed when the appeal is based on the filing of a notice of appeal or application for leave, rather than when the trial judge certifies that the case is fit for appeal. In the latter situation, the case will proceed to the full hearing.

(i) Time limits

Section 18(2) of the Criminal Appeal Act 1968 imposes a time limit of 28 days within which the notice of appeal or application for leave must be given. Time begins to run on the day of the conviction or sentence to which the appeal relates. It is important to note that, where a case is adjourned for reports prior to sentence following a conviction, time runs in respect of the appeal against conviction from the date of the conviction, not the date of sentence. However, s 18(3) of the Act allows the Court of Appeal to extend the time limit either before or after it expires.

(ii) The notice

Rule 2 of the Criminal Appeal Rules 1968 (SI 1968 No 1262) requires that the proper notice together with grounds be served on the appropriate officer of the Crown Court. There is a standard form, which asks for items of information and an indication as to which of the various applications the appellant is making. The notice must be signed by the appellant or on behalf of the appellant (which requires that instructions to appeal be given).

(iii) Grounds of appeal

(a) General style of grounds

Grounds of appeal are required, and must be served with the notice. They may be varied with the leave of the Court of Appeal. The Guide to Proceedings in the Court of Appeal Criminal Division indicates:

> "Grounds must be settled with sufficient particularity to enable the Registrar and subsequently the court to identify clearly the matters relied upon ... A document containing a mere formula such as 'the conviction is unsafe and unsatisfactory' ... will be ineffective as grounds and time will continue to run against the defendant. Reasons must be given as to why the court is invited to come to such a conclusion.

Relevant particulars should be given in the grounds, e.g. names, dates and places. Statutory provisions or case law should be cited".

The Court of Appeal prefers cases to be cited from the Criminal Appeal Reports.

(b) Reference to bases for Court of Appeal intervention

The grounds should indicate why they should cause the Court of Appeal to intervene. Section 2 of the Criminal Appeal Act 1968 indicates that the Court of Appeal is required to allow an appeal against conviction if:

(i) the conviction is unsafe or unsatisfactory in all the circumstances of the case;

(ii) the judgment of the trial court should be set aside because of a wrong decision on any question of law;

(iii) there was a material irregularity in the course of the trial.

These mandatory provisions are subject to "the proviso"—namely that the court may decide the appeal point in favour of the appellant but dismiss the appeal if it considers that there has been no actual miscarriage of justice. The grounds can therefore indicate why there has been a miscarriage of justice.

(c) Common grounds

Typical grounds include the following:

(i) *Defects in the indictment:* If the issue was raised at trial and the judge ruled against the defence, a mistake by the judge is a wrong decision on a matter of law; otherwise, a defect in the indictment is a material irregularity. If the defect in the indictment is such that the indictment is a nullity—for example, because it was not signed or contained counts which were not properly joined—the conviction must be quashed under the court's inherent powers rather than under the statute. This may be important to the appellant because, if there has been no valid trial, there is no power to apply the proviso to s 2 of the Criminal Appeal Act 1968 and dismiss an otherwise meritorious appeal because there has been no actual miscarriage of justice.

(ii) *Mistaken reception of evidence:* If the judge has allowed evidence to go before the jury which it should not have heard, either because the evidence was inadmissible or because the judge should have exercised a discretion to exclude the evidence—under s 78 of the Police and Criminal Evidence Act 1984, for example—the Court of Appeal may intervene.

(iii) *Mistaken exclusion of evidence:* Similarly, the Court of Appeal may intervene if the defence has been prevented from adducing evidence or has been stopped from following a particular line of cross-examination.

(iv) *Rejecting a submission of no case to answer:* Such a submission raises a question of law, and a mistake by the judge is a wrong decision on a matter of law.

(v) *Errors in the summing-up:* The judge may have an important impact on the jury's deliberations because, after the speeches of counsel, the judge will have the last word before the jury retires to consider its verdict. What is said during the course of the summing-up should always be reviewed carefully by defence counsel.

(vi) *Inconsistent verdicts:* If the jury has reached decisions on different counts which no reasonable jury could have reached, the Court of Appeal will intervene.

(iv) Request for assistance from the Registrar:

In some circumstances, it may be difficult for the grounds of appeal to be completed without assistance from the Registrar of Criminal Appeals, for example in obtaining a transcript of part of the proceedings. In such circumstances counsel should send with the grounds a "Note to the Registrar" setting out the matters requiring assistance.

The advice on appeal which has been prepared by counsel may also be sent to the Registrar, though there is no requirement that that be done.

(v) Initial action by the Registrar

The Crown Court sends the notice and grounds to the Registrar of Criminal Appeals. The Registrar will consider whether a transcript is required, and if so how extensive a transcript is required. Any note from counsel indicating the need for a transcript will be considered by the Registrar. If there is any dispute as to the extent of the transcript required, the Registrar may refer the matter to a judge.

Where a transcript is obtained, the Registrar may invite counsel to amend the grounds in the light of the transcript—a process known as "perfecting the grounds". The perfected grounds should refer to the appropriate parts of the transcript, and identify any exhibits to which reference is made. The Registrar will usually request that perfection be completed within 14 days. If counsel does not attend to the task in the time set, the Registrar may use the unperfected grounds for the next stage of proceedings.

Perfecting allows the original grounds to be reconsidered; if counsel has changed his view and now believes the appeal should be abandoned, a fresh advice should be prepared and sent to the solicitors instructed at the trial. The Registrar should be informed that this has been done, but should not be sent a copy of the advice. The solicitors will then take the instructions of their client.

(vi) Frivolous appeals

The Registrar has power under s 20 of the Criminal Appeal Act 1968 to refer a notice of appeal or application for leave to appeal to the Court of Appeal for summary determination. This is to be done if there is no substantial ground of appeal. The court can summarily dismiss the appeal without a hearing if it considers that it is frivolous or vexatious. This power will usually be used to filter appeals on points of law; if the appeal is one of fact or mixed fact and law, there is a filter in any event because of the need to obtain leave.

(vii) Consideration by the single judge

The next stage is invariably that the matter is placed in front of a single judge of the Court of Appeal, who is empowered by s 31 of the Criminal Appeal Act 1968 to exercise some of the powers of the full court. The single judge will usually consider the application solely on the papers, though he may order a hearing in open court or chambers to assist the determination of the issues raised. In the event of a hearing, the judge or the Registrar may grant legal aid for the purpose of the hearing.

The Registrar may refer the case directly to the Court of Appeal, which may, of course, exercise all the powers of the single judge. This will be appropriate if the notice is within time and the sole ground of appeal is a matter of law and there are no ancillary applications which have to be considered before the appeal is heard. The single judge may also refer the case to the full court.

Although the main function of the single judge is to consider the question of leave to appeal in those cases which require leave, often there are various ancillary matters to be considered.

(viii) Ancillary matters

Section 31 of the Criminal Appeal Act 1968 refers to various powers exercisable by the single judge (in addition to granting leave to appeal and extending the time limits for filing the notice of appeal or application for leave).

(a) Presence of the appellant at the appeal

An appellant who is in custody is not entitled to be present at the hearing of a full appeal where the sole ground is one of law, or at the preliminary stages of an appeal or application for leave, unless he is given leave: s 22 of the Criminal Appeal Act 1968. Leave is sought by completing the appropriate part of the notice of appeal and giving reasons on the prescribed form. If the appellant is not in custody, there is no bar to his attendance at any hearing in open court; if the appellant is in custody and the appeal is one of fact or of mixed law and fact, there is a right to be present. In the latter situations, there is no requirement to be present.

(b) Attendance of witnesses

The Court of Appeal is empowered by s 23 of the Criminal Appeal Act 1968 to hear evidence, whether or not it was heard in the Crown Court, and review documents and exhibits; this power is exercisable if it is "necessary or expedient in the interests of justice". The court must hear fresh evidence—subject to a proviso—if it is likely to be credible, would have been admissible in the Crown Court in relation to an issue which is the subject of the appeal, and there was a reasonable explanation for it not being adduced at the Crown Court (s 23(2)). The proviso is that the court need not hear such evidence if satisfied that it would not give reason for allowing the appeal.

Whilst the decision as to receiving evidence is for the court, the single judge may grant an order that a witness attend for examination. The appropriate box on the standard notice of appeal or application for leave to appeal is rather confusing in that it refers to "leave to call a witness" whereas the only power of the single judge is to order attendance. Again, a standard form must be completed giving reasons for the application.

(c) Bail

The single judge may also exercise the powers provided by s 19 of the Criminal Appeal Act 1968 to grant bail to an appellant pending the hearing of the appeal. There are standard forms for this application; if no application is made, the Registrar of Criminal Appeals may refer the matter to the court if he feels that bail ought to be considered.

Bail may be of considerable importance if the appellant received a short custodial sentence, since there is a clear risk of injustice if the wrongful detention of the person is corrected at a time when he has already served most or all of the sentence imposed. However, the court indicated in *Watton* (1978) 68 Cr App R 293 that bail will be granted only if there are exceptional circumstances which are such that justice can only be done if bail is granted. An alternative practice which finds favour is administrative action to ensure that the appeal is heard more quickly than usual.

It should be recalled that the Crown Court can grant bail if it also certifies that the case is fit for an appeal. Pursuant to *The Practice Direction (Crown Court: Bail Pending Appeal)* of 10 November 1983, [1983] 1 WLR 1292, the judge in deciding the question of bail may take into account the length of time before the hearing of an appeal. However, the Practice Direction encourages the Crown Court judge to have the court clerk contact the Listing Co-ordinator of the Criminal Appeal Office to have an assessment of the waiting time.

The Practice Direction goes on to state

"Where the defendant's representative considers that bail should be applied for as a matter of urgency the application should normally be made, in the first instance, to the trial judge, and the Court of Appeal may decline to treat such an application as urgent if there is no good reason why it has not been made to the trial judge".

(d) Legal aid

The grant of legal aid for the purposes of trial includes advice on whether there are reasonable grounds of appeal and, if so, assistance in preparing the appropriate notice of appeal or application for leave. Section 2(4) of the Legal Aid Act 1988 defines "representation" to include advice and assistance as to any appeal, and a grant of legal aid for representation in the Crown Court must be so interpreted.

The Court of Appeal may grant further legal aid, under ss 19 and 20 of the Legal Aid Act 1988. The power to grant legal aid may be exercised by the single judge. The Registrar of Criminal Appeals may also grant legal aid, but may not refuse to grant it; if not minded to grant legal aid, the Registrar must refer the matter to the court or a single judge (reg 22 of the Legal Aid in Criminal and Care Proceedings (General) Regulations 1989).

There is a specific power under s 21(8) of the Act to grant aid limited to the question of whether there are reasonable grounds of appeal and advice in preparing the notice of appeal or application for leave. This will be useful in the case of an appellant who was not legally aided at the Crown Court, or who has decided to change representation after the trial. The Guide to Proceedings in the Court of Appeal Criminal Division makes it plain that in the latter case the Registrar of Criminal Appeals will require cogent reasons for the grant of legal aid and an explanation of the change of solicitors. It may also be wise to apply to the Registrar for a fresh grant of legal aid where the initial steps will involve an unusual amount of expenditure.

Legal aid for proceedings in the Court of Appeal after the notice of appeal or application for leave has been filed will invariably be limited to the services of counsel only, because the appeal will usually turn on the consideration of the papers available and argument based on those papers: so there is nothing for a firm of solicitors to do. However, there are instances when there is need for a solicitor to be assigned also, particularly when fresh evidence is to be adduced. The Guide indicates that it must be shown that there is work required which only a solicitor can undertake; a written application from counsel is expected.

(e) Directions on loss of time

A further power of the single judge is to exercise the court's powers under s 29 of the Criminal Appeal Act 1968. Under this section, time in custody pending appeal counts as part of the sentence "subject to any direction which the Court of Appeal may give to the contrary". The power exists to deter appeals which are without merit, since the effect of a direction is that the prisoner serves extra time in custody.

In *The Practice Direction (Crime: Sentence: Loss of Time)* of 14 February 1980, [1980] 1 WLR 270, the court noted that meritorious appeals are delayed by the lodging of hopeless appeals, and that a reminder of the power to direct that time be lost was necessary; steps were taken to draw the terms of the Practice Direction to the attention of prisoners contemplating an appeal.

Reasons are to be given for the direction, and the power may not be exercised if the appeal is brought pursuant to the certificate of the trial judge. Similarly, the power will not be used if counsel has advised in favour of appeal. It was noted in the Practice Direction that there is an obligation on counsel not to advise in favour of appeal or settle grounds of appeal unless they are properly arguable; consequently, it would not be appropriate to penalise a prisoner who has received advice to appeal even if the single judge considered the appeal to be hopeless.

(ix) Appeal from the single judge

An appellant who is not satisfied by the decision of the single judge may renew his application in front of the court. Notice of such a course of action must be given on the appropriate form within 14 days or such longer time as a judge may allow (s 31(3) of the Criminal Appeal Act 1968 and rule 12 of the Criminal Appeal Rules 1968).

4. Appeals against a verdict of insanity or unfitness to stand trial

A verdict of not guilty by reason of insanity may have important consequences for the defendant. Consequently, there are provisions in ss 12 and 13 of the Criminal Appeal Act 1968 which allow an appeal as of right on a matter of law, and with leave on a question of fact or of mixed law and fact; the trial judge may avoid the need for leave by certifying that the matter is fit for appeal. There are provisions requiring the Court of Appeal to set aside the finding if the verdict is unsafe or unsatisfactory, based on a wrong decision on a question of law, or there was a material irregularity; there is also a "proviso" allowing the court to uphold the finding if, despite the existence of grounds of appeal, there has been no miscarriage of justice.

Section 15 of the Act contains equivalent provisions with respect to appeals against a finding that a person is under a disability under the Criminal Procedure (Insanity) Act 1964.

Procedurally, appeals on the above grounds are similar to appeals against conviction.

5. Appeals against sentence: ss 9 to 11 of the Criminal Appeal Act 1968

(a) Introduction

A person convicted of an offence on indictment may appeal against the sentence imposed; such an appeal also lies in respect of any summary offences dealt with in the Crown Court pursuant to s 41 of the Criminal Justice Act 1988. These rights, granted by s 9 of the Criminal Appeal Act 1968, are subject to the need to obtain leave from the court pursuant to s 11 of the Act. Leave is required even if the appeal is based on a point of law.

Under s 10 of the Act—which is also subject to the requirement of leave—there are rights of appeal in respect of sentences imposed at the Crown Court following a committal for sentence (under any of the powers of committal for sentence) after a summary conviction. Similarly, if the summary conviction takes place during the operational period of a Crown Court order for conditional discharge, community order or suspended sentence and the magistrates do not commit for sentence but, instead, inform the Crown Court which then requires the offender to appear before the Crown Court and be further dealt with for the original offence, there is a right to appeal. However, this right applies only if one of the following circumstances is present:

(i)   a custodial sentence of more than six months is imposed; or

(ii)   the sentence is beyond the powers of the magistrates' court; or

(iii)   the Crown Court makes a recommendation for deportation, disqualifies the offender from driving, makes an order in respect of a suspended sentence (either activating in whole or in part the suspended sentence, or imposing a fresh period of suspension), or makes a restriction order under the Football Spectators Act 1989.

(b) Certificate of the trial judge

The requirement for leave is avoided if the trial judge certifies that the case is fit for an appeal: s 11(1A) of the Criminal Appeal Act 1968. Consequently, an advocate who believes that there is a clear point of appeal should consider applying for a certificate from the trial judge. If the person convicted is in custody, the Crown Court's jurisdiction to grant bail pending appeal is dependent on the granting of a certificate that the case is fit for appeal. *The Practice Direction (Crown Court: Bail Pending Appeal)* of 10 November 1983, [1983] 1 WLR 1292, requires that there be a particular and cogent ground of appeal; a certificate should not be issued if it relates to mitigation to which the trial judge has given due weight.

(c) Procedure

(i) Time limits

Section 18(2) of the Criminal Appeal Act 1968 imposes a time limit of 28 days within which the notice of application for leave must be served on the Crown Court. Time begins to run on the day of the sentence to which the appeal relates. However, s 18(3) of the Act allows the Court of Appeal to extend the time limit either before or after it expires.

(ii) The notice

Rule 2 of the Criminal Appeal Rules 1968 (SI 1968 No 1262) requires that the proper notice together with grounds be served on the appropriate officer of the Crown Court. There is a standard form, which asks for items of information plus an indication of which of the various applications the appellant is making. The notice must be signed by the appellant or on behalf of the appellant (which requires that instructions to appeal be given).

(iii) Grounds of appeal

(a) General style of grounds

Grounds of appeal are required, and must be served with the notice. They may be varied with the leave of the Court of Appeal. The Guide to Proceedings in the Court of Appeal Criminal Division indicates:

> "Grounds must be settled with sufficient particularity to enable the Registrar and subsequently the Court to identify clearly the matters relied upon ... A document containing a mere formula such as ... 'the sentence is in all the circumstances too severe' will be ineffective as grounds and time will continue to run against the defendant. Reasons must be given as to why the Court is invited to come to such a conclusion".

As with appeals against conviction, dates and other relevant particulars should be given, statutes and case law should be cited (the latter from the Criminal Appeal Reports or Criminal Appeal Reports (Sentencing) if possible).

(b) Reference to bases for Court of Appeal intervention

The grounds should indicate why they should cause the Court of Appeal to intervene. Section 11 of the Criminal Appeal Act 1968 allows the court to quash any sentence or order in respect of which there is an appeal and substitute any sentence or order which is appropriate. Case law indicates that this general discretion is likely to be exercised in the following situations.

(i) *Sentence wrong in law:* If the Crown Court has sentenced an

159

offender in a manner which is not provided for by law—such as exceeding the maximum permitted term—then the sentence must be quashed.

(ii) *Irregularities in sentencing:* This situation includes failure properly to establish the factual basis of the sentence; the taking into account of material which is irrelevant to sentence (such as the choosing of trial on indictment when the magistrates were willing to accept summary jurisdiction); the failure to obtain a pre-sentence or other report as required by ss 3 and 4 of the Criminal Justice Act 1991; or the failure to differentiate between co-offenders where there are proper reasons for differentiation. It may also be possible to appeal where the defendant has a legitimate sense of grievance as a result of what has occurred in the sentencing procedure. This may occur if, for example, what is said to the offender when the case is adjourned for a pre-sentence report raises a legitimate expectation of a non-custodial sentence, but a custodial sentence is given even though the reports are favourable.

(iii) *Sentence "wrong in principle/manifestly excessive":* The Court of Appeal has taken the opportunity to issue guidelines to sentencing judges in respect of a number of commonly occurring offences—such as *Aramah* (1982) 76 Cr App R 190 in respect of drugs offences; *Barrick* (1985) 81 Cr App R 78 in respect of theft in breach of trust. Many of these guidelines were issued prior to the changes in parole brought about by the Criminal Justice Act 1991, and should be read in the light of the Practice Direction reported at (1992) 95 Cr App R 456, discussed in Chapter 7.

If a sentencer exceeds the appropriate range of sentences, rather than imposing a sentence which is severe but within the permissible range, then the court will intervene to correct the sentence.

(iv) Initial action

The Crown Court sends the notice and grounds to the Registrar of Criminal Appeals. As with appeals against conviction, it may be difficult in some circumstances to complete the grounds of appeal without assistance from the Registrar of Criminal Appeals, for example in obtaining a transcript of the sentencing remarks. Counsel should in such circumstances send with the grounds a "Note to the Registrar" setting out the matters requiring assistance. The Registrar will consider the matter. Usually, the transcript in an appeal against sentence will be limited to the sentencing remarks.

The advice on appeal which has been prepared by counsel may also be sent to the Registrar, though there is no requirement that that be done.

As with appeals against conviction, the Registrar may invite counsel to amend the grounds in the light of any transcript or other documentation obtained—a process known as "perfecting the grounds".

Perfecting allows the original grounds to be reconsidered; if counsel has changed his view and now believes the appeal should be abandoned, a fresh advice should be prepared and sent to the solicitors instructed at the trial. The Registrar should be informed that this has been done, but should not be sent a copy of the advice. The solicitors will then take the instructions of their client.

(v) Frivolous appeals

As with appeals against conviction, the Registrar has power under s 20 of the Criminal Appeal Act 1968 to refer a notice of appeal or application for leave to appeal to the court for summary determination. This is to be done if there is no substantial ground of appeal. The court can summarily dismiss the appeal without a hearing if it considers it to be frivolous or vexatious. This power will rarely be used in appeals against sentence alone, because hopeless appeals are filtered by the need to obtain leave to appeal.

(vi) Consideration by the single judge

The next stage is that the matter be placed in front of a single judge of the Court of Appeal, who is empowered by s 31 of the Criminal Appeal Act 1968 to exercise some of the powers of the full court. The single judge will usually consider the application solely on the papers. The procedures and ancillary applications are as with appeals against conviction, as described above. The question of bail may be of particular importance if the argument on appeal is that a shorter sentence is appropriate. If the application for leave is refused, it may be renewed in front of the full court.

(d) Appeals against conviction and sentence

Naturally, there are circumstances in which the person convicted in the Crown Court will wish to appeal against both conviction and, in the event that the conviction is upheld, against sentence as well. In such a case, the procedure will be as any other appeal requiring leave; the grounds of appeal will contain one section dealing with the appeal against conviction and another section covering the grounds of appeal against sentence.

6. Appeals on reference from the Home Secretary

The Home Secretary may refer a case to the Court of Appeal where a person has been convicted on indictment (or found not guilty by reason of insanity or found to be under a disability); equally, the Home Secretary may seek an opinion on a particular point arising in a case. The case then proceeds as if leave to appeal had been granted.

Typically, this method is used when fresh evidence has come to light which casts doubt on the correctness of the original decision. An alternative route in such a case is to seek the leave of the Court of Appeal to bring an appeal out of time and call fresh evidence.

7. Appeals following action by the Attorney-General

(a) Reference on point of law

The Attorney-General may refer cases to the Court of Appeal in two circumstances. The first is the power under s 36 of the Criminal Justice Act 1972 to seek the opinion of the Court of Appeal in respect of a point of law which arose during the course of a case which resulted in the acquittal of the defendant. This is of no relevance to the defendant who was acquitted as the verdict remains. However, the decision of the Court of Appeal on the point of law is authority for future cases.

(b) Increasing unduly lenient sentences

Of more relevance to a defendant is the power granted to the Attorney-General by ss 35 and 36 of the Criminal Justice Act 1988 to refer a case to the Court of Appeal, requesting it to increase the sentence imposed on the particular defendant. The Attorney-General must consider that the sentence was unduly lenient (which condition may be satisfied if the judge erred in law as to his sentencing powers: s 36(2)). The power exists in respect of indictable-only offences. It is, of course, hoped that the Attorney-General will not simply act when the media demands action.

The Court of Appeal must grant leave in the case. The procedures are outlined in Schedule 3 of the 1988 Act. Briefly, the Attorney-General's application for leave must be made within 28 days of the sentence. Naturally, the defendant whose sentence is under review is entitled to be present and to be represented at the hearing.

The Court of Appeal has made it plain in the course of references that it will intervene only if public confidence would be affected by an error of principle in the sentence, that it will take account of the fact that mercy is part of the art of sentencing, that it has a discretion whether or not to increase the sentence even if it was unduly lenient, that its discretion includes imposing a different type of sentence (such as probation instead of a suspended sentence of imprisonment), and that the ordeal of being resentenced is mitigation itself.

8. Appeals against rulings at preparatory hearings

(a) General

Section 9(11) of the Criminal Justice Act 1987 allows an appeal against any order or ruling of a judge at a preparatory hearing in a serious fraud case (see Chapter 3). The rulings might be on matters of admissibility or other issues of law, or orders that the defence reveal the basis of its case. The appeal requires the leave of the trial judge or of the Court of Appeal, and it is heard before the trial on indictment: it is an interlocutory appeal, governed by the Criminal Justice Act 1987

(Preparatory Hearings) (Interlocutory Appeals) Rules 1988 (SI 1988 No 1700).

(b) Seeking leave from the Crown Court

The application to the Crown Court judge must be made within two days of the relevant order or ruling, and written notice with grounds must be served on the parties to the trial and the Crown Court. The requirement for written notice can be avoided if the application for leave is made orally immediately after the order or ruling against which there is an appeal.

If leave is given by the Crown Court, then the notice of appeal must be served within seven days of the order or ruling on all parties, the Crown Court and the Registrar of Criminal Appeals. This time limit may be extended by the Court of Appeal.

(c) Seeking leave from the Court of Appeal

If the application for leave is made to the Court of Appeal, notice of application for leave must be served within seven days of the order or ruling on the parties, the Crown Court and the Registrar of Criminal Appeals. The Court of Appeal may extend this time limit.

(d) Information required by the Court of Appeal

The notice of appeal or application for leave must specify the relevant question of law and any facts necessary to consider the question; it must summarise the arguments and specify any authorities to be cited. Copies of any necessary documents or other items must be supplied.

(e) Notice by respondent

If the appeal is opposed, the respondent must within seven days of receipt of the notice of appeal or application for leave serve a notice on the Registrar of Criminal Appeals, the other parties and the Crown Court. The time limit can be extended by the Court of Appeal. The notice must summarise the counter-arguments and specify any authorities.

(f) Other matters

In other respects, the appeal is similar to an appeal against conviction. A person in custody who is a party to the appeal is entitled to be present at the hearing of the appeal; a co-defendant in custody who is not a party to the arguments in the Court of Appeal requires the leave of the court to be present. A single judge of the Court of Appeal is entitled to grant the relevant leaves and can extend the time limits for the steps to be taken.

PART VI:
GOOD PRACTICE

Chapter 9

Good practice

Advocates and courts are becoming less formal as time goes on. However, there are still formalities and rules of etiquette which advocates are expected to follow. Some judges can still demonstrate a fondness for archaic procedures and formalities; advocates should be aware of the possible gripes from the bench.

There are also various other rules of good practice which those who practise in the Crown Court should bear in mind. None of these is written in stone, and what follows is inevitably a personal selection.

1. Modes of address

A Practice Direction was issued on 12 January 1982 setting out how to address a judge in open court ([1982] 1 WLR 101). The basic rule is that Crown Court judges will be addressed as "Your Honour". This applies equally to circuit judges, recorders and assistant recorders. The exceptions to this rule are as follows:

(i)   If the judge is a High Court judge sitting in the Crown Court, he or she will be addressed as "My Lord/Lady" or "Your Lordship/Ladyship".

(ii) All judges who sit at the Central Criminal Court—whatever their judicial rank—are addressed as "My Lord/Lady" or "Your Lordship/Ladyship".

(iii) The Recorder of Manchester and the Recorder of Liverpool are entitled to the same treatment as an Old Bailey judge.

When the court is sitting in chambers or the advocate sees the judge in his or her private room, those who would be addressed as "Your Honour" are addressed as "Judge"; those who would be addressed as "My Lord/Lady" remain so addressed.

When hearing appeals against conviction and sentence in the magistrates' court, the judge will sit with justices; the advocate should address the judge, but may where appropriate refer to "Your Honour's Colleagues" (or "Your Lordship's or Ladyship's Colleagues").

If it becomes necessary to describe the judge in writing—in a notice of appeal, for example—the following rules apply. A High Court judge will be described as "The Honourable Mr/Mrs Justice A". Circuit judges are described as "His/Her Honour Judge A" and deputy circuit judges as "His/Her Honour BA, sitting as a deputy circuit judge". Recorders are described as "Mr/Mrs Recorder A" and assistant recorders as "Mr/Mrs/Miss BA, sitting as an assistant recorder". Strangely enough, there is no formal provision in the terms of the Practice Direction for unmarried female recorders or for female recorders who do not wish to reveal their marital status. Naturally, there should be no complaint if an advocate describes a recorder as Miss or Ms.

There are also rules relating to how to describe other advocates in court. When the case begins, the first advocate to speak—who will usually be the prosecutor—introduces the other advocates and indicates who they represent. Similarly, when the prosecutor makes his opening speech to the jury, the other advocate(s) will be introduced to the jury. Other advocates should be referred to as "my learned friend" or "my friend". Fortunately, it is becoming acceptable to refer to "Mr/Ms/Mrs/Miss A, who appears for B" or simply to give the name of the advocate and any other description as is necessary to identify the person in question. This has the clear benefit of being less pompous.

It used to be the case that when advocates saw the judge in chambers, other advocates were referred to by their surnames only. This custom was from an era when there were no female advocates; traditionalist males who call other males by their surnames will refer to female advocates as "Mrs/Miss/Ms" in chambers. The better practice is to use the appropriate prefix whatever the gender of the advocate. It will be found that, particularly outside London, there are some judges who are sufficiently familiar that they will address the advocates in their chambers by their first names.

Other court officials are usually referred to by their title—usher, dock officer and so on—except the clerk of the court, who will sometimes be called "the learned clerk" or "Mr/Madam clerk".

2. Seeing the judge in private

(a) Procedure

There are occasions when the advocates may wish to see the judge in private; the reasons for this can vary. Some judges are more amenable to private meetings than others; some will meet in the court room which has been closed and marked "Sitting in Chambers" whilst others will call the advocates into their room. The usual approach is to indicate to the clerk that there are matters on which counsel wish to see the judge; the clerk may ask for an indication as to the substance of the issue to be discussed. The judge will then indicate, via the clerk, whether he is prepared to see advocates in private and whether that will be in a closed court or in a private room. To denote that the matter is not in open court, wigs may be removed.

(b) Private mitigation

The basic rule is that justice must be done openly, but there are occasions when it is not appropriate to reveal information in public. Two simple examples can demonstrate this. It might be part of the mitigation to be put forward on behalf of a particular accused that he is suffering from a terminal illness of which he is not aware; that should be known by the judge, but should not be revealed in open court. In any event, reports prepared for mitigation—pre-sentence reports, medical reports and so on—are read by the judge rather than being given in evidence and heard by the public.

Similarly, it may be part of the mitigation for a client that he has provided useful information to the police; since it might endanger the client for this to be known amongst the wider public, it should be communicated to the judge in the judge's private room (usually in the form of a written letter from a suitably senior police officer).

There can be no doubt that there should be free access to the judge to raise matters of mitigation which ought not to be in the public domain.

(c) Indications as to sentence

There are occasions when the criminal process can be expedited considerably if the judge's attitude towards sentencing can be assessed reliably in advance. Quite simply, some defendants wish to know what sort of credit they will receive for entering a guilty plea to an appropriate count or series of counts on the indictment or to lesser offences: this can have a considerable impact on whether they will plead guilty or not, and hence whether there will be the expense of a trial. Some judges are more willing than others to give an indication in advance of the likely sentence they will impose.

One of the problems which has arisen with regard to seeking an indication of the likely sentence is whether this imposes an obligation on the judge and creates an expectation in the mind of the defendant which will cause the Court of Appeal to intervene if the judge then hands down a more severe sentence. It is clear that a plea of guilty should be voluntary, and a promise of leniency which is not then put into effect will cause a defendant to have a legitimate sense of grievance.

There are also problems of miscommunication, where what has been said or intended by the judge is not conveyed accurately to the defendant. Some judges overcome this problem by agreeing to see counsel only if the defendant is also present. Most judges will require the clerk or a shorthand writer to record what occurs in the private meeting.

It is to be hoped that private access to the judge will continue in appropriate circumstances. As long as it is for proper purposes, and the defence advocate has taken instructions from the client as to whether the client would like counsel to seek a judicial indication, then the dangers of improper pressure on a client to enter an involuntary plea of guilty are limited.

3. Preparation of a case

Advocates in criminal cases, whilst usually not as well paid as their contemporaries who specialise in civil matters, are nevertheless well paid. They are also professional. The case should therefore be prepared well; the possibility of a wasted costs order must also be borne in mind. The fact that a brief fee is usually not obtained unless the advocate makes a court appearance should not cause an advocate to wait until he knows that he will appear in court the next day before the necessary preparation is undertaken.

Of course, there will inevitably be circumstances in which an advocate makes an appearance on short notice when he has not had the opportunity to prepare a case properly. However, if the brief is obtained in time, it should be reviewed and any necessary advice on evidence should be written. If points of law are at issue, references to or photocopies of relevant statutes or cases should be included. If the case against the defendant rests on evidence which might be excluded, then that should be considered: defence advocates should remember that the prosecution must prove its case beyond reasonable doubt on the basis of admissible evidence. If the brief relates to more than one defendant, consideration should be given to whether there is a potential conflict between the defendants, since each individual defendant is entitled to have his best interests represented.

The lay client is entitled to a conference with his advocate: an appearance in court as a defendant, with the possibilities of a finding of guilt and punishment, may be a very worrying time and it is not always helped by the fact that the defendant has not had the opportunity to meet his advocate. The listing of cases means that it is not possible to guarantee that the advocate who has the conference will appear in court in due course: in such a situation, being represented by a colleague of the advocate who has had a conference is usually the next best alternative from the point of view of the client.

4. Advocacy

Advocacy is often said to be an art. There are different styles of advocacy, and particular cases require a different approach (and perhaps a different advocate). In certain circumstances, the defence requires that the prosecution witnesses be cross-examined forcefully; in other circumstances, the best course of action might be a more gentle undermining of the prosecution case. Some advocates can adopt to whatever style is required for the particular case, but many cannot. Those who brief an advocate should consider what their client requires; equally, advocates should be aware of their own limits and should be prepared to recommend someone else if the interests of the lay client require such a course.

Whatever style of advocacy is adopted, certain things must be done. Taking a witness through their evidence in chief involves asking a series of questions that allow the witness to tell their story to the jury. Questions should be phrased in a neutral fashion—that is, they should not suggest the answer or put words into the mouth of the witness. This rule against "leading questions" does not apply to formal and introductory matters, and the permission of opposing advocates may be sought as to whether a witness can be led through other non-controversial issues. The judge should be informed if this permission has been given so that he does not interpose to prevent such a question. It is not always possible to define a leading question; as with the rule against duplicity, it is something lawyers are supposed to recognise when they come upon it.

Cross-examination also has basic aims, whatever the style of the advocate. Information to support the defence case is to be sought; at the very least, the accuracy of the facts which form the prosecution case should be undermined. If the prosecution witnesses are adamant about the facts, then the fall-back position is to undermine their credibility as witnesses—either their veracity, the correctness of their recollection, or the possibility that they might be mistaken. If there is to be evidence from the defence, the factual basis of that case should be put to appropriate prosecution witnesses so that they have a chance to comment on it.

Prosecution advocates must follow the same ground rules in cross-examination, but must always recall that their function is not to obtain a conviction but to present facts in a more neutral fashion than the defence advocate: the latter is supposed to do as much as is ethical to secure an acquittal.

Defence advocates cannot ask questions which are merely scandalous, but otherwise must put the case that the client has asked them to put. A lawyer can advise a client that a particular line of defence is not wise, but should always recall that instructions come from the client; if necessary, an advocate can have a client endorse on the brief the fact that the client wishes a particular line of questioning to be followed and going against the advice of his advocate. There are statutory limitations on cross-examination in rape cases, and one should always be prepared to justify the line of questioning if objections are raised by the judge or opposing counsel.

Advocacy is also relevant when submissions are made on points of law, or in mitigation, or in making a speech to a jury. Clarity is usually the most important feature. It is also vital to know what the tribunal requires, and be sufficiently flexible to deliver that.

When being addressed on a point of law, some judges prefer the advocates to refer to case authorities which support the position being put forward; others prefer arguments on principles without the clutter of cases. Some require one thing one day and another thing the next. An advocate must be sufficiently flexible to adapt to what will work best on a particular day. The same applies to mitigation. With a plea in mitigation it is important that the factual basis for the sentence is established, the current circumstances of the client are explained (together with any improvements made since the time of the offence), and a concise statement of any matters for which the client can receive credit are made plain. If the Court of Appeal has issued a guideline on sentencing, it will often indicate what factors aggravate the offence and what might mitigate: the absence of aggravating factors and the presence of mitigating factors can often be structured accordingly.

Speeches to juries are more effective if the advocate appears to believe what he is saying. As a professional advocate, whether one actually believes the defendant to be innocent or not is irrelevant. The decision on that matter is the task of the jury, and the function of the advocate is to ensure that the defendant's case is presented well. The prosecutor is in a different position, and is supposed to be disinterested.

5. Professional ethics; the "cab-rank" rule

The supposed independence of barristers, and their acceptance of briefs from anyone who requires a lawyer, is often mentioned. This also means that one can appear for the prosecution one day and a defendant the next. This is part of the "cab-rank" principle.

In reality, not all barristers appear regularly for both prosecution and defence, and there will usually be a legitimate reason for not accepting a particular brief. The Crown Prosecution Service requires advocates to put their names forward; they will graduate to more difficult cases in accordance with how much work they have done and how well they are seen to have done it. An advocate who does not put himself on the CPS list is unlikely to receive prosecution work (though it is not impossible). Similarly, some solicitors prefer their work to be done by advocates who appear solely for defendants.

There are clearly arguments in favour of barristers being willing to represent both the prosecution and the defence; for example, such a system is said to enable the barrister to give the objective advice which a defendant requires regarding the strength of the case against him. There are also arguments in favour of defence advocates who always identify with the defendant: it is said that they become more adept at presenting the defence case with an element of passion. There are people who will only defend, some who will happily do either, some who would prefer to defend only but have to prosecute for simple financial reasons, and others who spend most of their time prosecuting. The arguments are many and varied, and it is difficult to do more than assert that one approach is better. Of course, you will always be able to find a lawyer who will assert the contrary.

Appendix

Just as styles of advocacy are personal, so are styles of written work. The following are personal suggestions for some commonly occurring situations which may require a written advice.

1. Advice on separate representation

In the Leicester Crown Court

R

v

Peter Lyons
Simon Boswell
Pauline Boswell

Advice on separate representation

---

1. I am asked to advise whether the above three defendants should be represented separately. I am of the opinion that they should be represented by separate counsel at the trial and when pleas are entered, but that on the papers currently available there is no conflict of a nature that requires that separate solicitors be instructed.

2. The current indictment contains five counts involving the three defendants plus a Mr Richard Benson. Messrs Lyons, Boswell and Benson are named in three counts alleging burglaries on 26 April, 4 May and 6 May 1992; Ms Boswell is charged with handling part of the proceeds of the burglary on 26 April; the final count is against Mr Benson only, and alleges a burglary on 2 November 1991. Mr Lyons' instructions are not clear;

Mr Boswell will admit the third burglary but not the earlier two; Ms Boswell's instructions are not clear.

3. Ms Boswell must be represented separately at all court hearings for the following reason. She is charged with receiving part of the proceeds of a burglary which Mr Boswell (and presumably Mr Lyons) deny committing. She makes somewhat ambiguous admissions in the course of interview and implicates Mr Lyons. The fact that she is related to Mr Boswell will obviously create suspicions against him. Whilst evidence against Ms Boswell is not strictly admissible against the others, it is clearly something which will prejudice the two men. Consequently, it would be of assistance to Messrs Boswell and Lyons if Ms Boswell were to plead guilty when the matter is listed for pleas. The advocate for Ms Boswell must therefore have a degree of independence from the other co-defendants.

4. As to the position of Mr Boswell and Mr Lyons, there is a hint in the course of Mr Boswell's interview that he may seek to place blame on the others who were also caught near the scene of the burglary. For this reason alone, it would not be appropriate for the two men to be represented by one advocate; since the appearance for pleas may be an effective disposal of the case—it not being known whether the Crown will allow the burglaries of 26 April and 4 May to lie on the file—it would be appropriate for separate counsel to appear when the matter is listed for pleas. Of course, if the Crown insist on a trial on these other matters, it would be appropriate for a not guilty plea to be entered to the 6 May burglary so as to avoid being remanded in custody as a convicted prisoner.

5. In addition, arguments will have to be made on behalf of the above three defendants to have severed from the trial of the three burglaries the allegation against Mr Benson only of a domestic burglary at his father's house. There is no clear nexus with this latter allegation.

6. Finally, it is usually appropriate for defendants with criminal records to be separately represented to avoid the loss of the shield of the Criminal Evidence Act 1898. The fact that one defendant is prepared to run a line of questioning which puts his or her character in issue should not prejudice the other defendants—which it will if they are represented by one counsel.

Camberwell Chambers   Kris Gledhill

2. Advice on need for leading counsel

In the Crown Court at Wood Green

R

v

David Charles Monmouth

Advice on seeking leading counsel

---

1. I have now received the indictment which has been preferred and upon which Mr Monmouth is to be arraigned at the start of the trial. The allegation of numerous rapes and buggeries on his daughter, plus an indecent assault on a friend of his daughter, is clearly very serious.

2. I am of the opinion that the case is one which merits the assignment of leading counsel. Consequently, I would advise that those instructing apply to the Chief Clerk at the Wood Green Crown Court for the current legal aid order to be amended to allow the assignment of leading counsel. Naturally, this should be done in a timely manner so that a suitable QC can be located. Naturally, those instructing should liaise with the authorities at the Crown Court as to any difficulties in the consideration of this application and so that, if necessary, the matter can be listed for mention in open court in front of a senior judge at the Court.

3. The basis for the application is that Regulation 48 of the Legal Aid in Criminal and Care Proceedings (General) Regulations 1989 (SI 1989 No 344) provides that two counsel may be assigned:

    "where it appears to the court or the person making the legal aid order that the case is one of exceptional difficulty, gravity or complexity and that the interests of justice require that the legally assisted person should have the services of two counsel".

4. This is plainly a case of exceptional gravity and, given the nature of the allegation and the fact that very experienced counsel is required to cross-examine the alleged victim of such an allegation, it is in the interests of justice that leading counsel be assigned:

Camberwell Chambers   Kris Gledhill

Appendix

3. Advice on plea and likely sentence

In the Harrow Crown Court

R

v

Roger Freeman

Advice

Introduction

1. Mr Freeman faces an indictment containing four counts. Three allege indecent assaults on his daughter, Joanna, and one alleges an assault on his daughter's friend, Louise. He was originally charged with two offences only, one relating to each girl. The first three counts are specimens and reflect the statement of Joanna, which alleges a course of assault over nine years. In his first interview, Mr Freeman admits assaults over a period of two years, stopping when Joanna began menstruating.

Plea

2. Mr Freeman concedes that his first interview is an accurate version of events, although he seemed to be withdrawing his confession at the outset of the second interview. In addition, he makes limited admissions to a social worker. There are no admissions with respect to the allegation involving Louise.

3. The first three counts cover 1983 to 1986, 1987 to November 1990 and December 1990 to April 1991; it seems that the admissions made cover counts 2 and 3. Mr Freeman is emphatic that nothing happened within the period covered by the first count. The fourth count covers Louise; Mr Freeman denies this allegation.

4. Consequently, it would seem that the appropriate pleas are guilty to counts 2 and 3 and not guilty to 1 and 4. Of course, it goes without saying that, in Mr Freeman's best interests, this indication of plea should not be given at this early stage. This point is developed below. It also is the case that

176

attempts should be made to have the Crown accept a plea of guilty to one count only—probably count 2.

5. Mr Freeman has asked what his best position is if there is a degree of intransigence on the part of the Crown to accepting guilty pleas to less than all counts. The simple fact is that it is substantial mitigation in a case such as this to avoid a trial and avoid having young women/girls giving evidence and being subject to cross-examination. There is also the danger of the jury believing the evidence given by the prosecution witnesses and convicting on all counts. Consequently, I am of the opinion that there are possible advantages in pleading guilty to the counts which are not admitted. The final decision, of course, is for Mr Freeman to make.

6. If the Crown are intransigent, before Mr Freeman enters pleas of guilty to matters he does not admit, the judge should be consulted. Explanation can be given that Mr Freeman makes no admissions as to the counts which are not admitted but does not wish the young women to have to give evidence. The judge can be asked to indicate whether any sentence imposed in respect of the disputed counts would be concurrent to the sentence imposed on the count or counts which are admitted. If they are to be concurrent—so that there is effectively no extra sentence for the guilty plea in respect of the matters which are not admitted—then this is a factor which Mr Freeman can take into account.

Likely sentence

7. It is, of course, impossible to make a proper prediction as to the sentence of the judge, since so much turns on the individual judge and the feeling of that judge on the day in question. The discretion given to the sentencing judge is wide; the Court of Appeal will intervene only when the sentence is manifestly excessive.

8. There are guidelines for offences of this sort, though it must be stressed that as such (namely, guidelines) they are in no way binding.

(i) At the more serious end of the scale is *Rolls* (1981) 3 Cr App R (S) 357, in which the Court of Appeal upheld a term of imprisonment of three years on a man who placed his penis in the mouth of his nine year-old daughter: this case is clearly more serious than Mr Freeman's offence.

(ii) At the lower end of the scale is *Helliwell* (1987) 9 Cr App R (S) 357, in which a sentence of nine months' imprisonment was deemed proper for a man who fingered his two daughters (aged four) in the region of the vagina on an isolated occasion.

(iii) A similar case is *Vinson* (1981) 3 Cr App R (S) 315, in which a man touched the private parts of his ten and eleven year-old nieces over a period of six months; his sentence was reduced on appeal to nine months' imprisonment.

(iv) In *Hessey* (1987) 9 Cr App R (S) 268, the Court of Appeal imposed a sentence of fifteen months' imprisonment in respect of three counts of indecently assaulting the twelve year-old daughter of the woman with whom he was living; the assaults involved fingering her vagina over a period of twelve months.

(v) In *Renouf* (1988) Cr App R (S) 157, a sentence of two years' imprisonment was deemed proper for frequent assaults over a period of twelve months on a step-daughter aged fourteen, involving fondling of breasts and vagina, rubbing his penis against her and persuading her to masturbate him and suck his penis.

It is noticeable that all the cases reported involve immediate custodial sentences. However, it should be noted that the cases which are heard by the Court of Appeal are, necessarily, ones in which the sentence imposed by the Crown Court has been a heavy sentence (since otherwise it would not have been appealed).

Listing

9. This is a matter in respect of which it is appropriate to have a fixed date for trial, given the involvement of young witnesses and the possibility of applications for the use of video-relays of evidence. The listing office should also be informed that there is a contested care hearing, and that the outcome of that hearing might have an impact on the plea and the evidence in this case.

Evidence

10. It is, of course, necessary to prepare this case for trial, since nothing is certain as to the eventual disposal. Consequently, those instructing should obtain:

(i)   any further unused material.

(ii) within the above head comes any previous statements, notes of interview, video-recorded interviews and the like of the prosecution witnesses.

(iii) a copy of the crime report.

(iv) copies of the material on the Social Services file.

(v)   copies of the tape recordings of Mr Freeman's interviews.

(vi) for use in mitigation, copies of assessments of Mr Freeman from the doctors he is seeing.

(vii) a letter of reference from his employers.

Camberwell Chambers   Kris Gledhill

4. Advice on evidence

In the Northampton Crown Court

R

v

Terence James Rogers

Advice on evidence

---

1. Mr Rogers has been committed to stand trial at the Crown Court on one count of domestic burglary. The evidence against him is entirely circumstantial and consists of two main links between the scene of the crime and Mr Rogers. (i) A Ford Capri was seen acting suspiciously in the vicinity of the burglary at a time when it is possible that the burglary occurred; the registered holder of this car indicates that he had sold it to Mr Rogers, though Mr Rogers indicates that he had sold it to someone else a couple of days before the burglary. (ii) A forensic examination of the soles of the shoes which Mr Rogers was wearing at the time of his arrest—the morning after the burglary—led an experienced Home Office scientist to conclude that there was a significant connection between the shoes and the burglary.

2. It is clear that the forensic evidence is the crux of the matter. It is therefore vital that the defence instruct a forensic scientist with the appropriate qualifications and experience to answer the questions which are posed in this advice. Legal aid should be obtained to cover this.

3. The burglary occurred some time between 8.45 a.m. and 7.10 p.m. on 9 January. Various items were taken. On 10 January, the television and video recorder taken in the burglary were identified by one of the occupiers of the burgled property, presumably at a police station. The CPS should be asked to supply all statements relating to how these items came to be in the possession of the police the day after the burglary.

4. A dark Ford Capri was seen near the scene of the burglary at around 5:15 p.m. It was seen again twice by police officers and on the second occasion drove away when the police flashed for it to stop. The registered owner of the car—Mr Khan—indicated that he had sold the car

to Mr Rogers, though Mr Rogers denies the accuracy of certain parts of his statement. Mr Rogers indicates that he sold the car a few days before this burglary; any corroboration of this from Mrs Rogers or anyone else would be of considerable value.

5. Mr Rogers indicates that the car was subsequently at West Drayton Police Station; he should be asked how he knows this and what proof he has. The Crown Prosecution Service should be asked to supply such information as they are able to about the whereabouts of the Capri, when it was taken into police custody and why. If they are not co-operative in this respect, Instructing Solicitors should contact West Drayton Police Station and ask about the car. If necessary, an appropriate senior officer can be summonsed to appear with the appropriate records relating to the car.

6. Some of the statements of the officers in the case are made several months after the burglary and several months after the forensic analysis was completed. Further, certain of the statements contain information which is not obviously significant until the forensic analysis was completed. Consequently, Instructing Solicitors should ask the CPS to supply copies of their original notebooks relating to the investigation of this burglary, including actions relating to any other suspects.

7. The standard request ought to be made that the CPS supply any unused material in this matter, the defendant's custody records and copies of the tape recordings of his interview, and a copy of the crime report.

8. In addition to that mentioned in paragraph 5 above, a further statement should be taken from Mr Rogers dealing with other relevant matters, together with statements from anyone who can provide corroboration of these facts. For example, he has indicated that the shoes which he gave to the police on the day of his first arrest were not those that he was wearing on the night of the alleged burglary. He has also indicated that he has been arrested several times since his release from prison in early 1989; he should provide further details on these instances. He indicates that on most occasions he has been taken to the same police station: custody records should be sought relating to every occasion when he was taken into custody. In addition, the alibi notice was given; if there is an alibi, the details should be supplied to the CPS as soon as possible.

9. I am of the opinion that it is best not to accuse the police of planting evidence when that can be avoided; this is especially the case when the defendant has a record such as Mr Rogers'. I would suspect that this is more particularly the case in Northampton than in an Inner London court, given likely differences in the attitudes of some jurors. It is therefore important to have express instructions from Mr Rogers as to whether he wishes to accuse the police of any form of improper conduct. If he decides against this, he will need to be very cautious when in the witness box not to lose his temper.

10. Whilst it is clear that there are grounds for arguing that evidence has in fact been planted, it may well be that the safer course of action is simply

to point out the inadequacy of the prosecution evidence. In order to do this, an independent forensic expert ought to be instructed. The starting point for his or her investigation ought to be the deposition of the Crown scientist. Further, it is important that the defence scientist have access to the original notes of the Crown scientist and the exhibits; the necessary arrangements for this will have to be made.

11. Mr Rogers works as a roofer. Consequently, he will come into contact with glass for various innocent reasons. If he has business records to indicate where he was working in the time immediately before the burglary, these places should be catalogued and photographs taken of them. Instructing Solicitors should also investigate the location of the burglary: is it a new estate of purpose-built houses? The value of some of this information is dependent upon the preliminary report of the defence forensic scientist; it might be necessary for a further advice on evidence to be given after that report is available.

12. A forensic scientist with some experience will be aware of the questions to investigate with respect to the methods and conclusions of the Crown scientist, with a view to testing their cogency and the conclusion reached. This should include (but not be limited to) the following:

   (a) are the shoes shown in the photograph taken at the scene the same size as those taken from Mr Rogers?

   (b) would one expect that some fragments of glass from a pane in a door would be embedded in the sole of the shoe of the burglar rather than merely be adhering to the sole?

   (c) are there any figures available showing the tonnage of glass made or imported which has the same refractive index, elemental composition and combination of index and composition as that identified by the Crown scientist? How common is this glass?

   (d) what are the proper procedures to be followed in a laboratory to ensure that sub-pinhead sized fragments of glass do not accidentally transfer from a sample of glass to the soles of a pair of shoes?

Camberwell Chambers   Kris Gledhill

5. Advice on appeal against sentence

In the Crown Court at Snaresbrook

R

v

Richard Andrew Johnson

Advice on appeal

---

1. Mr Johnson was sentenced to thirty months' imprisonment for an offence of false imprisonment, and six months' concurrent for Taking and Driving Away.

2. On the basis of the facts admitted, the factors for which Mr Johnson could legitimately claim credit, and reported authorities, the sentence was quite clearly excessive. I strongly advise Mr Johnson to appeal.

3. Draft grounds of appeal are enclosed.

Camberwell Chambers   Kris Gledhill

In the Court of Appeal

The Queen

and

Richard Andrew Johnson

Draft grounds of appeal

On 27 January 1993, the appellant appeared before Her Honour Judge Graham sitting at the Crown Court at Snaresbrook. He faced an indictment which initially contained three counts; leave was given for two further counts to be admitted. Pleas of not guilty were entered to counts of kidnapping, robbery and theft; pleas of guilty were entered to false imprisonment and taking a conveyance without authority. These pleas were accepted by the Crown; the counts to which not guilty pleas were entered were ordered to lie on the file on the usual terms.

The guilty pleas were based on admissions in interview. In the early hours of Saturday, 26 June 1992, the Appellant, who was depressed and under the influence of alcohol, asked the victim for a lift outside the Enfield Golf Club; the victim had also been drinking at the Golf Club. The Appellant then forced himself into the car, thereby causing the victim to move into the passenger seat of the car. The Appellant then drove the car, which had already been started. After a few moments, the victim jumped from the car, sustaining minor injuries and damage to his clothing. The Appellant then drove the car to Ipswich; he was arrested two days later whilst taking the car to Ipswich city centre to abandon it.

Allegations that the Appellant used a knife or any further force were specifically denied. The Appellant's actions were motivated by a desire to return to his wife in Ipswich, who suffered from acute pre-menstrual tension and had on that day asked the Appellant to leave the matrimonial home, combined with panic. The victim did not state for how long he was falsely imprisoned; in court it was stated that it was approximately ten minutes.

The Appellant was sentenced to immediate custody for thrity months for the offence of false imprisonment and twelve months for the offence of taking a conveyance without authority, the latter sentence to run concurrently.

When it was pointed out to the learned judge that the maximum sentence for the offence of taking without authority was six months, the sentence was modified to a concurrent term of six months' imprisonment.

The grounds of appeal against sentence are:

1. The sentence was too severe in all the circumstances of the case; in particular:

    (i) the Appellant had no convictions for an offence of like nature to false imprisonment and had no convictions since February 1989;

    (ii) the crime was committed by the Appellant acting alone, on the spur of the moment in a time of stress, did not involve threats of violence to the victim, and involved false imprisonment of at most ten minutes;

    (iii) the Appellant had employment and had recently been promoted to foreman with his employers;

    (iv) the Appellant's wife was economically dependent upon her husband, being unable to work on account of acute pre-menstrual tension.

    The Appellant will rely on the cases of *Mattan* (1985) 7 CAR(S) 415 and *Ahmad and Wooley* (1985) 7 CAR(S) 433; it will be submitted that the facts of the Appellant's crime are less serious than the facts of the crimes in the reported decisions.

2. The learned judge failed to give any or any sufficient weight to the recommendation in the pre-sentence report that the appellant be given a community service order.

3. The learned judge failed to give any or any sufficient weight to the impact of an immediate custodial sentence on the wife of the Appellant.

4. The learned judge failed to give sufficient credit to the Appellant for his co-operation with the police and his plea of guilty on being arraigned.

5. A sentence of imprisonment was wrong in principle since non-custodial alternatives were appropriate.

6. Further or in the alternative the sentence was excessive in that the judge appeared to give little or no thought as to whether any sentence of imprisonment could be suspended either in part or in full, or whether the imposition of a community service order as a direct alternative to custody was appropriate.

<u>Camberwell Chambers</u>   Kris Gledhill

6. Advice on appeal against conviction

In the Crown Court at Birmingham

The Queen

and

. Gail Ann Pratt

Advice

---

1. I am asked to advise on the merits of an appeal in the above case, in which the defendant entered a plea of guilty following a ruling from His Honour Judge Wright that defence objections to the admissibility of evidence which the Crown sought to adduce were not well-founded.

2. I am of the opinion that the learned judge was wrong in ruling that the disputed evidence was admissible. He should have exercised his discretion at common law or pursuant to s 78 of the Police and Criminal Evidence Act 1984 to exclude the evidence.

3. It is unusual to have an appeal against conviction following a plea of guilty. However, it is well-established that the Court of Appeal can hear an appeal against conviction based on a guilty plea induced by an incorrect ruling on law.

4. In the circumstances of the case, the sentence was wrong in principle: a non-custodial alternative should have been employed.

5. Grounds of appeal are enclosed.

Camberwell Chambers   Kris Gledhill

In the Court of Appeal

The Queen

and

Gail Ann Pratt

Grounds of appeal

On 15 February 1993, the defendant appeared before His Honour Judge Wright sitting at the Crown Court at Birmingham. On a previous occasion, she had entered pleas of not guilty to counts of offering to supply a controlled drug of Class 'B', supplying a controlled drug of Class 'B' and attempting to possess a controlled drug of Class 'B'.

The defendant had been arrested during the execution by police officers from the drugs squad of a warrant issued under the Misuse of Drugs Act, and was interviewed after her arrest. Count 1 was based on an offer to supply what was thought to be a controlled substance to an undercover police officer, DC Burton; count 2 was based on admissions made during interview; count 3 was based on admissions during interview.

During the proceedings prior to the hearing on 15 February, it was not admitted that an undercover police officer had been involved. Notice of additional evidence, namely the statement of the undercover officer, was served on the defence shortly before the trial and after the defence had obtained a witness summons against the officer concerned.

The learned judge was asked to rule on the admissibility of the defendant's interview and of the statements of the officers who executed the warrant. Following his ruling that the prosecution evidence was admissible, the defendant changed her pleas to guilty on all counts. She was sentenced to nine months' immediate imprisonment on each of counts 1 and 2 and three months' immediate imprisonment on count 3, all sentences to run concurrently.

The grounds of appeal against conviction are:

1. The learned judge erred in law in ruling that he possessed no discretion at common law to exclude evidence obtained as a result of the activities of DC Smith, the undercover police officer, and, further, incorrectly failed to exercise his discretion to exclude the evidence obtained as a result of the activities of DC Smith.

2. Alternatively, the learned judge, in the exercise of his discretion under s 78 of the Police and Criminal Evidence Act 1984, should have ruled that the evidence of DC Smith was inadmissible. In the circumstances, particularly the part played by DC Smith in encouraging the commission of the offence and the refusal of the prosecution to acknowledge to the defence the existence of DC Smith and his role until after the defence had obtained a witness order to compel his attendance and the failure of the prosecution to ensure that the defence was informed of the details of the evidence of DC Smith until the day before the trial was listed for hearing, the admission of the evidence of DC Smith and of all other prosecution evidence had such an adverse impact on the fairness of the proceedings that it ought not to have been admitted.

3. In all the circumstances of the case, the appellant's conviction is unsatisfactory.

The grounds of appeal against sentence are:

1. The sentence was too severe in all the circumstances of the case; in particular:

   (i) the defendant had never been sentenced to a period of imprisonment before;

   (ii) the defendant had only one previous conviction, and for an offence of a different nature, for which she had received a conditional discharge;

   (iii) the defendant had a stable employment record and was highly thought of by her employers and by her trades union.

2.   The learned judge failed to give any or any sufficient weight to the recommendation in the pre-sentence report that the appellant be given a community service order.

3.   The learned judge failed to give any or any sufficient weight to the impact of an immediate custodial sentence on the aged and unwell parents of the appellant.

4.   The learned judge failed to give sufficient weight to the fact that proceedings against a further suspect, who was arrested at the same time and in the room where the drugs were found on the table and who was said by the appellant to have been the supplier of the drugs, were withdrawn.

5.   The learned judge failed to give sufficient credit to the appellant for her co-operation with the police.

6.   A sentence of imprisonment was wrong in principle since non-custodial alternatives were appropriate.

7.   Further or in the alternative the sentence was excessive in that the Learned Judge appeared to give little or no thought as to whether any sentence of imprisonment could be suspended either in part or in full.

<u>Camberwell Chambers</u>   Kris Gledhill

Index

Index

UNDERSTANDING THE LAW OF CONTRACT

THE EASYWAY

Ronald Skinner

Easyway Guides

Easyway Guides

© Straightforward Publishing 2018

British Cataloguing in Publication data. A catalogue record is available for this book
from the British Library.

ISBN
978-1-84716-838-2

Pri   co.uk

Whilst every ... in this book is
accurate at th... :cognise that the
information can ... the understanding
that no responsi... sponsibility is held

Contents

Table of cases

3

4

5

****

Table of cases

Ch. 1

Introduction

This latest book in the Straightforward Guides Series, A Straightforward Guide to Contract Law, Revised Edition, updated to 2017 is a comprehensive and easy to understand introduction to the complex area of contract law. The book covers key changes to contract law that arise from the introduction of the Consumer Rights Act 2015.

These changes relate to sale and supply law in the context of consumer contracts-in particular the implied promises made by a trader, and the corresponding rights of the consumer. Certain pre-contract information supplied by a trader in a B2C (buyer to consumer) contract may also become terms.

Other significant changes affecting contract law include the changes to consumer law governing unfair contract terms, with the enactment of a single regime governing B2C contracts in Part 2 of the Consumer Rights Act 2015 and the separation of the legislative regulation of exemption clauses in B2B contracts within UCTA 1977. Parts 1 and 2 of the Consumer Rights Act 2015 consolidate and replace the Unfair Terms in Consumer Contracts Regulations 1999 (UTCCRs) and relevant provisions of the Unfair Contract Terms Act 1977 (UCTA).

The Unfair Contract Terms Act 1977 applies only to exemption clauses covering business liability and, since the CRA 2015, does not cover any exemption clauses that would be covered by the Act, i.e. in contracts between a trader and a consumer. The CRA 2015 defines a 'trader' as a person acting for purposes relating to that persons trade, business craft or profession. A 'consumer' is defined as an individual acting for purposes that are wholly or mainly outside the indiviual's trade, business, craft or profession .

The other main statutory amendment is that of the Consumer Protection Amendment Regulations 2014, which adds a system of 'civil 'rights to redress' for consumers in B2C contracts in relation to misleading actions (misrepresentations)

Many people, either knowingly or unknowingly, enter into contracts without fully understanding the implications of what they are doing. Contracts can cover a number of areas, from hire purchase agreements to more complex finance agreements, contracts for construction of buildings, contracts for work around the house or contracts to supply goods. Notwithstanding the type of contract or what area of life it relates to, there is a comprehensive framework of law, both in statute and also common law, which covers parties to a contract. This book will enable the reader, whether layperson or professional, to obtain the basic facts about contract law and also to see clearly where they stand in relation to their rights and obligations. Throughout the book there is reference to relevant court cases.

The necessity of contract law

Contract law is necessary because the law only enforces certain types of promises, basically those promises that involve some sort of exchange. A promise for which nothing is given in return is called a gratuitous promise, and is not usually enforceable in law (the exception being where the promise is put into some sort of document, usually a deed). The main reason that we need contract law is because of the complex society we live in, a capitalist society. In capitalist society people trade freely on many different levels. There are many complex interactions, from small business endeavors to massive projects, such as construction projects where binding agreements are essential.

Contract law is there to provide a framework to regulate activities. Contract law will rarely force an individual or company to fulfill contractual promises. What it does do is to try to compensate innocent parties financially, usually by attempting to put them in a position that they would have been in if the contract had been performed as agreed.

Contract law-a brief history

Contract law, or the origins of contract law, goes back more than three hundred years. However, because of the very fast innovations in technology and the industrial revolution generally, the main body of contract law was established in the nineteenth century. Before that, contract law barely existed as a separate area of law.

Before the nineteenth century there were many areas of life where free negotiation was not an issue. Activities such as buying goods and then selling them on in the same market were illegal and were criminal offences. There was a basic right to a reasonable standard of living and no one was expected to negotiate that standard for them- selves. A similar, though less humane approach was taken to relationships between employer and employee, or master and servant as they were then called. Today, we all expect to have an employment contract detailing hours of work, duties and pay. This is the most basic of perceived rights.

We may, in most cases, not be able to negotiate the terms, but at least it is a contract. In a status society (as it was called), employment obligations were quite simply derived from whether you were a master or a servant: masters were entitled to ask servants to do more or less anything, and an employee who refused would or could face criminal sanctions. Employers had less onerous obligations that could sometimes include supplying food or medical care. Both sets of obligations were seen as fixed and non-negotiable.

Along with the development of contract law within a rapidly changing laissez faire society, came a rapidly changing political consciousness. The view arose that society was no more than a collection of self-interested individuals, each of whom was the best judge of their own interests, and should as far as possible be left alone to pursue those interests. This laissez faire approach gave birth to the law of contract, as we know it, in that, as we have seen, where people make their own transactions, unregulated by the state, it is important that they keep their promises.

Freedom of contract

Its origins in the laissez faire doctrine of the nineteen-century have had enormous influence on the development of contract law. The most striking reflection of this is the importance traditionally placed on freedom of contract. This doctrine promotes the idea that since parties are the best judges of their own interests, they should be free to make contracts on any terms they choose-on the most basic assumption that no one would choose unfavorable terms. The courts role is to act as umpire holding the parties to their promises, not to ask whether the bargain made was a fair one.

However, there are many problems with the freedom of contract:

- Inequality of bargaining strength between the two parties
- The acceptance of implied terms
- The use of standard form contracts
- Statutory intervention to protect consumers; and
- The obligation to implement EU law.

Over the years, courts have moved away from their reluctance to intervene, sometimes through their own making sometimes through parliament, notably the Unfair Contract Terms Act 1997.

Contracts and the notion of fairness

Traditional contract law lays down rules that are designed to apply in any contractual situation, regardless who the parties are, their relationships to each other and the subject matter of a contract. The basis for this approach is derived from the *laissez-faire* belief that parties should be left alone to make their own bargains. It was thought that the law should be required simply to provide a framework, allowing parties to know what they had to do to make their agreements binding.

This framework was intended to treat everyone equally, since to make different rules for one type of contracting party than for another would be to intervene in the fairness of the bargain. As a result the same rules were applied to contracts in which both parties had equal bargaining power as to those where one party had significantly less economic power, or legal or technical knowledge, such as a consumer contract.

This approach, often called procedural fairness, or formal justice, was judged to be fair because it treats everyone equally, favoring no one. There are, however, big problems inherent in this approach in that, if people are unequal to begin with, treating them equally simply maintains the inequality.

Over the last century the law has, to some extent at least, moved away from procedural fairness, and an element of substantive fairness, or distributive justice has developed. Substantive fairness aims to redress the imbalance of power between parties, giving some protection to the weaker one. For example, terms are now implied into employment contracts so that employers cannot simply dismiss employees without reasonable grounds for doing so. Similar protections have been given to others, such as tenants and consumers.

18

The objective approach

Contract law claims to be about enforcing obligations that the parties have voluntarily assumed. Bearing in mind that contracts do not have to be in writing, it is clear that enforcing contract law might be a problem. Even where contracts are in writing important areas may be left out. Contract law's approach to this problem is to look for the appearance of consent. This approach was explained by Blackburn J in Smith v Hughes (1871)-

" if, whatever a man's real intentions may be, he so conducts himself that a reasonable man would believe he was assenting to the terms proposed by the other party and that other party upon that belief enters into the contract with him, the man thus conducting himself would be equally bound as if he had intended to agree to the other party's terms".

It can be seen that the area of contract law is complex and yet is governed by basic principles.

In this book we cover, amongst other areas:

- Contracts and the law generally
- The formation of a contract
- The terms of a contract
- Implied terms
- Misrepresentation
- Remedies if a contract is breached.

A basic understanding of contracts will prove invaluable to any person who takes the time to understand more. This brief book will enable the reader to obtain that basic understanding.

****

2

Forming a Contract

In this chapter we look at the main principles underpinning forming a contract. We look at the nature of contracts and the notion of offer and acceptance plus certainty of contract and terms implied into a contract. The intention to create legal relations is examined along with different types of contract and capacity to enter into a contract.

Underpinning all contracts are four main principles:

1) A contract is an agreement between the parties to that contract-one person makes an offer and the other accepts that offer

2) Both parties have an intention to be legally bound by the agreement-this is usually known as an intention to create legal relations

3) Parties to the agreement need to be absolutely clear as to the terms of the agreement – this is the main area of contention with contracts, as we will see later

4) There must be consideration provided by each of the parties to the contract – this means that one person promises to give or deliver and the other promises to pay. The offer and the payment – either monetary

or in kind - is the consideration. When making a contract, or entering into a contract all parties to the contract must have the legal capacity to enter into a contract. Very importantly, a contract, in most cases, does not have to be in writing – a piece of paper is not necessary, the agreement and evidence of that agreement forms the basis of contract. There are a few important exceptions, including contracts relating to interests in land (Law of property (Miscellaneous Provisions) Act 1989, s 2(1)) and consumer credit (Consumer Credit Act 1974). We will outline those contracts that do need to be in writing later on in this chapter.

Other factors affecting formation include:

- Form-the way the contract is created (e.g. the sale of land can only be made in the form of a deed) Form is an issue with specialty contracts but not with simple contracts
- Privity of contract and the rights of third parties-generally a contract is only enforceable by or against a party to it, subject to exceptions and certain third party rights are now protected in the Contracts (Rights of Third Parties) Act 1999.

The nature of contracts – unilateral and bilateral contracts
The majority of contracts entered into are known as bilateral contracts. This quite simply means that each party to a contract agrees to take on an obligation. This obligation is underpinned by a promise to give something to the other party. A unilateral contract will arise where one party to the contract will make a promise to do something (usually to

pay a sum of money) if the other party carries out a certain task. Examples of this are where you might undertake to pay someone a sum of money if they shave off their hair for charity or give up smoking. Estate agents enter into unilateral contracts whereby a percentage of sales go to the agent if they sell the property. However, the agent is not legally bound to sell the property, just to try to sell it.

The notion of offer and acceptance

As we have seen, for a contract to have legal status, usually one of the parties to the contract must have made an offer and the other party must have accepted the offer. Once the contract is accepted the agreement will be legally binding. The person making the offer is called the offeror and the person to whom the offer is made is known as the offeree. An offer may be express or implied. Express means that there is an express intention to offer goods and for X to pay an amount for the goods. Implied may mean, for example, when purchasing something from a store. The act of taking goods to a checkout means that there is an implied offer to buy those goods.

When dealing with contracts, or the formation of a contract most offers are made to specific parties. However, offers can also be made to a group of people or to the public at large. One such example is where a reward is offered for information following a crime.

One famous case dealing with offers to the public at large is Carlill v Carbolic Smokeball (1893) the defendants in this case were the manufacturers of 'smokeballs' popular at the time, which they claimed could prevent flu. They published adverts to this effect stating that anyone using their smoke balls and not being cured of flu would receive £100.

One person buying their smokeballs was a Mrs Carlill. It did not work and she claimed the £100. The manufacturers argument was to claim that their advert did not constitute a contract, since it was impossible to contract with the whole wide world. They claimed that they were not legally bound to pay the money. The court, needless to say, rejected this argument, which held that the advert did contract with the world. Mrs Carlill accepted the offer and duly claimed the £100. A contract such as the one above is usually a unilateral contract.

The invitation to treat

Certain kinds of transactions between parties might involve a preliminary stage where one party to the contract invites the other party to make an offer. This preliminary stage is known as 'invitation to treat'.

One such case that demonstrates this is that of Gibson v Manchester City Council (1979). In this case, a council tenant of Manchester City Council expressed an interest in buying their house. The application was duly completed and sent to the council. A letter was received from the council stating that it may be prepared to sell the house to the tenant for £2180. The tenant, Mr Gibson, queried the purchase price pointing out that the path to the house was in bad condition. The council refused to alter the price, stating that the valuation reflected the condition of the property and the current property market. Mr Gibson then wrote asking the council to continue with the sale. Following a change in the control of the council, and a new political approach, it was decided to stop the sale of houses to tenants. Mr Gibson was informed that his application had been declined, notwithstanding the initial offer. Legal proceedings were brought against the council claiming that the letter received by Mr Gibson, with the offer of sale at a price, constituted a contract, and was an offer which he duly accepted. The House of Lords, however, ruled that the council had not made an offer, the letter stating the purchase price was merely one step in the negotiations for a contract and amounted only to an invitation to treat. Its purpose in the first instance was quite simply to invite the making of a formal application, amounting to an offer, from the tenant.

Retailers websites

These are probably invitations to treat, although this has no clear definition at the moment. Regulation 12 of the E-Commerce (EC Directives) Regulations 2002 suggests that the customers order may well be the offer so that the website is an invitation to treat.

Offers of sale in shops

Goods in shop windows marked with a price are generally regarded as invitations to treat, rather than offers to actually sell the goods at the price displayed. One such case highlighting this is Fisher v Bell (1961) where a shopkeeper was prosecuted under the Offensive Weapons Act 1959 for 'offering for sale' an offensive weapon. The shopkeeper was displaying a flick knife with a price attached in the window. It was held that the display of the flick knife was an invitation to treat, rather than an offer, thus the shopkeeper was found not guilty of the offence.

Where goods are sold on a self-service basis, the customer will make an offer to purchase on presenting the goods at the till and the shopkeeper may reject or accept that offer. One case which highlights this is Pharmaceutical Society of Great Britain v Boots Cash Chemists (Southern) Limited 1953. Boots were charged with an offence concerning the sale of items, medicines that could only be sold under the supervision of a qualified pharmacist. Two customers in a self-service shop selected the items, which were marked with a price from a shelf in the shop. The shelves were not supervised by a pharmacist but the pharmacist was instructed to supervise at the cash desk. The issue was whether the sale had taken place at the shelf or the cash desk. The Court of Appeal decided that the shelf display was like an advertisement and was therefore an invitation to treat. The offer was made by the customer when the items were placed in a basket and was only accepted when the goods were taken to the cash desk. A pharmacist was supervising at that point so no offence was committed.

Following on from this principle, shops do not have to sell goods at the marked price and a customer cannot insist on buying a particular good on display. Displaying the goods is not an offer so a customer cannot accept it making a binding contract. (In reality, if shops do display goods at a price they generally sell it at that price although, as we have seen they do not have to).

Contracts and advertisements

A distinction is generally made between advertisements for unilateral contracts and advertisements for bilateral contracts. Advertisements for unilateral contracts will include those such as described in the case of Carlill and Carbolic Smokeball Co or those offering a reward for information or for lost property. They are usually treated as offers on the basis that no further negotiations are need between the parties to the offer and the person making the offer will usually be bound by it. One case is that of Bowerman v Association of British Travel Agents Ltd (1996) in which a school had booked a skiing holiday with a travel agent, which was a member of ABTA. Any member of ABTA has to display a notice as follows:

Where holidays or other travel arrangements have not yet commenced at the time of failure of the tour operator, ABTA arranges for you to be reimbursed the money you have paid for your holiday.

In this case the tour operator became insolvent and all holidays were cancelled. The school was refunded the money paid for the holiday but not the cost of the travel insurance taken out, which was significant. The case was taken to court and ABTA lost because the notice constituted an offer which h the school accepted by contracting with the ABTA member.

Bilateral contracts

Bilateral contracts are the types that advertise specified goods at a certain price such as those found in shop windows and in magazines.

They are usually considered invitations to treat on the grounds that they may lead to further bargaining. One such case that highlights this is Partridge v Crittendon (1968). An advertisement in a magazine stated 'Bramblefinch cocks and hens 25shillings each'. As the Bramblefinch was a protected species, the person who placed the advert was charged with unlawfully offering for sale a wild bird which was against the Protection of Birds Act 1954, but the conviction was quashed on the grounds that the advertisement was not an offer but an invitation to treat.

Communication of offers

A valid offer must be communicated to the offeree. It would be unfair for a person to be bound by an offer of which he had no knowledge. This is reflected in Taylor v Laird 1856. The offeree must have clear knowledge of the existence of an offer for it to be enforceable. This is reflected in Inland Revenue Commissioners v Fry 2001.

An offer can be made to one individual or to the whole world, when the offer can be accepted by any party who had genuine notice of it. In addition, the terms of the contract must be certain. The parties must know in advance what they are contracting over, so any vague words may invalidate the agreement. this is reflected in Guthing v Lynn 1831.

The length of time an offer should last

An offer may cease to exist in any of the following circumstances:

-Where an offeror states that an offer will be open for a specified time

-Where the offeror has not specified how long the offer will remain open, the offer will lapse after a reasonable length of time has passed. How much time can be deemed reasonable will depend on whether the offer was communicated quickly and also on the subject matter.

Some offers are made subject to certain specified conditions, and if these conditions are not in place, the offer may lapse. An offer may lapse if and when the offeree rejects it. For example, if A offers to sell B a car on Tuesday, and B says no, B cannot come back on Wednesday and insist on accepting the offer

A counter offer can terminate the original offer. One case that highlights this is Hyde v Wrench (1840) where the defendant offered to sell his farm for £1000 and the plaintiff responded by offering to buy it at £950-this is termed making a counter offer. The farm owner refused to sell at that price and when the plaintiff later tried to buy the farm at £1000, the original asking price, it was held that this offer was no longer available. The counter offer had terminated the original offer

The death of the offeror can affect the offer. If the offeree knows of the death of the offeror then the offer is terminated. If they did not, the offer still stands, although this is one area of law that is still unclear. It very much depends on the circumstances at the time

An offer may be revoked, withdrawn, at any time until it has been accepted. This is the basic rule, although there are a number of other principles. It is not enough for an offeror simply to change his or her mind about an offer. The offeror must notify the offeree that the offer has been revoked. Revocation does not specifically have to be communicated by the offeror, it can be by another reliable party.

Acceptance of an offer

Acceptance of an offer must be unconditional, accepting the precise terms of the offer. Where the process of negotiation is long and difficult, it might be difficult to pinpoint exactly when an offer has been made and accepted. In such cases a court will examine the precise course of negotiations to ascertain whether the parties have reached agreement, if at all and when. This process can be complicated when the so-called 'battle of forms' occurs. Rather than negotiating terms each time a contract is made many companies try to use standard conditions, which will be printed on headed stationary, such as order forms and delivery notes. The 'battle of forms' occurs when one party sends a form stating that the contract is on their terms, and the other party responds by sending back the forms and stating that the contract is on their terms. The general rule in these cases is that the 'last shot' wins the battle. Each new form issued is treated as a counter offer, so that when one party performs its obligation under the contract the action will be seen as acceptance by the other side. One simple case that illustrates this is British Road Services v Crutchley (Arthur V) Ltd (1968). The plaintiffs delivered some whisky to the defendants for storage. The BRS driver handed the defendants a delivery note, which listed the company's terms of carriage. The note was accepted and stamped with Crutchley's terms and conditions and the court held that by accepting this, the BRS driver had accepted a counter offer.

Although many cases are simple, other more recent case law has held that the last shot will not always succeed.

It is a basic assumption that there is no acceptance until the act has been thoroughly performed. However, in some cases, part performance may amount to acceptance. In Errington v Errington (1952) a father bought a house in his own name for £750, borrowing £500 of the price from a building society. He bought the house for his son and daughter in law to live in, and told them that they must meet the mortgage repayments. If they met the payments the house would be signed over to them on completion of the term. The couple moved in and began to pay the mortgage, but they never in fact made the promise to continue with the payments until the mortgage was paid off, which meant that the contract was unilateral.

When the father later died, the people in charge of his affairs sought to withdraw the offer. The Court of Appeal held that it was too late to do this. The part performance of the son and daughter in law constituted an acceptance of the contract and the father and his representatives after death were bound by the resulting contract unless the son and daughter in law ceased the payments, in which case the offer was no longer binding.

A request for information about an offer does not constitute a counter offer, so the original offer remains open. If an offeree has to accept an offer in a specified manner, then only acceptance by that method or an equally effective one will be binding

31

Communicating acceptance of an offer

An acceptance will not usually take effect until it is clearly communicated to the offeror. However, there are some circumstances where acceptance may take effect without it being communicated to the offeror. An offer may clearly state, or indeed imply, that acceptance need not be communicated to the offeror. An offeror who fails to receive an acceptance through their own fault may be prevented from claiming that the non-communication means they should not be bound by the contract.

The general rule for acceptances by post is that they take effect when they are posted, rather than when they are communicated. The postal rule was laid down in the case of Adams v Lindsell (1818), when on the 2nd of September 1817, the defendants wrote to the plaintiffs, who were in the wool processing business, offering to sell them a quantity of sheep fleeces, and stating that they required an answer 'in course of post'. However, the defendants did not address the letter correctly and it did not reach the plaintiffs until the evening of September the 5th. The plaintiffs posted their acceptance the same evening, and it reached the defendants on the 9th of September. If the original letter had been correctly addressed it would have reached the plaintiffs by the 7th of September. Because it was incorrectly addressed it did not and no reply was received and the wool was sold to a third party. The issue was whether a sale had been made before the sale of the wool to the third party. The court heard that the contract was concluded as soon as the acceptance was posted and that the defendants were bound from the evening of 5th September so should not have sold the wool to a third party. There are certain exceptions to the postal rule. The offeror may avoid the postal rule by making it a specific term of their offer that acceptance will only take effect when it is communicated to them.

The postal rule has limited application to modern communications technology. In Entores Ltd v Miles Far East Corp, offer and acceptance communicated by telex were valid because the method was so instantaneous that the parties were deemed to be dealing as if face-to-face, even though they were in different countries. The time when these forms of communication are used may cause problems in determining if a contract is made, as when a fax is sent out of office hours. Now offer and acceptance in the case of electronic communication is governed by the Consumer Protection (Distance Selling) Regulations 2000. This gives the buyer the right to be informed of the right to cancel within seven days, description, price, arrangements for payment and identity of seller, and to be given written confirmation, without which a contract is not formed. Under EU Electronic Commerce Directive 2000/31 no contract can be made electronically until the buyer has received acknowledgement of his acceptance. the Directive has been implemented through the Electronic Commerce (EC Directive) Regulations 2000.

Ignorance of the offer
It is generally accepted that a person cannot accept an offer of which they are unaware, because in order to create a binding contract, the parties must reach agreement. This is a very important principle.

Tenders, auctions and the sale of land

The rules outlined above also apply to the sale of land and to sales by tender and auction. If a large organization, such as a company or government department needs to contract a supplier of goods or services, it will, more often than not, advertise for tenders, i.e., bids. Organizations wishing to supply goods or services will reply, detailing price for these services. The advertiser will choose from the replies and contact the successful tender. As a general rule, the request for tenders is regarded as an invitation to treat, (see previous) so there is no specific obligation to accept any of the tenders sent. The tenders themselves are offers and a contract does not come into existence until one is accepted. However, where a party has issued an invitation to tender, it is bound to consider all correctly submitted tenders. One such case highlighting this is Blackpool and Fylde Aero Club v Blackpool Borough Council (1990). Blackpool BC invited tenders from people who were interested in operating leisure flights from the local airfield. Tenders had to be submitted to the town hall by a stated deadline. The Aero Club submitted its application on time but the council refused to consider it, as due to an error on their part, they mistakenly believed that the tender had been submitted after the deadline.

It was held that the council's invitation to tender was a unilateral offer to consider all tenders which fell within its rules. The tender constituted an offer which had been accepted by the Aero Club. The offer was accepted by any party who put in a tender. Thus the council were obliged to consider all tenders (acceptances) to their offer, including the Aero Club tender. They were not, of course, obliged to accept the tender. In some cases however, an invitation for tenders may in itself be an offer. The main example of this is where the invitation to tender makes it clear that the lowest tender (or highest) will be accepted. The implications of choosing to accept a tender depend on what sort of tender is involved.

Specific tenders

Where an invitation to tender specifies that a particular quantity of goods is required on a particular date, or between certain dates, agreeing to one of the tenders submitted will constitute acceptance of an offer, creating a contract between the parties.

Non-specific tenders

Some invitations to tender are not specific, and may for example simply state that certain goods may be required, up to a particular maximum quantity, with deliveries to be made if and when requested. For example, an invitation to tender made by a hospital may ask for tenders to supply goods, if and when required. In this case, taking up one of the tenders submitted does not amount to acceptance of an offer in the contractual sense and there is no contract. The hospital may take the goods all at one, some at a time or none at all. It is not bound.

Auction sales

The parties to an auction sale are the bidder and the owner of the goods. The auctioneer supplies a service and is not party to the contract between buyer and seller.

Sale of land

The standard rules of contract apply to the sale of land, including buildings. However, the court applies the rules strictly in the case of land, tending to require very clear evidence of an intention to be bound before they will state that an offer has been made.

In Harvey v Facey (1893) the plaintiffs sent the defendants a telegram asking 'will you sell us Bumper Hall Pen? Telegraph lowest cash price'. The reply arrived back stating 'Lowest price for Bumper Hall pen £900'. The plaintiffs then sent a telegram saying 'we agree to buy Bumper Hall Pen for £900. Please send us your title deeds'. On these facts, the Privy Council held that there was no contract. They regarded the telegram from the defendants as a statement of price only. It was therefore not an offer which could be accepted by the third telegram.

In practice there are rigid procedures involved in the sale of land. The first is the 'sale subject to contract', where the parties agree to the sale and the implication is that there is a good deal of proving and other work before a contract is in existence. The next stage is the exchange of contract, where the buyer and seller agree to the terms of the formal contract. Once the contracts are exchanged then the contract is binding and any backing out can result in a claim for damages and lost deposit.

Certainty of contract

In order to be viewed as a binding contract, an agreement must be absolutely certain. That is, it should not be vague or incomplete. One such case that amplifies this is that of Scammell v Ouston (1941) where the parties agreed that Ouston could buy a van from Scammell, giving his lorry in part exchange paying the balance over two-years on hire purchase terms. Scammell decided to back out and claimed that there was no contract between the parties.

The House of Lords agreed, pointing out that the courts would uphold an agreement if there really was one, in this case the terms were too vague, particularly the agreement to pay on Hire Purchase Terms.

In certain cases, parties may leave details vague, particularly when dealing with fluctuating prices and other factors. Provisions should be in the contract stating how they should be clarified.

Terms implied into contract by statute

In some cases, statute will override contract and will provide that certain provisions should be read into contracts even though they have not been specifically agreed between the parties. For example, under the Consumer Rights Act 2015, an agreement for the sale of goods can become binding as soon as the parties have agreed to buy and sell, with the details of the contract being laid down by law, or determined by the standard of reasonableness. In such a case, the parties do not even have had to agree on a price. The buyer is entitled to pay a reasonable price. Terms implied by statute will be examined further on in this book.

Intention to create legal relations

One major principle of contract law is that of intention to create legal relations. If two or more parties make an agreement without the

37

intention of being legally bound by it, the agreement will not be regarded as a contract. As far as intent to be legally bound is concerned, contracts can be divided into domestic and social agreements on one hand, and commercial agreements on the other. Where the agreement falls into the former category there is an assumption that the parties do not intend to create legal relations. The reverse is true when it comes to commercial agreements.

Domestic and social agreements

Where a husband and wife who are living together as one household make an agreement, the courts will assume that they do not intend to be legally bound, unless the agreement states other wise. In Balfour v Balfour (1919) the defendant was a civil servant stationed in Sri Lanka. Whilst the couple were on leave in England, Mrs. Balfour was taken ill, and it became clear that her husband would have to return by himself. He promised to pay her maintenance of £30 per month. They eventually separated and the husband refused to make any more payments. The Court of Appeal decided he was not bound to make further payments, as when the agreement was made there was no intention to create legal relations. Likewise, agreements between parents and children are assumed not to be legally binding.

Social agreements

The presumption that an agreement is not intended to be legally binding is also applied to social relationships between people who are not related. With both the above though, there can be exceptions.

Commercial agreements

There is a strong presumption in commercial agreements that the parties intend to be legally bound, and unless clear words are used this presumption stands. Where the words of a business agreement are ambiguous, the courts will favor the interpretation that suggests that the parties did intend to create legal relations.

The capacity to enter into a contract

There are categories of people in society whose power to make contracts is limited by law. The main categories are minors and people considered incapable of contracting due to mental disorders or some other condition of incapacity such as drunkenness or under influence of certain drugs. In addition, the contracting capacity of a company or corporation will also have a bearing, i.e. the legal capacity to enter into a contract in the first place.

The basic common law rule is that contracts do not bind minors. In some cases however, as in much of contract law, there are contracts that will bind minors. The main contracts binding on a minor are contracts to supply 'necessaries'. Under the Sale of Goods Act 1979, now replaced by the Consumer Rights Act 2015, necessaries means 'goods suitable to the condition in life of the minor or other person concerned and to his actual requirements at the time of sale and delivery'. When deciding if a contract is one for necessaries, the courts first of all determine whether the goods or services are capable of amounting to necessaries in law, and then consider whether they are necessary for the minor in question. Two cases highlight this point. In Nash v Inman

(1908) a student purchased 11 silk waistcoats while still a minor. He argued that they comprised 'goods suitable to his condition in life, and to his actual requirements at the time of sale and delivery'. It was held that the silk waistcoats were suitable to the conditions of life of a Cambridge undergraduate at that time, but they were not suitable to his actual needs as he already had a sufficient supply of waistcoats.

A more recent case was that of Proform Sports Management Limited v Proactive Sports management Limited and Another (2006). In this case, footballer Wayne Rooney signed a two year management and agency agreement with the claimant when he was aged 15. Rooney later terminated the contract. It was held that the agreement was not a contract of apprenticeship, education or service substantially to the footballer's benefit thus he was entitled to avoid it.

Mental incapacity

This category covers people who suffer from mental disability, and those who are drunk when the contract is made. In general terms, contracts made with people in either state will be valid unless, very importantly, at the time the contract was made, the person is incapable of understanding the nature of the transaction and the other party knows this. In such circumstances, the contract is voidable. The party suffering the disability can choose to void it. Where one party is incapable, through disability as described, of understanding the nature of the contract, but the other party is unaware, the courts will ignore the disability. One important case highlighting this is Hart v O'Connor (1985) the Privy Council held that a person of unsound mind was bound by his agreement to sell some land because when the contract was made the buyer did not realize that the buyer had any mental incapacity. The fact also that language may be a barrier does not render a person incapable of making a contract.

Corporations

A corporation is a legal entity that is treated by law as having a separate identity from the persons who constitute it. There are three main types of corporation: registered companies, corporations established by statute and chartered corporations. Each has a different level of contracting ability.

Registered companies

These are companies registered under the Companies Act 1985 (as amended) most commercial companies. When registering, companies must supply a document that regulates their activities called a memorandum of association, which contains information including an objects clause, laying down the range of activities that their company can engage in. Under the 1989 Act a company can be liable for a contract made outside its stated activities if the other party has acted in good faith.

Statutory companies

These corporations are created by an Act of Parliament, for specific purposes, the Independent Broadcasting Authority is an example, as are local authorities. The statute creating the particular corporation will specify the purposes for which that corporation may make contracts.

Any contracted outside of these purposes is null and void.

Chartered corporations

These are corporations set up by Royal Charter, which means that their rights are officially granted by the Crown. Examples are charities and some universities and other educational institutions. They have the same contractual capacity as an adult human being.

Formalities

We have discussed the fact that an agreement does not have to take a specific written form in order to be deemed a binding contract. A contract can be oral. One famous recent case involving an oral contract was Hadley v Kemp (1990) where Gary Kemp was the songwriter in the group Spandau Ballet. He was sued by other members of then group for royalties received for the group's music. The basis of the claim was that there was an oral agreement to share royalties. They were unable to prove the existence of any oral agreement and their claim failed.

Contracts which must be made by deed

The Law of Property Act 1925 states that a contract for a lease of more than three years must be made by deed, which basically means that it must be put into a formal document, signed in front of witnesses.

Contracts which must be in writing

Some statutes lay down that certain types of contract must be in writing. Most contracts involving sales of land must be in writing, under the Law of Property Act 1989. Other contracts that need to be in writing are those involving the transfers of shares in a limited company (Companies Act 1985 (as amended), bills of exchange; cheques and promissory notes (Bills of Exchange Act (1882); and regulated consumer credit agreements, such as hire purchase agreements (Consumer Credit Act 1974).

Contracts which must be evidenced in writing

Contracts of guarantee (where one party guarantees the obligations of another, such as parents guaranteeing a sons or daughters overdraft) are required to be 'evidenced in writing'. Contracts for sale or disposition of land before 27th September 1989 are still covered by the old law prior to the Law of Property Act 1989. Evidenced in writing means that although the contract itself may not be a written one, there must be written evidence of the transaction. The evidence must have existed before one party tried to enforce the contract against the other, and it must be signed by the party against whom the contract is to be enforced.

****

Main points from chapter two

Underpinning all contracts there are four main principles:

- A contract is an agreement between the parties to that contract – one person makes an offer and the other accepts that offer
- Both parties have an intention to be legally bound by the agreement – this is usually known as an intention to create legal relations
- Parties to the agreement have to be very clear as to the terms of the agreement
- There must be consideration provided by each of the parties to the contract.

Other aspects of contracts are:

- Contracts do not have to be in writing
- A contract must be clear and certain in its intent
- People must have the capacity to enter into an agreement

3

Consideration and Contracts

In this chapter we look at the notion of consideration which is central to contract law. We look at the different types of consideration

As we saw in chapter 2, English law states that a contract is not usually binding unless it is supported by consideration. Consideration is usually said to mean that each party to a contract must give something in return for what is gained from the other party. Very basically, if there is a dispute and you wish to enforce someone's promise to you must prove that you gave something in return for that promise.

Consideration may be goods or services, a thing or a service. Many problems concerning consideration arise not when a contract is made but when one or other of the parties to the contract seeks to modify it, such as paying a lower price than agreed or supplying a different good or service.

Promisor and Promisee

In most contracts, it is the case that two promises will be exchanged, so each party to the contract is promisor and promisee. In a contract case, the claimant will often be arguing that the defendant has broken the promise made to the claimant and therefore the claimant will usually be the promisee. One example is if A contracts to build a conservatory and B promises to pay £5000 for the conservatory, there are two promises in this contract. A's promise to build a conservatory and B's promise to pay. If A fails to build the conservatory B can sue him. If the issue of consideration arises, B will seek to prove that his promise to pay £5000 was consideration for A's promise for building the conservatory. In that action, A will be the promisor and B the promisee. However, reverse the situation and B fails to pay, then A will sue and, if consideration is at issue, A will have to prove that his promise to build the conservatory was consideration for B's promise to pay. In that action, A will be the promisee and B the promisor.

'Executory' and 'executed' consideration

Consideration can fall into two categories: executory and executed. Executed consideration is the performance of an act in return for a promise. Executory consideration is when the defendant makes a promise, and the plaintiff offers a counter promise – you promise to deliver goods to me and I promise to pay for them when they arrive, the promise is executory because it is something to be done in the future.

Consideration must be given in return for the promise or act of the other party. Something done, given, or promised beforehand will not be counted as consideration. A classic case concerning this arose in Roscorla v Thomas (1842). The defendant sold the plaintiff a horse. After the sale was completed, the defendant told the plaintiff that the animal was 'sound and free from any vice'. This was not the actual truth and the plaintiff sued. The court held that the defendants promise was unenforceable, because it was made after the sale. If the promise about the horse's condition had been made before, the plaintiff would have provided consideration for it by buying the horse. As it was made after the sale, the consideration was past, for it had not been given in return for the promise.

There are two exceptions to the rule that past consideration is no consideration. The first is where the past consideration was provided at the promisors request, and it was understood that payment would be made. The second is the bill of exchange. Under s27 of the Bills of Exchange Act 1882, an antecedent debt or 'liability' may be consideration for receipt of a bill of exchange.

The rules of consideration

Consideration need not be adequate

The law of contract regulates the making of bargains. As freedom of contract is vital, the law is not concerned with whether a party has made a good bargain or a bad one. Adequacy is given its normal meaning-the contract is enforceable even if the price does not match the value of what is being gained under the agreement.

One such case that reflects this is Thomas v Thomas (1842). before he died Thomas expressed a wish that his wife should be allowed to remain in his house although there was no mention of this in his will. The executors carried out his wish but charged the widow a nominal ground rent of £1 a year. When they later tried to dispossess her they failed.

Consideration must be sufficient

Consideration offered is sufficient provided that:

- It is real (White v Bluett (1853)
- It is tangible (Ward v Byham (1956)
- It has some discernible value (Chappel v Nestle (1960); and
- Economic value is measured against benefit gained.

Consideration must not be past

Consideration must follow rather than precede agreement. This prevents coercion by suppliers of goods and services.

Consideration must be of economic value

What this principle basically means is that there must be some physical value, rather than just an emotional or sentimental value.

Consideration can be a promise not to sue

If one party has a possible civil claim against the other, a promise not to enforce that claim is good consideration for a promise given in return. One clear example is if A crashes into B's car then A can promise not to sue if B pays for the damage.

Performance of an existing duty

Where a promisee already owes the promisor a legal duty, then in theory performing that duty should not in itself be consideration. If the promisee does nothing more than they are already obliged to do, they are suffering no detriment and the promisor is only getting a benefit to which he or she is entitled.

Existing duties can be divided into three categories: public duties; contractual duties to the promisor; and contractual duties to a third party.

Existing public duty

Where a person is merely carrying out duties they are legally bound to perform – such as police officer or juror, doing that alone will not be consideration. However, where a promisee is under a public duty, but does something beyond the call of that duty, that extra act amounts to consideration. In Glasbrook Brothers v Glamorgan County Council (1925) the owners of a South Wales Mine asked the police to place a guard at their colliery during a strike. The police suggested that regular checks by mobile patrol would be adequate but the owners replied that they wanted something more intensive and the police agreed at an extra cost of £2,200. After the strike the owners refused to pay saying that the police had a duty to protect their property. The courts held in favor of the police saying that the police did not have a duty to supply the cover they did, only the cover they deemed sufficient. Anything over and above was deemed consideration.

Existing contractual duty to the promisor

The position on contractual duties and consideration has changed from the traditional position whereby the performance of an existing contractual duty owed to a promisor was not consideration. In Stilk v Myrick (1809) two sailors deserted a ship during a voyage and the captain was unable to find replacements. The remaining crew-members were promised extra wages for sailing the ship back to London but the captain refused to pay on arrival and the sailors sued with the court holding that there was no consideration as the sailors had already contracted to sail the boat back to its destination. In Hartley v Ponsonby (1857) half the crew deserted and the remaining crew were offered extra wages to carry on the journey. At the end the captain refused to pay and the crew sued and won, as the courts held that there was consideration as the crew were to small to sail the boat adequately and extra money was justified.

An exception to the rule that performance of an existing contractual obligation owed to the promisor will not amount to consideration will occur where a party can be seen to receive an extra benefit from the other party's agreement to carry out his existing obligations. One such case that highlights this is that of Williams v Roffey Brothers (1991). In this case the defendants (the main contractors) were refurbishing a block of flats. They sub-contracted the carpentry works to the plaintiff. The plaintiff ran into financial difficulties, whereupon the defendants agreed to pay the plaintiff an additional sum if they completed the work on time. It was held that where a party to an existing contract later agrees to pay an 'extra bonus' in order that the other party performs his obligations under the original contract, then the new agreement is binding if the party agreeing to pay the bonus has thereby obtained some new practical advantage or avoided a disadvantage. In this particular case, the advantage was the avoidance of a penalty clause and the expense of finding new carpenters, among other factors.

Existing contractual duty to a third party

In some cases two parties make a contract to provide a benefit to a third party. If one of the parties (A) makes a further promise to that third party to provide the benefit they have already contracted to provide, that further promise can be good consideration for a promise made by the third party in return-even though nothing more than the contractual duty is being promised by A.

One case that illustrates this is Scotson v Pegg (1861). Scotson contracted to supply a cargo of coal to a third party, X, or to anyone X nominated. Scotson was instructed by X to deliver the coal to Pegg, and Pegg promised to unload the coal at a stated rate of pay. He subsequently failed to do the agreed unloading. Scotson sued Pegg, claiming that their promise to deliver coal to him was consideration for his promise to unload it. Pegg claimed that this could not be consideration, since Scotson was already bound to supply the coal under the contract with X. The court upheld Scotson's claim: delivery of the coal was consideration because it was a benefit to Pegg, and a detriment to Scotson in that it prevented them from having the option of breaking their contract with X.

Waiver and Promissory estoppel

These are ways of making some kind of promise binding even where there is no consideration. Waiver has traditionally applied where one party agrees not to enforce their strict rights under the contract by, for example, accepting delivery later than agreed. One case that illustrates the doctrine of waiver is that of Hickman v Haynes (1875). A buyer

51

asked the seller to deliver goods later than originally agreed and then when the delivery was made refused to accept it. The seller sued for breach of contract, the buyer responded by arguing that the seller was in breach, for delivering later than specified. The courts rejected the buyer's argument on the ground s that the delivery was made at the buyer's request.

Promissory estoppel (stopping the contract on the basis of a promise) is a newer doctrine than waiver, developing the concept. It was introduced by Lord Denning in the Central London Property Trust Ltd v High Trees (1947) where owners of a block of flats had promised to accept reduced rents in 1939. There was no consideration for their promise but Lord Denning nevertheless stated that he would estop them from recovering any arrears. He based his case on the decision in Hughes v Metropolitan Railways (1875). In this case, under the lease the tenants were obliged to keep the premises in good repair, and in October 1874, the landlord gave them six months notice to do some repairs stating that if they were not done in time, the lease would be forfeited. In November the two parties began to negotiate the possibility of the tenants buying the lease, the tenants stating in the meantime that they would not carry out the repairs. By December the negotiations had broken down and at the end of the six-month notice period, the landlord claimed that the lease was forfeited because the tenants had not done the repairs. The House of Lords (now Supreme Court) held however, that the landlord's conduct was an implied promise to the tenants that he would not enforce the forfeiture at the end of the notice period, and in not doing the repairs, the tenants had been relying on this premise. It was seen that the six-month notice period began again when negotiations broke down.

The exact scope of the doctrine is a matter of debate, but certain requirements must be met:

- Estoppel only applies to the modification of discharge of an existing contractual obligation. It cannot create a new contract.
- It can only be used as a 'shield' and not a 'sword'.
- The promise not to enforce rights must be clear and unequivocal.
- It must be inequitable for the promisor to go back on his promise.
- The promisee must have acted in reliance on the promise, although not necessarily to his detriment.

Agreement by deed

There is one other way in which a promise can be made binding without consideration: it can be put into a document called a deed. An agreement by deed is often described as a 'formal' contract. Other types of contract are known as simple contracts. The procedure for making a contract by deed is laid down in s.1 of the Law of Property (Miscellaneous Provisions) Act 1989 and usually involves signing a formal document in the presence of a witness. Deeds are usually used to give legal effect to what otherwise might be a gratuitous gift, which could be unenforceable for lack of consideration.

****

Main points from chapter three

- English law states that a contract is not usually binding unless it is supported by consideration

- Consideration is usually said to mean that each party to a contract must give something in return for what is gained from the other party

- Consideration may be goods or services, a thing or a service.

4

Terms of Contracts

In this chapter we look at the main terms of contracts and what must be inherent in a contract before it can be legally binding. Express terms of contract and implied terms are examined along with collateral agreements and unfair contract terms. Finally, we look at misrepresentation, duress and undue influence. Illegality of contract is dealt with in chapter 6.

Once a contract has been formed, it is necessary to define the scope of the obligations which each party incurs. Terms of contracts describe the respective duties and obligations of each party to the contract. As well as the contractual terms laid out and agreed by parties to a contract, called express terms, there may also be implied terms – terms that are 'read into' a contract because of the facts of the agreement and the apparent intention of the parties or the law on specific types of contract.

Express terms of contract
Oral statements

In all transactions, with the exception of the simplest, there will be some negotiations before a contract is made. These are usually oral statements or based on oral statements. Problems can arise following oral statements when parties cannot agree whether the statement was intended to be binding. In considering questions such as these a court will classify statements made during negotiations as either representations or terms. A representation is a statement that may have encouraged one of the parties to make the contract, but is not itself part of the contract, while a term is an undertaking that is part of the contract.

Representation can also be construed as misrepresentation, which is a common cause of dispute. Whether a statement is either a representation or a term is mainly a question of the party's intentions. If the parties have indicated that a particular statement is a term of their contract, then the court will carry out that intention.

Written terms of a contract

Written terms can be incorporated into a contract in three different ways: by signature, by reasonable notice and by a previous course of dealing.

The parol evidence rule

Under this rule, where there is a written contract, extrinsic (parole) evidence cannot change the express terms laid down in that document. Extrinsic evidence includes oral statements and written material such as draft contracts or letter, whether relating to pre-contract negotiations or the parties post contractual behavior. One case that illustrates the parole evidence rule is Henderson v Arthur (1907). The plaintiffs and the defendant were parties to a lease that contained a covenant for the payment of rent quarterly in advance, although before the lease was drawn up the parties agreed that the rent could be paid in arrears. When the tenant was sued for not paying quarterly in advance, he pointed out this prior agreement. The court held that the terms of prior oral agreement could not be substituted for the terms of a later formal contract covering the same transaction. There are a few exceptions to the parol evidence rule, the following being the main ones:

Rectification
Where a document is intended to record a previous oral agreement but fails to do that accurately, evidence of the oral agreement will be admitted.

Partially written agreements
Where there is a written agreement, but the parties clearly intended it to be qualified by other written or oral statements, the parol evidence rule is displaced.

Implied terms
The parol evidence rule only applies where a party seeks to use existing evidence to alter the express terms of a contract. Where a contract is of a type that is unusually subject to terms implied by law and statute, parol evidence may be given to support, or to deny, the usual implication.

Collateral agreements
There is a way in which an oral statement can be deemed binding, even though it conflicts with a written contract and does not fall within any

of the exceptions to the parol rule. If one party says something like 'I will sign this document if you will assure me that it means....' The courts may find that two contracts have been created, the written agreement and a collateral contract based on the oral statement.

Construction of express terms in contracts

The courts will sometimes have to determine the construction of an express term within a contract. The courts will have to 'seek the meaning which the document would convey to a reasonable person having all the background knowledge which would have reasonably been available to parties at the time of entering into the agreement'. The courts start by presuming that the parties meant what they said. The courts would also look at the outcome of the words and meaning to see if they create an absurdity or are inconsistent with the rest of the contract.

Implied terms

As well as the express terms laid down in the contract, further terms may be sometimes read into the contract by the courts. These implied terms are divided into four groups: terms implied by fact, terms implied by law, terms implied by custom and terms implied by trade usage.

Terms implied by fact are terms not laid out in the contract, but which it is assumed both parties would have intended to include if they had thought about it, they may have left them out by mistake. In order to decide what the intention of the parties was, the courts have developed two tests, the 'officious bystander test, and the 'business efficacy' test.

The officious bystander test was laid down in Shirlaw v Southern Foundries (1926). The Judge said, ...'that which in any contract is left to be implied and need not be expressed is something so obvious that it goes without saying: so that, if while the parties were making their bargain, an officious bystander were to suggest some express provision for it in the agreement, they would testily suppress him with a common 'oh, of course'. The business efficacy test covers terms which one side alleges must be implied to make the contract work, to give it business efficacy.

Terms implied by law are terms which the law dictates must be present in certain types of contract-in some cases whether the parties intended them or not. In Liverpool Council v Irwin (1977) the defendants lived in a council maisonette that was part of a high-rise block in Liverpool. The block was in a bad condition and tenants withheld rent and the case went to court with the tenants arguing that the council was in breach of contract (tenancy). The council argued that there was no agreement to keep the block in good condition and the courts argued that good repair and safety were implied terms of contract. The council lost the case.

Other implied terms may arise from contracts governing the supply of goods and services, such as the Consumer Rights Act 2015.

Terms implied by custom can be implied into a contract if there is evidence that under local custom they would normally be there.

Terms implied by trade usage would normally be part of a contract made by parties in a particular trade or business.

The classification of contractual terms

There are three types of contractual terms, conditions, warranties and innominate terms.

A condition is a term that the courts would regard as important in that it would clearly have negative consequences if breached.

Where a condition is breach the injured party can regard the contract as repudiated, and need not render any further performance, and can also sue for damages.

Warranties denote contractual terms that can be broken without highly important consequences. This would be a minor term and would not entitle the party to terminate the contract it merely entitles him to sue. The Sale of Goods Act 1979 designates certain terms as warranties breach of which does not allow the buyer to treat the contract as discharged, but merely to sue for damages, for example, the right to quiet enjoyment.

One such case that illustrates the above is that of Bettini v Gye (1876) where a singer was engaged to sing for a whole season and to arrive six days in advance to take part in rehearsals. He arrived only three days in advance. It was held that the rehearsal clause was a warranty, as it was subsidiary to the main clause. The management were therefore not entitled to treat the contract as discharged. They should have kept to the original contract and sought damages for the three days delay.

Innominate terms are terms that can be broken with either important or trivial consequences, depending on the nature of the breach.

Innominate terms were illustrated in Hong Kong Fir Shipping Co Ltd v Kawasaki Kisen Kaisha (1962) in which the defendants had chartered a ship for two years from the claimants. Twenty weeks of the charter were lost due to condition of ship and incompetent staff. The agreement contained a clause stating that the ship was 'in every way fitted for ordinary cargo service'. There was no doubt that the defendants were entitled to bring an action for damages but instead decided to terminate the contract. The claimants counter sued, claiming that the breach did not entitle the defendants to terminate, only to claim damages. The Court of Appeal agreed, stating that the question to be asked was that whether as a result of the breach the defendants had been deprived of the whole of the benefit of the contract. As this was not the case, the termination was unjustified.

Unfair contract terms

Contract terms can be considered to be so unfair to one of the contracting parties that the courts have had to intervene to prevent an injustice. This has usually arisen within the context of exemption clauses and is controlled both by common law and the exemption clauses in contracts. Parts 1 and 2 of the Consumer Rights Act 2015 consolidate and replace the Unfair Terms in Consumer Contracts

Regulations 1999 (UTCCRs) and relevant provisions of the Unfair Contract Terms Act 1977 (UCTA). The Unfair Contract Terms Act 1977 applies only to exemption clauses covering business liability and, since the CRA 2015, does not cover any exemption clauses that would be covered by the Act, i.e. in contracts between a trader and a consumer. The Act defines a 'trader' as a person acting for purposes relating to that persons trade, business craft or profession. A 'consumer' is defined as an individual acting for purposes that are wholly or mainly outside the indiviual's trade, business, craft or profession (see Overy v Paypal (Europe) Ltd 2012.

In certain cases, one party to a contract may seek to avoid incurring liabilities for breach of contract, or may specify that their liability for such a breach will be limited, usually to a specific amount of damages. However, a clause that seeks to exclude all liability for uncertain breaches is called an exclusion clause. There are many examples such as holiday companies seeking to exclude all liability for holidays gone wrong or cancelled. Over the past 40 years the law has sought to control the use of these clauses, first by the efforts of judges and also by legislation such as the Unfair Contract Terms Act 1977 and the Unfair Terms in Consumer Contracts Regulations 1999, now consolidated as described above by the CRA 2015.

Misrepresentation in contracts
Even in cases where a contract clearly meets the requirements of offer and acceptance, consideration and intent to create legal relations, it will still not be binding if, at the time the contract was made, certain factors

were present which meant that there was no genuine concern. These are known as vitiating factors (because they vitiate, or invalidate, consent). The vitiating factors that the law recognizes as preventing a contract are misrepresentation, mistake, duress, undue influence and illegality. In these cases, the innocent party may set the contract aside if he wishes. If one party has been induced to enter into a contract by a statement made by the other party, and that statement is untrue, the contract is voidable and the innocent party may also be able to claim damages. For a misrepresentation to be actionable it must be untrue, a statement of fact not opinion, and it must have induced the innocent party to enter into the contract.

It is worth noting that, following the amendments to the Consumer Protection from Unfair Trading Regulations 2008 (CPRs 2008) made by the Consumer Protection Amendment Regulations 2014, after October 1st 2014 consumers who entered into a contract for the sale or supply of a product by a trader or who entered into a contract to sell a product to a trader (for example selling a car to a dealer) or made a payment to a trader for the supply of a product, and that trader engaged in a prohibited practice in relation to that product, for example by giving misleading information, have an extended range of specific consumer 'rights to redress' under the CPRs (right to unwind, right to a discount, and specific rights to damages).

This regime is separate to the consumers general remedies but the consumer cannot make a claim twice for the same product. In addition, there is an amendment to s.2 of the Misrepresentation Act 1967 which removes the ability of consumers to recover damages under that legislation where they have a right to redress under the CPRs in respect of the misrepresentation,

There are four different types of misrepresentation, fraudulent misrepresentation, where there is clear deceit, negligent, where misrepresentation arises through acts of negligence but not deceit and innocent misrepresentation which is not fraudulent but is still clear misrepresentation. The effect of a misrepresentation is generally to make a contract voidable, rather than void, so the contract will continue to exist unless or until the injured party chooses to have it set aside by the courts by means of rescission. Rescission is an equitable remedy that sets the contract aside and puts the parties back in the position where they were before the misrepresentation. An injured party who decides to rescind the contract may do so by notifying the other party or, if this is not possible owing to the conduct of the party, by taking some reasonable action to indicate the intention to default. A case that illustrates this is Car and Universal Finance Co Ltd v Caldwell (1965) where the defendant sold and delivered a car and was paid by cheque. The cheque bounced, by which time the car and buyer had disappeared. The defendant notified the police and the Automobile Association. While the police were investigating the buyer sold the car to a dealer who knew that the car was not the buyer's to sell. Finally, the car dealer sold the car to the claimants who bought it in good faith. The court of Appeal held that by contacting the police and the AA the claimant had made his intention to rescind the contract clear. As soon as this happened the ownership of the car reverted to him. This meant that at the time the car was sold back to the claimant the car was not anyone's to sell.

Another case illustrating this is Whittington v Seale-Hayne (1900) where the plaintiff's, breeders of prize poultry, were induced to take a lease of the defendant's premises by his innocent representation that the premises were in a sanitary condition. Under the lease, the plaintiff's covenanted to execute any works required by any local or public authority. Owing to the insanitary conditions of the premises, the water supply was poisoned, the plaintiff's manager and his family became very ill, and the poultry became valueless for breeding purposes or died.

The court rescinded the lease, and held that the plaintiffs could recover an indemnity for what they had spent on rates, rent and repairs under the covenants in the lease, because these expenses arose necessarily out of the contract. It refused to award compensation for other leases, since to do so would be to award damages, not an indemnity, there being no obligation created by the contract to carry on a poultry farm on the premises or to employ a manager, etc.

Representation and terms of a contract

Section 1 of the Misrepresentation Act 1967, s.2 as amended by The Consumer Protection Amendment Regulations 2014, described above, provides that where a misrepresentation becomes a term of the contract, the innocent party may bring an action for both misrepresentation and breach of contract. Under section 3 of this Act, as amended by the Unfair Contract Terms Act 1977, as amended by the CRA 2015, exemption clauses that attempt to exclude or limit liability for misrepresentations are operative only if reasonable. This provision is illustrated in Walker v Boyle (1982) where the seller of a house told the buyer that there were no disputes regarding the boundaries of the property. This was not true. This misrepresentation appeared to entitle the buyer to rescind the contract and notwithstanding a clause seeking to deny this, the court granted a rescission.

Mistake

The general rule is that a mistake has no effect on a contract, but certain mistakes of a fundamental nature, sometimes called operative mistakes, may render a contract void at common law. If the contract is rendered void, then the parties will be returned to their original positions, and this may defeat the rights of innocent third parties who may have acquired an interest in the contract.

The reluctance of the courts to develop the common law doctrine of mistake is probably due to the unfortunate consequences for third parties that can result from holding a contract void. Equity at one stage intervened to create a more flexible doctrine, but this has been overruled. We discuss mistakes in more depth in the next chapter.

Rectification

Where there has been a mistake, not in the actual agreement but in reducing it in writing, equity will order rectification of the document so that it coincides with the true agreement of the parties. The main conditions for this are that:

- The document does not represent the intention of both parties; or

- One party mistakenly believes that a term was included in the document and the other party knew of this error.

- There must have been a concluded agreement but not necessarily an enforceable contract. Rectification is an equitable remedy and is available at the discretion of the court.

Refusal of specific performance

Specific performance will be refused when the contract is void at common law. Equity may also refuse specific performance where a contract is valid at law, but only 'where a hardship amounting to injustice would have been inflicted upon him by holding him to his bargain' (Tamplin v James (1879)).

Duress

This requires actual or threatened violence to the person. Originally, it was the only form of duress recognized by the law. This is highlighted by the case of Barton v Armstrong (1975) where a managing director was threatened with death if he did not purchase a former chairman's shares. The managing director was happy to purchase the shares notwithstanding the threats that had been made. It was held that the threats constituted duress and the contract was set aside. We will look at duress in more depth in chapter 7.

****

Main points from chapter four

- The terms of a contract describe the respective duties and obligations of each party to the contract

- As well as the contractual terms laid out and agreed by parties to a contract, called express terms, there may also be implied terms – terms which are 'read into' a contract because of the facts of the agreement and the apparent intentions of the parties or the law on specific types of contract

- Contracts can be considered to be so unfair to one of the contracting parties that the courts have had to intervene to prevent an injustice. The Unfair Contract Terms Act 1977, as amended by the CPA 2015, along with common law will regulate this area

- Misrepresentation in contracts can render a contract voidable

5

Errors and Contracts

In this chapter we look at the effect that an error or errors in a contract has on the parties involved. We take a look at general principles and common mistakes and also rectification.

The general rule is that a mistake has no effect on a contract, but certain mistakes of a fundamental nature, sometimes called operative mistakes can render a contract void at common law.. However, the law in this area operates quite rigidly.

The general principles

There are two types of mistake within contract law, Common mistake and cross-purpose mistake. Both are underpinned by general rules. There is an objective principle, or test that the court will apply when considering mistakes within contracts. The courts do not ask the parties to the contract what they thought they were entering into but rather they consider what an onlooker would have thought it was each party was agreeing to. This is very much akin to the 'officious bystander test' referred to earlier.

Another key principle is that in order to void a contract the mistake must be made before the contract is completed. One case that illustrates this is Amalgamated Investment and Property Co Ltd v John Walker and sons Ltd (1977). In this case, a contract was made for the sale of a warehouse, for £1,710,000. The sellers knew that the purchasers were buying the warehouse with the intention of redeveloping it. The day after the contract was signed, the Department of the Environment, as it was then, made the property a listed building. This made it more difficult for the buyers to get permission to redevelop. Without this permission the warehouse would be worth considerably less. Neither party to the contract had been aware that the DOE were going to list the building.

The Court of Appeal held that the contract was valid as at the time of the agreement both parties were perfectly correct in their belief that the building was not listed, so there was no operative mistake. In the past, only a mistake of fact could negate a contract not a mistake of law. However, in the light of certain key cases, this is not now the case.

Common mistake

Having explored the general principles underpinning the treatment of mistakes in contract it is now time to explore the two types of mistake more thoroughly.

Common mistakes are also known as identical mistakes, shared mistake or mistake nullifying consent. In this situation both parties make the same mistake-for example if A buys an antique from B which both parties think is rare and valuable, such as Wedgwood Pottery, but which is in fact a fake, they have made a shared mistake which would only render the contract void if the mistake relates to one of three subjects which the courts consider fundamental to the contract: the existence of the subject matter, its ownership and, in limited cases, its quality. A mistake as to the existence of subject matter will usually only concern goods to be sold-if for example A purports to sell a motorbike to B, and it is then discovered that the motorbike has been destroyed by fire, the contract will not be valid. It can apply equally to other subject matter. The main test is, do the goods or other exist at the time of a contract. One case that illustrates this is Scott v Coulson (1993). A life insurance policy was taken out, covering a person's death. In fact the person was already dead so the contract was null and void.

It is not always the case that the non-existence of subject matter will render the contract null and void. There have been several cases that obscure this general principle. One such case was Couturier v Hastie (1856) that involved a contract to buy a cargo of corn, which, at the time the contract was made was supposed to be on a ship sailing to England from the Mediterranean port of Salonica. In fact by that time the corn had already been sold by the master of the ship to a buyer in Tunis because the corn had started to deteriorate and go off. This is a common occurrence and the master's action was the usual accepted solution. For the purposes of the original contract the corn had ceased to exist. The sellers claimed that the buyers still had an obligation to pay as per the contract. The House of Lords held that the buyer did not have to pay for the corn, as the goods did not exist. There was no mistake; quite simply the corn did not exist.

Mistake as to title

Very rarely, a situation will arise in which one party agrees to transfer property to the other but unknown to both party's, the latter already owns that property. In such a case, the contract will be void for mistake. This is obviously very rare but has happened on occasion.

Mistaken identity

There is a presumption that a contract is valid even where one party has made a mistake as to the identity of the other. However, this presumption can be denied or negated by the party who has made the mistake. If this is done the contract is void at common law. In order to achieve this the mistaken party must prove that they intended to deal with a person other than the person who was in fact the other party to the contract, and that the identity of the other party was regarded as of fundamental importance.

One key case that illustrates this is Cundy V Lindsey (1878). The claimants received an order for a large number of handkerchiefs from a Mr Blenkarn of 37 Wood Street, Cheapside. Mr Blenkarn rented a room at that address, and further down the road at 123 Cheapside, were the offices of a firm called Blenkiron and Co. Blenkarn signed his name so it looked liked Blenkiron. The claimants sent off their goods addressed to Blenkiron and Co. Mr Blenkarn received them and by the time that the fraud was discovered he had sold them to the defendants, Cundy, who had bought them in good faith. The claimants sued the defendants to get the money back, and their success in this depended on whether it could be proved that there was a contract between the claimants and Blenkarn. The House of Lords held that there was no contract between Blenkarn and the claimants, because they had intended all along to deal with Blenkiron and Co. The court very importantly held that 'between him and them there was no consensus of mind which could lead to...any contract whatsoever.

Mistake over the terms of the contract

Where one party is mistaken as to the terms of the contract, and the other knows this, the contract will be void, regardless of whether the term is fundamental.

Mistakes relating to documents

Where a mistake relates to a written document there are two special remedies in existence, *non est factum* and rectification. Although the general principle is that a contract becomes effective when a person signs it, regardless of whether they understood it, *non est factum* (this is not my deed) becomes operative where a person signs a document believing it to be something totally different from what it actually was. This remedy may make the contract void. In order to void the contract the person seeking this remedy must prove three things: that the signature was induced by a trick or a fraud, that they made a fundamental mistake as to the nature of the document and that they were not careless in signing it. The mistake made by the signee must concern the actual nature of the contract and not just its legal effect.

Mutual and unilateral mistakes

These mistakes negate consent, that is they prevent the formation of an agreement. The courts adopt an objective test in deciding whether agreement has been reached. It is not enough for one of the parties to allege that he was mistaken. Mistake can negate consent in the following cases.

Mutual mistakes concerning the identity of the subject matter

In these cases the parties are at cross-purposes, but there must have been some ambiguity in the situation before the courts will declare the contracts void. One such case that illustrates this is Raffles v Wichelhaus (1864) where a consignment of cotton was bought to arrive on the ship *Peerless* from Bombay. Two ships, both called Peerless, were due to leave Bombay at around the same time. It was held that there was no agreement as the buyer was thinking of one ship and the seller was referring to the other ship.

Unilateral mistake concerning the terms of the contract

Here, one party has taken advantage of the other party's error. In Hartog v Colin and Shields (1939) the sellers mistakenly offered to sell goods at a given price per pound when they intended to offer them per piece. All the preliminary negotiations had been on a per piece basis. The buyers must have realised that the sellers had made a mistake. It was held that the contract was void.

Unilateral mistakes as to the identities of other parties to the contract

Where the identity of the other party is of fundamental importance, and there has been a genuine mistake, the contract will be void. In

Cundy c Lindsey (1878) a Mr Blenkarn ordered goods from Lindsey signing the letter to give the impression that the order came from Blenkiron and Co, a firm known as Lindsey and Co. It was held that the contract was void. Linsey and Co had only intended to do business with Blenkiron and Co. there was therefore a mistake concerning the identity of the other party to the contract.

A mistake as to attributes or credit-worthiness will not render a contract void. In Kings Norton Metal Co v Edridge Merrett and Co Ltd (1872) a Mr Wallis ordered goods on impressive stationary which indicated that the order had come from Hallam and Co, an old established firm with branches all over the country. It was held that the contract was not void. The sellers intended to do business with the writer of the letter; they were merely mistaken as to his attributes, that is, the size and credit worthiness of his business.

Another case illustrating this is Boulton v Jones (1857) where the defendant sent an order for some goods to a Mr Brocklehurst unaware that he had sold his business to his foreman, the plaintiff. The plaintiff supplied the goods but the defendant refused to pay for them as he had only intended to do business with Brocklehurst, against whom he had a set off. It was held that there was a mistake concerning the identity of the other party and the contract was therefore void.

Mistake in equity

The narrow approach taken by the common law towards remedies for mistake (that is that it renders the contract void) is supplemented by the more flexible approach of equity. The following remedies may be available in equity: rescission (discussed above); rectification and refusal of specific performance.

Rectification

Where some aspect of a written document is alleged not to reflect accurately the will of the parties, the remedy of rectification may in certain instances allow the written document to be altered so that it coincides with the true agreement of the parties. In order for this remedy to be applied, three conditions must be satisfied: the parties must have agreed about the point in question; the agreement on that aspect of the contract must have continued unchanged up to the time it was put into writing and the written document must fail to express the parties agreement on that point.

****

Main points from chapter five

- In certain cases, a mistake within a contract can render that contract void. However, the law in this area operates quite rigidly

- There are two types of mistake within contract law – common mistake and cross-purpose mistake

- In order to void the contract the mistake must have been made before the contract was entered into

6

Contracts-Illegality

In this chapter we look at the concept of legally unenforceable contracts and the effect of this on parties to a contract. We look at modes of performance and breaches of common law and legislation generally, plus contracts prejudicial to public safety.

Although a contract, on the face of it may contain all the elements of a valid agreement, such as offer and consideration, that contract may still be legally unenforceable.

Contracts may be illegal at the time of their formation or because of the way they have been performed. A contract may be illegal when entered into because the contract cannot be performed in accordance with its terms without committing an illegal act. For example, a contract may involve a breach of the criminal law, or it may be a statutory requirement for the parties to the contract to have a license that they in fact do not have. A case that illustrates this is Levy v Yates (1838). In this case, there existed a statutory rule that a royal license was required to perform a play within 20 miles of London. In that case the contract was between a theatre owner and an impresario for the performance of a theatrical production where no royal license had been obtained. The contract was thus illegal at the time of its formation.

Illegal mode of performance

In some cases a contract may be perfectly legal when it was made, but may be carried out in an illegal manner. A case that illustrates this is Anderson Ltd v Daniel (1924). In this case, a statute provided that a seller of artificial fertilizer had to supply buyers with an invoice detailing certain chemicals used in its manufacture. The sellers failed to provide the invoice needed. Although not against the law to sell fertilizer it was against statutory rules not to supply an invoice. As a result the sellers were unable to claim the price when the defendants refused to pay. A contract is obviously illegal if it involves a contravention of the law. However, a contract is also regarded as being illegal where it involves conduct that the law disapproves of as contrary to the interests of the public, even though the conduct is not actually unlawful. In both cases the transaction is treated as an illegal contract and the courts will not enforce it.

Contracts violating legal rules

Breach of common law

There are a number of factors that may make a contract illegal at common law, the most important where there is a contract to commit a crime or tort (negligent act). These are obvious breaches of the law. However, another very important area is contracts in restraint of trade. The issue of restraint of trade commonly arises and concerns those contracts that limit an individuals right to use their skills for payment, or to trade freely.

These contracts fall into four groups:

- Contracts for the sale of a business where the vendor promises ot to compete with the purchaser
- Contracts between businesses by which prices or output are regulated
- Contracts in which an employee agrees that on leaving employment they will not set up in business or be employed in such as way as to compete with their employer or ex employer. This is most common in business where personal skills and reputation attract custom, such as advertising and the ex-employee may take with them valuable customers
- Contracts where a person agrees to restrict their mode of trade by, for example, only accepting orders from one particular company. This is sometimes called a 'solus' agreement and is frequently used for petrol stations, in return for the land or lease the trader promises to use the product of the seller (Esso Petroleum v Harper's Garage (Stourport) 1968).

Any of the above can be held to create a restraint of trade, a general restraint if the contract completely prohibits trading, or a partial restraint if it limits trading to a certain time or area.

Breach of legislation
Some types of contract are expressly declared void by statute. The two most important examples of contracts that are expressly declared void by statute are contracts in constraint of trade and wagering contracts.

Contracts in restraint of trade

As stated above, these are arrangements by which one party agrees to limit his or her legal right to carry out a trade, business or profession. A contract that does this is always viewed as *prima facie* void for two reasons:

- To prevent people signing away their livelihoods at the request of a party with stronger bargaining power
- To avoid depriving the public of the person's expertise.

These contracts are of several possible types as mentioned above-employee restraints, vendor restraints-preventing the seller of a business from unfairly competing with the purchaser and agreements of mutual regulation between businesses.

However, these agreements might be upheld as reasonable:

- as between the patties-so the restraint must be no wider than to protect a legitimate interest
- in the public interest-so the restraint must not unduly limit public choice.

The reasonableness of the restraint is also measured against factors such as duration and geographical extent.

Employee restraints

An employer can legitimately protect trade secrets and client connection, but not merely prevent the employee from exercising his or her trade or skill.

Reasonableness is measured against certain criteria:

- A restraint in a highly specialised business is more likely to be reasonable. In the case of Forster and Sons Ltd. v. Suggett (1918) 35 TLR 87 the works manager of the plaintiff who were chiefly engaged in making glass and glass bottles was instructed, in certain confidential me those concerning inter alia the correct mixture of gas and air in the furnaces. He agreed that during the five years following the determination of his employment he would not carry on in the United Kingdom or be interested in glass bottle manufacture or in any other business connected with glass making as conducted by the plaintiffs. The restraint for protection of trade secrets was held to be reasonable.
- Restraint of an employee in a key position is more likely to be reasonable.

An employer is not entitled to protect itself against the use of the skill and knowledge which the employee acquired during his or her employment. Those belong to the employee, who must be free to exploit them in the market place. Neither can an employer seek protection from competition per se since it is against the public interest that employees should be deprived of the opportunity to earn their living or to use their personal skills to the ultimate benefit of the community as a whole:

Herbert Morris Limited v Saxelby
[1916] AC 688.

Instead the employer must demonstrate that the covenant protects a legitimate business interest. In the Herbert Morris case, Lord Parker defined this as "some proprietary right, whether in the nature of a trade connection or in the nature of trade secrets, for the protection of which such a restraint is reasonably necessary". The concept was further developed by Lord Wilberforce in Stenhouse Australia Limited v Phillips [1974] 1 All ER 117, who said:

"The employer's claim for protection must be based on the identification of some advantage or asset inherent in the business which can properly be regarded as, in a general sense, his property, and which it would be unjust to allow the employee to appropriate for his own purposes, even though he (the employee) may have contributed to its creation".

In other words, the employer is entitled to prevent the employee taking unfair advantage of confidential information and business connections to which he had access in the course of his/her employment

An employee may be significant to the business without even being a member of staff as demonstrated in Leeds rugby Ltd v Harris (2005).

The duration of the extent must not be too long (Home Counties Dairies v Skilton (1970) and the geographical extent too wide (Fitch v

Dewes (1921). Similarly, the range of activities that the restraint covers must be no wider than is necessary to protect legitimate interests (J A Mont (UK) Ltd v Mills (1993).

Soliciting of clients can be prevented by such clauses, if not too wide (M&S Drapers v Reynolds (1957). Also, including clients not within the original scope of the restraint is not unreasonable (Hanover Insurance Brokers Ltd and Christchurch Insurance Brokers Ltd v Shapiro (1994). Attempting a restraint by other means is also void, including making contractual benefits subject to a restraint (Bull v Pitney Bowes Ltd (1966) and restraints in rules of associations (Eastham v Newcastle United FC Ltd (1963).

Vendor restraints

These are void for public policy to prevent an individual from negotiating away his or her livelihood and also because the public may lose a valuable service. Restraints are more likely to be upheld as reasonable since businesses deal on more equal bargaining strength, even is restraint is very wide (Nordenfelt v Maxim Nordenfelt Co (1894).

The restraint must still protect a legitimate interest to be valid (British Concrete Ltd v Schelff (1921).

Agreements between merchants, manufacturers or other trades

If the object is regulation of trade then they are void unless both sides benefit (English Hop Growers v Dering (1928). So they are void when the parties have unequal bargaining strength (Schroder Publishing Co Ltd v Macaulay (1974)-unless public policy dictates otherwise Panayiotou v Sony Music International (UK) Ltd (1994).

Wagering contracts

Wagering agreements are bets, and are rendered void by The Gaming Act 1845. Section 18 of the Act provides:

"All contracts or agreements, whether by parole or in writing, by way of gaming or wagering, shall be null and void, and no suit shall be brought or maintained in a court of law or equity for recovering any sum of money or valuable thing alleged to be won upon any wager..."

The Act does not make wagering agreements illegal it simply provides that neither party to such an agreement can legally enforce it. For the provisions of the legislation to apply, a wagering contract must be one in which there are two parties and the terms of the agreement are such that one party wins and the other loses. This means that football pools, for example, are not covered as its promoters take a percentage of the stake money and so gain by the transaction regardless of whether players win as well.

The Act also covers gaming, which is defined by the Betting, Gaming and lotteries act 1963 as 'the playing of a game of chance for winnings in money or money's worth'. Games of chance include games that depend partly on skill and partly on chance. Athletic games and sports are excluded.

Competition law

Common law lays down certain controls on contracts in constraint of trade. These controls give only limited protection and actual legislation provides more adequate protection. One of the main goals of the European Union, through Article 85, is to promote free trade between member states and clearly restrictive trade can affect this policy. Where a restrictive trade agreement could affect trade between member states it will only be valid if allowed under both EU and English law. In terms of contracts in English law, the relevant legislation is now contained in the Competition Act 1998. This Act prohibits a number of anti-competitive practices. The 1998 Act applies to agreements between undertakings, decisions by associations of undertakings or concerted practices that (a) may affect trade and (b) have as their object or effect the prevention, restriction or distortion of trade. For the Act to prohibit an agreement the effect of the agreement must be significant and not minor.

Contracts against public policy

There exist a wide-range of contracts that are considered to be illegal because they are against public policy. As we discussed, public policy really means the interest of society at large and the contract must contravene it. Contracts promoting sexual immorality for example are seen as contravening public policy.

One case that illustrates this is Armhouse Lee Ltd v Chappell (1996) concerning a contract under which the defendants paid the plaintiffs to place adverts for telephone sex lines in magazines. When regulation concerning such publicity was tightened the defendants terminated the contract, as they no longer wished to advertise their services in this way. The plaintiffs brought an action for the money due under the contract and the defendants argued that the contract was illegal and unenforceable as it promoted sexual immorality. This defense was rejected by the Court of Appeal. The court held that though the adverts were distasteful the sex lines were generally accepted by society and were regulated by the telephone industry. There was no evidence, in the eyes of the Court of Appeal that any 'generally accepted moral code' condemned these telephone sex lines. It considered that contracts should only be found illegal under this heading if an element of public harm clearly existed.

Contracts prejudicial to public safety

The main types of contracts found illegal on these grounds are contracts with those living in an enemy country, contracts to perform acts which are illegal in a friendly foreign country and contracts which are damaging to foreign relations.

The effect of an illegal contract

The effect of an illegal contract will depend on whether it is illegal due to a statute or due to the common law. Where the contract is illegal due to a statute, in some cases the statute provides for the consequences of any illegality. Under common law an illegal contract is void and courts will not order it to be performed. The precise effects of an illegal contract depend on whether the contract is illegal at the time of formation or is illegal due to the way in which it was performed.

Contracts illegal at the time of formation are treated as if they were never made, so the illegal contract is unenforceable by either party. Contracts illegal as performed are slightly different as to their effect. It will be possible to enforce the illegal contract if the illegal act was merely incidental to the performance of the contract. For example, a contract for the delivery of goods may not be tainted by illegality when the lorry driver is caught speeding or under the influence of drink. Where the contract is merely illegal because of the way it was performed, it is possible for either both or only one of the parties to intend illegal performance. If both parties are aware that a contracts performance is illegal, the consequences for this type of contract are the same as for a contract that was illegal at the time of its formation. When one party did not know of the illegal performance of the contract by the other party, the innocent party can enforce it.

In some cases, it is possible to divide the illegal part of a contract from the rest and enforce the provisions which are not affected by the illegality-this is called severance. The illegal parts of the contract can be severed if they are relatively unimportant to the contract and if the severance leaves the nature of the contract unaltered.

****

Main points from chapter six

- Although a contract may contain all the elements of a valid agreement, such as offer and consideration, that contract may still not be legally enforceable.

- Contracts may be illegal at the time of their formation or because of the way they have been performed.

- In some cases, a contract may be perfectly legal when made, but may be carried out in an illegal manner

- Contracts may breach common law, legislation, competition law or public policy

7

Duress and Undue Influence

In this chapter we look at the effects that duress and undue influence have on the parties to a contract. We also look at inequality of bargaining power.

As we have seen, contracts are only binding if parties voluntarily consent to them. If one party is forced to sign under duress, the contract is invalid. As is usual, the law has developed two doctrines to deal with duress: the common law of duress and the equitable one of undue influence.

Duress

Although traditionally, common law has dealt with duress in terms of physical or psychological duress exerted when signing a contract, the doctrine has now been extended to economic duress. This, as the term implies, is where one party is forced into the contract due to economic pressure. Economic duress first arose in North Ocean Shipping Co v Hyundai Construction Co (The Atlantic Baron) (1979) that concerned a contract for the building of a ship. As is commonly the case where duress is raised, the dispute concerned not the formation of the contract, but a supposed modification of its terms. Such a modification can only be binding if both parties consent to it. If one party's consent is achieved by duress the contract is void. Although the price of the ship had been fixed at the outset˘ while it was being built the sellers decided to raise the price by ten per cent, due to a drop in the exchange rate of the dollar. The buyers were not happy about this but were unwilling to risk delaying completion of the ship as they were already negotiating for it to be chartered by a major oil company. They therefore agreed to pay the increased price.

Eight months after the ship was delivered the buyers tried to sue the sellers claiming back the ten per cent because they said that it had been extracted from them under duress. The judge agreed that economic power constituted duress, the question being whether there had been 'compulsion of will'. This compulsion could stem from economic pressure as well as physical force. In this particular case the buyers were not allowed to recover the extra ten per cent. This was not because duress did not play a part as it did, but that they waited so long after delivery to sue, implying acceptance.

Economic duress will be present where there is compulsion of will to the extent that the party under threat has no practical alternative but to comply, and the pressure used is regarded by the law as illegitimate.

Compulsion or coercion of the will
In Pau v Lau Yiu Long (1980) Lord Scarman listed the following indications of compulsion or coercion of the will:

- Did the party coerced have an alternative course open to him

- Did the party coerced protest
- Did the party coerced have independent advice?
- Did the party coerced take steps to avoid the contract?

Undue influence

Undue influence is an equitable doctrine, which applies where one party uses their influence over another to persuade them to make a contract. Where a court finds that a contract was made as a result of undue influence, it may set it aside, or modify its terms. In Bank of Credit and Commerce International SA v Aboody (1990) The court distinguished between two classes of undue influence: actual and presumed.

Class 1. Actual undue influence arises where the claimant can prove that they entered into the transaction as a result of undue influence from the other party. An example is where a person promises to either pay money or give goods in exchange for a promise not to report them for a criminal offence. The party claiming duress must prove that they were influenced (Williams v Bayley (1886)).

Class 2. Presumed undue influence will arise where there is a pre-existing relationship between the parties to a contract, as a result of which one places trust in another, and the contract between them is obviously disadvantageous to the one placing trust in another. Such a relationship of trust is called a fiduciary relationship and it may arise in two ways. It may fall into a category in which a relationship of trust is presumed to exist, such as parent and children (Lancashire Loans Co v

Black (1933)) patient-doctor, solicitor and client, trustees and beneficiaries (Benningfield v Baxter (1886)) and spiritual leaders and followers (Allcard v Skinner (1887)). Where a relationship does not fall into obvious categories then a relationship of trust may well be established through, for example, effluxion of time or inherent trust such as an ongoing successful business relationship.

Where there has been a long relationship of trust and confidence between the parties, and the transaction is not readily explicable by the nature of the relationship, for example, between husband and wife or where one party had been accustomed to rely for advice and guidance on the other, the presumption in these cases of trust and confidence is irrebuttable. The presumption of undue influence where the transaction 'calls for explanation' is rebuttable. The stronger party can rebut the presumption of undue influence by showing that:

- full disclosure of all material facts was made
- the consideration was adequate
- the weaker party was in receipt of independent legal advice

One example of a fiduciary relationship is in the case of Lloyds Bank v Bundy (1974). The plaintiff and his son both used the same bank. The son ran into business difficulties and the father was asked to guarantee the overdraft. He did this, putting up his farm as a guarantee and the bank tried to repossess the farm. The farmer claimed that the contract had been obtained by undue influence, on the basis that he had banked with Lloyds for a long time, and in that time had placed considerable trust in their advice, yet they had made no effort to warn him that it was not in their interest to give the guarantee. The Court of Appeal agreed that the presumption of undue influence had been raised. There was a relationship based on trust over time and the bank lost the case.

The transaction must be extremely disadvantageous (manifestly so) to give rise to a presumption of undue influence. This will be the case where it would have been 'obvious to any independent and reasonable persons who considered the transaction at that time with knowledge of all the relevant facts'. (Bank of Credit and Commerce International SA v Aboody (1989)).

Inequality of bargaining power

In Lloyds Bank v Bundy, as described above, Lord Denning suggested that economic duress was simply an example of a general principle of inequality of bargaining power. He argued that this principle allows English law to give relief to anyone who, without taking independent advice, makes a contract on unfair terms, or sells property for much less than it is worth because their own bargaining power is seriously compromised by ignorance, infirmity or need. Clearly, this is a key principle when negotiating and entering into contracts, more pertinent than simple undue influence as there is no suggestion that the other party had behaved improperly.

Illegitimate pressure

There must be some element of illegitimacy in the pressure exerted, for example, a threatened breach of contract. The illegitimacy will normally arise from the fact that what was threatened is unlawful. Economic duress is often pleaded together with lack of consideration in cases where a breach of consent is threatened by the promisor, unless he receives additional payment.

One case that illustrates this is Atlas Express v Kafco (1989) where Kafco, a small company which imported and distributed basketware, had a contract to supply Woolworths. They contracted with Atlas for the delivery of the basketware to Woolworths. The contract commenced, then Atlas discovered that they had underpriced the contract, and told Kafco that unless they paid a minimum sum for each consignment, they would cease to deliver. Kafco were heavily dependent on the Woolworth contract, and knew that a failure to deliver would lead both to the loss of the contract and an action for damages. At that time of year, they could not find an alternative carrier and agreed, under protest, to make the extra payments. Atlas sued for kafco's non-payment.

It was held that the agreement was invalid for economic duress, and also for lack of consideration..

Manifest disadvantage

In any claim of presumed undue influence, the agreement must be manifestly disadvantageous. In deciding whether an agreement is manifestly disadvantageous the courts will look at whether the disadvantages of the transaction outweigh the advantages.

Effect of undue influence on a third party

A bank may be deemed to have constructive knowledge of an impropriety if it has been placed 'on inquiry' that one of the parties has unduly influenced the other into entering into the contract. The leading case on undue influence is Royal bank of Scotland v Etridge (2001). This appeal concerned eight cases of undue influence. In seven cases, the wife had permitted the family home, of which she had part ownership to be used as surety against her husband's personal or business debts. In all cases, the husband had defaulted and the bank had sought possession of the family home. The wife claimed that the bank had been placed on enquiry that the agreement had been elicited as a result of the husband's undue influence. It was held that three appeals were dismissed and five allowed. Moreover, the House of Lords provided important guidance for banks on how to avoid constructive knowledge of undue influence. The HOL also held that in that situation the third party could discharge his duty by making clear to the party concerned the full nature of the risk he or she is taking on.

****

Main points from chapter seven

- Contracts are only binding if the parties to that contract voluntary consent to the terms

- If one party is forced to sign under duress the contract can be void

- Duress can be physical, psychological or economic

8

Third Party Rights

In this chapter we look at the rights of third parties to a contract. We also look at the notion of assignment.

A third party to any contract is a person who is not a party to the contract and has not provided consideration for the contract but has an interest in the performance. There has been a rule, long established in contract law, that only the parties to the contract could incur rights and obligations under it. This is known as 'privity of contract' this principle meaning that third parties could neither sue nor be sued under the contract.

There are two main aspects to the rule of privity. The first is that the third party cannot be made the subject of a burden imposed by the contract. The second is that a third party cannot enforce a benefit purported to be granted by the contract. This second rule has been heavily criticized, as it is inherently unjust and can lead to hardship and resulted in much debate and eventual reform leading to the Contracts (Rights of Third Parties) Act 1999. The privity rule has now only very limited effect. The Act has made changes in the way that contracts can be enforced by third parties.

The rights of third parties

The Contract (Rights of Third Parties) Act 1999 enables third parties to enforce contractual terms in certain situations. The Act applies to contracts made on or after 11th May 2000 or to contracts made during the six-month period after Royal Assent (11th November 1999) if the contract expressly states that the Act applies. Under the Act, third parties can sue in two situations:

- The contract expressly provides that they may do so; or
- The contract purports to confer a benefit on them, unless it is clear -that the term was not intended to be enforceable by the third party.

Express provision in the contract

Section 1 of the Act deals with this area. This enables the parties to expressly identify the third party in the contract.

The contract purports to confer a benefit on a third party

This is subject to an important provision that it will not apply if the contract expressly outlines this. The contract must specifically state that third parties will not benefit. In the absence of this then there may be a purported benefit to a third party inherent in the contract.

Under either of the above it is not necessary for the third party to be named. Nor need the person be in existence at the time of the contracts formation. The Act also provides that third parties are able to rely on a contracts exclusion or limitation clauses that are intended to cover them.

Consent to variations

The rights conferred under the Act would be of limited value if the contracting parties could at any time change their minds and remove the promised benefit. Section 2 of the act deals with the issue of amending and canceling contracts. The section states that unless the contract states otherwise, the parties to the contract may not rescind the contract, or vary it, so as to extinguish the third parties rights without their consent if the third party has either:

- Communicated to the promisor their assent to the relevant term;
- Relied on that term and the promisor knows of that reliance; or
- Relied on the term and the promisor can reasonably be expected to have foreseen that reliance.

If one of these three situations applies, then any variations or cancellations can only take place with the consent of the third party. Third parties to a contract have remedies that are available to them as if they were contracting parties.

Common law exceptions

Agency

The term 'agent' has a specific meaning in this context, and applies to an individual who makes a contract on behalf of someone else who is know as the principal. In the contractual sense, an agent is viewed by the law as an intermediary of the principal rather than a true party to the contract. In practice, one party to a contract made by an agent is usually a corporation of one kind or another, such as a PLC or a Local Authority, and the agent is their employee. There are three circumstances in which a party will be treated as an agent: where there is express authority; where there is implied authority; and where there is apparent authority. Express authority means that the agent has specifically asked the agent to make the contract in question. Implied authority arises where the agent is asked to do something where by implication a contract is to be made. Apparent authority is more problematic and arises where the principals past behavior gives the party to the contract reason to believe that the agent has authority to contract on the agent's behalf.

Assignment

It is possible to assign the benefit of the contract without the permission of the other party. A common example is where a small business with cash flow problems sells the debts owed to them to others who are factoring businesses.

Collateral contracts

Where one party makes contracts with two others, the courts will sometimes use the device of 'finding' a collateral contract between the two others to evade the privity rule. An example of this is Shanklin Pier Ltd v Detel Products Ltd (1951). The plaintiffs owned Shanklin Pier, and needed it repainting. They contracted Detel to inquire about the qualities of its paint, and were told that it lasted between 7-10 years. The plaintiffs employed other contractors and told them to use Detel paint. The paint started to peel after three months and the Plaintiffs could not sue the contractors, as it was not they who had stated that the paint would last 7-10 years. The pier owners had no contract with Detel since the paint was bought by the contractors. However, the court held that there was in fact a collateral contract between the pier owners and Detel as Detel had told them that the paint would last, and the Pier owners request that the painters should use Detel paint was collateral for that promise.

****

Main points from chapter eight

- A third party to any contract is a person who is not party to the contract and has not provided consideration for the contract but has an interest in the performance

- The long established rule has been that only the parties to the contract could incur rights and obligations under it. This is known as 'privity of contract, this principle meaning that third parties could neither sue nor be sued under the contract

- This longstanding rule has been amended through The Contract (Rights of Third Parties Act) 1999 that enables third parties to enforce contractual terms in certain situations. In addition those who are party to the contract cam bring an action against the third party.

9

Discharge of a Contract

In this chapter we look at the ways that a contract is effectively discharged and also frustration of contract. We look at the effects on the contract when it becomes impossible to fulfill and we look at the death of either party to a contract. Other areas are also explored.

A contract is said to be discharged when the rights and obligations in it come to an end. There are four ways in which a contract can come to an end: performance under the contract, i.e., natural end, end by mutual agreement, breach of contract and frustration. We should look at these areas in turn.

Performance under contract

This is the most obvious way of parties discharging their obligations and bringing the contract to a satisfactory end. In many cases, it is uncomplicated but there are some cases where one party may claim to have discharged their obligations and the other party disagrees. The law then has to look at the question of what constitutes performance.

The obvious and general rule is that performance must exactly match the requirements laid down in the contract. This is known as entire performance. If the first party fails to perform then the other party need pay nothing at all, even if the shortfall actually causes no hardship. This is the simple rule and obviously contracts can be more complicated, with claim and counter claim. The case of Cutter v Powell (1795) demonstrates the difficulty. A sailor had contracted to serve on a ship traveling from Jamaica to Liverpool. He was to be paid 30 Guineas for the voyage, payable when the ship arrived in Liverpool. However, he died during the journey. His widow sued for wages up until he died, but her claim was unsuccessful, as the court held that the contract required entire performance.

Similarly, in Bolton v Mahadeva (1972) a central heating system gave out less heat than it should, and there were fumes in one room. It was held that the contractor could not claim payment; although the boiler and pipes had been installed, they did not fulfill the primary purpose of heating the house.

The rule can also allow parties to escape from what has become an unprofitable contract to do so by taking advantage of the most minor departures from its terms. In Re Moore and Co Ltd and Landaur and Co (1921) the contract concerned the sale of canned fruit that were to be packed into cases of 30 tins. On delivery it was discovered that although the correct number of tins had been sent, almost half the cases contained only 24 tins in each. This made no difference to the market value of the goods, but the buyers pointed out that the sale was covered by the Sale of Goods Act, which stated that goods sold by description must correspond with that description. The delivery did not, and the buyers were within their rights to reject the whole consignment.

Mitigation of the entire performance rule

Substantial performance

This doctrine allows a party who has performed with only minor defects to claim the price of the work done, less any money the other party will have to spend to put the defects right.

Severable contracts

A contract is said to be severable where payment becomes due at various stages of performance, rather than in one lump sum when performance is complete. Most contracts of employment are examples of this. Also, major building contracts also operate in this way, allowing for stage payments. In a severable contract the money due at the end of each stage may be claimed and the person carrying out the work under the contract can refuse to continue if the payments are not made.

Prevention of performance by one party

Where one party performs one part of the agreed obligation, and is then prevented from completing the rest of the contract because of a fault of the other party, a quantum meruit can be claimed from the other party. Quantum meruit is an assessment of the amount performed to date and a reasonable price arrived at.

Breach of terms concerning time

The judgment here will be that of an assessment of whether 'time is of the essence' and the effect that completing the contract out of time has on the other party.

Frustration of contract

The basic principle underlying frustration of contract is that, after a contract is made, something happens, through no fault of the parties own, to make fulfillment of the contract impossible. Although there are many situations that can make it impossible to fulfill a contract only certain cases can be seen as genuine frustration. When a contract is discharged by frustration both parties are excused performance of their future obligations and the application of the Law Reform (Frustrated Contracts) Act 1943 determines what happens to advance payments (such as deposits and any other payments due) made before the frustrating event and claims for reimbursement for contractual expenses and performance conferred prior to frustration.

The modern doctrine of frustration arose from Taylor v Caldwell (1863). The parties in the case had entered into an agreement concerning the use of Surrey Gardens and music hall for a series of concerts and day and night fetes. Six days before the planned date for the first concert, the building was burnt down, making it impossible for the concerts to go ahead. The party planning to put on the concerts was sued for breach of contract but the action failed, as fulfillment of the contract was impossible.

The concept and practice of frustration of contract can be placed in three categories: events that make performance or further performance impossible; events that make performance illegal; and those that make it pointless.

Impossible to fulfill contract

A contract may become impossible to perform because of destruction or unavailability of something essential for the contract to be performed.

Death of either party to the contract

Unavailability of party. Contracts which require personal performance will be frustrated if one party, for example, is ill or is imprisoned, providing that the non-availability of the party substantially effects performance

Method of performance impossible

Where a contract lays down a particular method of performance and this becomes impossible, the contract may be frustrated. A contract is unlikely to be frustrated simply because performance has become more expensive or more onerous than expected.

The leading modern case on frustration is Davis Contractors Co Ltd v Fareham UDC (1956). Davis, a construction company contracted to build 78 houses for a local authority. The job was to take eight months, at a price of £94,000. In fact, labor shortages delayed the work, which ended up taking 22 months and cost the builders £22,000 more than they had planned for. The defendant was willing to pay the contract price in spite of the delay, but Davis sought to have the contract discharged on the grounds of frustration arguing that labor shortages made performance fundamentally different from that envisaged in the contract (it intended to seek payment on a quantum meruit basis to cover costs).

However, the House of Lords decided that the events that caused the delays were within the range of changes that could reasonably be expected to happen during the performance of a contract for building houses and the change of circumstances did not make performance radically different from what was expected. Therefore, the contract was not frustrated. Lord Radcliffe explained:

'it is not hardship or inconvenience or material loss which itself calls the principle of frustration into play. There must be as well such a change in the significance of the obligation that the thing undertaken would, if performed, be different from that contracted for'.

Illegality

If, after a contract is formed, a change in the law makes its performance illegal, the contract will be frustrated.

Performance made pointless

A contract can be frustrated where a supervening event makes performance of a contract completely pointless, though still technically possible. A contract can be rendered pointless if there has been such a drastic change of circumstances as to dramatically alter the nature of the contract.

Time of frustrating event

In order to frustrate a contract, the event in question must occur after the contract is made.

Limits to the doctrine of frustration

The doctrine of frustration will not be applied on the grounds of inconvenience, increase in expense or loss of profit. The case above that highlights this is Davis Contractors Limited v Fareham UDC (1956). It will also not apply where there is express provision in the contract covering the intervening event or where the frustration is self-induced.

A contract will not be frustrated if the event making performance impossible was the voluntary action of one party. If the party concerned had a choice open to him, and chose to act as to make performance impossible, then frustration will be self induced and the court will refuse to treat the contract as discharged. One such case that highlights this is The Superservant Two (1990). In this case one of the two barges owned by the defendants and used to transport oil rigs was sunk. They were therefore unable to fulfill their contract to transport an oil rig belonging to the plaintiff as their other barge (superservant one) was already allocated to other contracts. It was held that the contract was not frustrated. The defendants had another barge available, but chose not to allocate it to the contract with the plaintiffs.

Where the event was foreseeable

If, by reason of special knowledge, the event was foreseeable by one party, then he cannot claim frustration. This was highlighted in Amalgamated Investment and Property Co v John Walker and Sons Ltd (1976) where the possibility that a building could be listed was foreseen by the plaintiff who had enquired about the matter beforehand. A failure to obtain planning permission was also foreseeable

111

and was a normal risk for property developers. The contract was therefore not frustrated.

Breach of contract

A contract is breached when one party performs defectively, or differently from the agreement or not at all (actual breach) or indicates in advance that they will not be performing as agreed (anticipatory breach). Where an anticipatory breach occurs, the other party can sue for breach straight away, it is not necessary to wait until performance falls due.

One case illustrating this is Frost v Knight (1872) where the defendant had promised to marry the plaintiff once his father had died. He later broke off the engagement before his father died, and when his ex fiancé sued him for breach of promise, he argued that she had no claim as the time for performance had not yet arrived. This argument was rejected and the plaintiff's case succeeded. Any effect of a breach of contract will entitle the innocent party to sue for damages but not every breach will entitle the wronged party to discharge the contract. If the contract is not discharged it will still need to be performed.

There are three main circumstances where the innocent party may wish to seek to discharge the contract:

Repudiation – this is where one party makes it clear that they no longer wish to be bound by the contract, either during its performance or before performance is due

Breach of a condition – Breach of a condition allows the innocent party to terminate the contract.

Serious breach of an innominate term- where the relevant term is classified as innominate, it will be the one that can be breached in both serious and trivial ways, and whether the innocent party is entitled to terminate or not will depend on how serious the results of the breach are. If the results are so serious as to undermine the foundations of the contract, the innocent party will have the right to terminate.

Even when one of these three types of breach occurs, the contract is not automatically discharged. The innocent party can usually choose whether or not to terminate. If the innocent party chooses to terminate this must be clearly communicated to the other party.

Agreement

In some cases, the parties to a contract will simply agree to terminate the contract, so that one or both parties are released from their obligations. A distinction is usually made between bilateral discharge where both parties will benefit from the ending by agreement and a unilateral discharge where one party benefits. In general an agreed discharge will be binding if it contains the same elements that make a contract binding when it is formed. Those that present the most problems are formality and consideration.

Consideration

Consideration is not usually a problem where both parties agree to alter their obligations since each is giving something in return for the change. Problems are most likely to occur when one parties obligations change. If the other party agrees to the change, their agreement will only be binding if put into the form of a deed, or supported by consideration. Where consideration is provided in return for one party's agreement to change this is called 'accord'. The provision of consideration is called 'satisfaction'. The arrangement is often termed accord and satisfaction.

Formalities

This issue arises in connection with certain types of contract (mainly concerning the sale of land) that must be evidenced in writing to be binding under the Law of Property Act (1925).

Remedies for breach of contract

There are a number of remedies available to the innocent party in the event of a breached contract. There are two main remedies, those under common law and equitable remedies. There is a third category that involves remedies arising from the party's own agreement. We will discuss remedies in more depth in the next chapter.

****

Main points from chapter nine

- A contract is said to be discharged when the rights and obligations in it come to an end. There are four ways in which a contract can come to an end – performance under the contract, end by mutual agreement, breach of contract and frustration

- A contract can be frustrated, the basic principle being that, after a contract has been made something happens through no fault of any party then the contract can be voided through frustration of its terms

- Contracts can be deemed to be frustrated on death

10

Remedies for Breach of Contract

Finally, in this chapter we look at the various remedies available when a contract is breached.

The principal remedy for breach of contract in English law is that of damages, which is compensation for loss suffered as a result of the breach. In the context of consumer contracts the Consumer Rights Act 2015 applies when statutory rights under a sale of goods, digital or services contract has not been met.

Damages

The usual remedy for breach of contracts is the award of damages to the innocent party. It aims to compensate for losses that result from not receiving performance that was due under the contract. In general the damages will cover both physical harm to the claimant and their property and also for any economic loss. There are very limited circumstances in which injury to feelings can be compensated for.

Damages can fall into the categories of unliquidated damages, which are damages assessed by the courts, the purpose of which is to compensate the victim for the loss he has suffered as a result of the breach and liquidated damages where the damages are set by the parties themselves.

General rule

When considering damages the general rule is that any damages are awarded innocent parties will place them in a position they would have been if the contract had been performed. There are, however, three limitations: causation, remoteness and mitigation.

Causation

A person will be liable only for losses caused by their own breach of contract. Acts intervening between the breach of contract and the loss incurred may break the chain of causation. One case illustrating this is County Ltd v Girozentrale Securities (1996) where the plaintiff's bank agreed to underwrite the issue of 26 million shares in a publicly quoted company. The defendants were stockbrokers who were engaged by the plaintiffs to approach potential investors in the shares. The brokers breached the terms of their contract and, in due course, the plaintiffs found themselves with 4.5 million shares on their hands which, the price of shares having fallen, represented a loss of nearly £7.5m. They sued the stockbrokers and the main issue in the case was whether the plaintiff's loss was caused by the defendant's breach of contract. In effect the plaintiffs would not have suffered their loss if there had not been a concurrence of a number of events of which the defendant's breach of contract was one. The Court of Appeal held that the broker's breach of contract remained the effective cause of the plaintiff's loss, the breach did not need to be the only cause. The defendants were liable for damages.

Remoteness

There are some losses that clearly result from the defendant's breach of contract, but are considered too remote from the breach for compensation to arise.

The rules concerning remoteness were originally laid down in Hadley v Baxendale (1854). The case concerned a contract for delivery of an important piece of mill equipment, which had been sent away for repair. The equipment, an iron shaft, was not delivered until some days after the agreed date, which meant that the mill, which could not work without it, stood idle for the period whilst awaiting the part. The mill owners attempted to sue for this loss. The courts held that the defendant could not be liable for the loss in this case.

Mitigation

Claimants cannot simply sit back, do nothing, and let losses pile up and expect compensation for the whole loss if there was something that could have been done to mitigate the loss. It is up to defendants in this case to prove that the loss could have been mitigated. Claimants need only do what is reasonable to mitigate the loss.

Calculating any loss

Once it has been established that there is a loss and the defendant is liable the court must quantify the damages. In 1936, two American academics, Fuller and Perdue came up with two main ways of calculating compensation:

Loss of expectation (also called loss of bargain). This is the usual way in which contract damages are calculated and it aims to put claimants in the position that they would have been if the contract had not been performed.

Reliance loss. There are some cases of loss that are very difficult to quantify and in this case, the court may award damages calculated to compensate for any expenses or other loss incurred by the claimant when relying on the contract.

Action for an agreed sum (debt claim)

Where a contract specifies a price to be paid for performance, and the party due to pay fails to do so, the party who has performed can claim the price owing by means of an action for the agreed sum. Although the claim is for money this is not the same as a claim for damages. The claimant is not seeking compensation, but simply enforcement of the defendants promise to pay. One such case illustrating this is White and Carter (Councils) Limited v McGregor (1962) which was an action in debt therefore there was no duty on the innocent party to mitigate by seeking to minimize the loss covered. However, where the claimant has suffered additional loss beyond not receiving the agreed price, damages can be claimed alongside the agreed sum. An action such as this can only be brought once the duty to pay has arisen

Restitution

Where money has been paid under a contract or purported contract and performance has not been received in return, or has not been adequate, the payer may want to claim the money back, rather than claiming damages (if, for example, no additional loss has resulted from the failure to perform). In general this will only be possible if there has been a total failure of consideration so that restitution will prevent undue enrichment. This means that the party paying the money has not received any of what was paid for.

An action for money had and received where there has been a total failure of consideration (no contractual performance) is an example of a restitutionary claim. In this case it was the price paid for non-existent work to an oil tanker in McRae v Commonwealth Disposals Commission (1951).

Equitable remedies

Where common law remedies are inadequate to compensate the claimant, there is a range of equitable remedies. However, these are not available as of right, merely because the defendant is in breach. They are provided at the discretion of the court, taking into account the behavior of both parties and the overall circumstances.

Specific performance

The common law will not force a specific party in breach to perform (except where performance is paying money only), even though this might be a fairly obvious solution to many contract problems. However, the equitable remedy of specific performance does compel a party in breach to perform. In practice, specific performance rarely applies as the making of such an order is subject to certain restrictions.

Specific performance is only granted if damages alone would be an inadequate remedy Specific performance is mainly applied to contracts to sell land since each piece of land is thought to be unique and impossible to replace. Where the damages are only nominal specific performance may be ordered to stop one party becoming unjustly enriched.

Because specific performance is a discretionary remedy the court will not apply it to cases where it could cause the claimant great hardship or unfairness. The courts will also allow the courts to refuse specific performance of a contract that has been obtained by unfair means. Some types of contract are unsuitable for specific performance, the two main types being contracts involving personal services (such as employment contracts) and contracts that involve continuous duties.

Key cases in respect of specific performance are Beswick v Beswick (1968) where a nephew had acquired his uncle's coal business and in exchange had promised his uncle that he would pay £5 a week annuity to the uncle's widow on the uncle's death. the nephew failed to pay and the court allowed specific performance, ordering the nephew to keep his promise. In Co-operative Insurance Society Ltd v Argyll Stores (Holdings) Limited (1997) the court allowed that a covenant in a lease of retail premises to keep open for trade during usual hours of business was not specifically enforceable because the courts would not make an order requiring a person to carry on a business. Any such order would require constant supervision and might cause injustice if keeping the business open caused a loss. In Warren v Mendy (1989) it was held that the court will not usually order specific performance of a contract involving personal services, such as a contract of employment.

Injunctions

Another remedy is that of the injunction. An injunction orders the defendant not to do a specific thing. Where the contract has already been breached the courts can make a mandatory injunction that will order the defendant to restore the situation to what it was before the breach.

Types of injunction

There are three main types of injunction, prohibitory injunction, which is an order commanding the defendant not to do something: mandatory injunction which orders the defendant to undo something he had agreed not to; interim injunction which is designed to regulate the position of the parties pending trial.

Injunctions are also discretionary remedies and are subject to the similar constraints of orders of specific performance. However, an injunction will be granted to enforce a negative stipulation in a contract of employment, as long as this is not an indirect way of enforcing the contract.

Two cases highlighting this are:
Warner Brother Pictures Inc v Nelson (1937) where the actress Bette Davis was contracted to WB exclusively for a one year period, with an option to extend the period. During the period of contract she agreed

to act for a competitor of WB. The court granted an injunction which prevented her from working for the competitor.

Page One Records v Britton (1968) where the 1960's pop group, The Troggs, were prevented indefinitely by their contract form appointing another person to work as their manager. The group were dissatisfied with their manager and appointed another. The courts refused to grant an injunction as it would prevent the group from working as musicians or would tie them to a personal contract against their wishes.

Consumer contracts and breaches of statutory rights relating to goods

In a consumer contract falling within the Consumer Rights Act 2015, the right to repair or replacement of:

- non-conforming goods (breaches of satisfactory quality, fitness for purpose, description, correspondence with sample or correspondence with a model seen and examined pre-contract) in a consumer contract; or
- goods incorrectly installed where installation forms part of a consumer contract and installation was the traders responsibility; or
- non-conforming digital content in a consumer contract,

is specifically provided for as a remedy available to the consumer rather than the option to reject and claim damages. But this remedy cannot be disproportionate when compared to other available remedies.

Remedies agreed by the parties (agreed damages)

Many contracts specify the kind of breach that will justify termination and the damages to be paid. There are two types of contractual clauses concerning damages: liquidated damages and penalty clauses. Liquidated damages is the term used where a contract specifies the amount of damages to be paid in the event of a breach, and this amount represents a genuine attempt to work out what the loss in the event if such a breach would be.

Penalty damages work in a different way. Some contracts, especially construction contracts, specify very high damages in the event of breach and they act as a deterrent, compelling the other party to perform. Where a court finds the damages laid down in contract act in this way, the relevant clause will be invalid and the party putting forward the clause must pursue damages in the usual way.

One case which illustrates this, and which provided for guidelines was that of Dunlop Pneumatic Tyre Co Ltd v New Garage and Motor Co Ltd (1915). The plaintiffs supplied tyres to the defendants under a contract providing that the defendants would not resell them at less than the list price. If they breached this provision they would be liable to pay £5 for every tyre sold at less than the list price. The House of Lords held that the provision was not penal and was in the nature of liquidated damages. Undercutting the list price would have been damaging to the plaintiff's business. Lord Dunedin described the factors to be taken into account when deciding whether damages were penal or not, damages would be considered penal if the sum laid down

125

was extravagantly greater than any loss that might conceivably result from the breach.

In Makdessi v Cavendish Square Holdings BV (2013) It was held that a penalty clause was unenforceable so that the claimant could recover his original loss.

****

Main points from chapter ten

- The usual remedy for breach of contracts is the award of damages to the innocent party

- When considering damages the general rule is that any damages that are awarded innocent parties will place them in a position that they would have been if the contract had performed

- Losses can be mitigated

- Parties can seek specific performance under the contract

- Parties can also apply for an injunction to force the other party to perform.

Glossary of terms

The following are common terms encountered when dealing with contracts.

Acceptance (of an offer) - agreement to all the terms of a contract. Can be oral or in writing.

Accord and satisfaction – this occurs where one party's obligations under a contract change and consideration is provided in return for the other party's agreement to the change.

Actionable misrepresentation- this is a false statement of fact made by one party to the other which induces the other to enter into the contract, rendering the contract voidable.

Affirmation - affirmation occurs when a party, with full knowledge of its ability either to terminate a contract for repudiatory breach or to rescind for actionable misrepresentation, continues performance of the contract or acts in such a way that an unequivocal intention to continue performance of the contract can be construed.

Agent – a person authorized to act on behalf of another who is known to the main party to the contract.

Agreed damages clause - the parties may provide in their contract for the amount of damages paid upon breach.

Bilateral contract – where each party takes on an obligation, usually for promising the other something.

Breach of a contract – where one party does not perform, or performs differently from the agreement.

Common mistake - when both parties enter into a contract based on the same fundamental mistake relating to a contractual term.

Condition – a term in a contract that is an important term and a breach of this term would have significant consequences to one party.

Consideration – something that must be provided by each of the parties in order to make a binding contract.

Contract – a legally binding agreement, written or unwritten Cross purpose mistake – where each party to the contract has a different view of the contractual situation.

Damages - damages are a financial remedy which aims to compensate the injured party.

Duress - duress is an equitable doctrine allowing a contract to be set aside because it was entered into under pressure or threat.

Economic duress – where one party is forced into a contract due to economic pressure.

Exemption clause - an exemption clause is a particular term which purports to exclude or limit the liability or the remedies which would otherwise be available to the injured party.

Exclusion clause – a clause that tries to exclude all responsibility for certain breaches of contract.

Freedom of contract – promotes the idea that parties should be allowed to bargain without interference from the courts.

Implied terms – terms which are not expressly used in a contract but which can be read into the contract.

Indemnity clause – provides that one party will reimburse the other in the event of any loss arising from the contract.

Innominate terms – these are terms that can be broken with either important or trivial consequences, depending on the nature of the breach.

Invitation to treat - an invitation to treat is an invitation to others to make offers as part of the negotiating process.

Limitation clause – this is where either party to the contract will seek to limit their liability for any loss.

Liquidated damages – this is where a contract specifies the amount of damages to be paid in the event of a breach.

Misrepresentation – where one party is induced to enter into a contract as a result of false statement of another.

Mitigation - the injured party has a 'duty' to minimise the losses it suffers following breach or misrepresentation.

Mutual mistake - a mutual mistake occurs when each party is fundamentally mistaken but each makes a different mistake, i.e. the parties are at cross purposes as to a term.

Offer – this is where communication is treated as an offer if it indicates the terms on which the offeror is prepared to make a contract and gives a clear indication that the offeror intends to be bound by the terms of the contract.

Privity of contract – this is where that only the parties to the contract incur rights and obligations under it.

Promissory estoppel - promissory estoppel is an equitable doctrine designed to prevent the promisor going back on his promise or representation that he would not insist on his strict legal rights under an existing contract where this would be inequitable because the promisee has relied on this promise or representation.

Quantum meruit – where a price has not been specified under a contract between parties but work has been done and a reasonable price can be claimed.

Remoteness - remoteness determines the scope of losses for which a party can be held responsible and so be liable to compensate the injured party in the event of breach of contract.

Representation - a representation is a statement which induces the contract but which does not involve any binding promise as to truth.

Repudiatory breach - every breach of contract will give rise to right to claim damages. However, unless the breach constitutes a repudiatory breach, the contract will remain in force.

Rescission - where a contract is voidable, for example for actionable misrepresentation, duress or undue influence, the remedy of rescission is available to the injured party.

Restitution - restitution allows for the recovery of money paid to the guilty party.

Severable contract – this is where a contract can be severed where payment becomes due at various stages of performance rather than in one lump sum.

Specific performance - this is an equitable remedy (and hence discretionary) which compels the party in breach to perform its obligations.

Subject to contract – parties do not intend to be bound by law until formal contracts are exchanged.

Terms of the contract – these describe the duties and obligations which each party has under the agreement.

Undue influence - this is an equitable doctrine allowing a contract to be set aside at the courts discretion.

Unilateral contracts – arises where only one party assumes an obligation.

Void contract – this is where a contract is declared void, the effect being that there never was a contract in the first place.

Voidable contract – this is where an innocent party to the contract can chose to terminate it.

Warranty – this describes a contractual term that can be broken without highly important consequences. If a warranty is breached, the innocent party can sue for damages but cannot terminate the contract.

****

Index